Hidden Holocaust?

*The Cassell Lesbian and Gay Studies list
offers a broad-based platform to lesbian, gay
and bisexual writers for the discussion of
contemporary issues and for the promotion
of new ideas and research.*

COMMISSIONING:
Steve Cook
Roz Hopkins

CONSULTANTS:
Liz Gibbs
Christina Ruse
Peter Tatchell

Hidden Holocaust?

Gay and Lesbian Persecution
in Germany 1933–45

Edited by Günter Grau
With a contribution by Claudia Schoppmann
Translated by Patrick Camiller

CASSELL

Cassell
Villiers House
41/47 Strand
London WC2N 5JE

387 Park Avenue South
New York, NY 10016–8810

Original German edition, *Homosexualität in der NS-Zeit:
Dokumente einer Diskriminierung und Verfolgung*,
© 1993 Fischer Taschenbuch Verlag GmbH, Frankfurt am Main
English translation © Cassell 1995

British Library Cataloguing-in-Publication Data
A catalogue record for this book is available from the British Library.

ISBN: 0–304–32958–4 (hardback)
       0–304–32956–8 (paperback)

Typeset by Fakenham Photosetting Ltd, Fakenham, Norfolk
Printed and bound in Great Britain by Mackays of Chatham plc

The editor, **Dr Günter Grau**, born in 1940, studied economics and psychology and is a sexologist specializing in the history of sex research. After a number of years at the Institute of Medical History at Leipzig University, he has been working since 1991 at the Institute of Medical History at the Charité, Humboldt University, Berlin.

Günter Grau has published several books. In 1991 the East Berlin publisher Dietz Verlag brought out a collection of articles on GDR policy towards homosexuals and prospects for the future: *Lesben und Schwule – was nun?* [Lesbians and Gays – What Now?].

Dr Claudia Schoppmann, born in 1958, studied history and German and is now a working historian. Her publications include a monograph on 'Nazi sexual policies and female homosexuality', which appeared in 1991.

'The exclusion of people with a homosexual character has a long and painful prehistory in our society. We regret that the Christian Church also bears a considerable share of the blame. The silence of Christians during the Nazi period about the murder of homosexuals in the concentration camps is one part of this shared guilt. We therefore have every reason to learn from history. Tolerance is necessary in relation to this minority too.'

From the statement by the Evangelical Church, Berlin-Brandenburg, on the violence against homosexuals, Berlin, 2 August 1991

Contents

List of Documents

Register of Persons

Astel, Professor Dr Karl

Doctor. From spring 1933 president of the Thuringia Regional Bureau for Race Affairs, Weimar; 1934 professor and director of the University Institute for Breeding Theory and Heredity Research (later the Training and Research Centre for Human Heredity and Race Policy); from 1934 to 1937 in charge of the Hereditary Health Supreme Court.

Axmann, Arthur

Reich Youth Führer. From 1933 director of the Social Department of the Reich Youth Leadership. Succeeded Baldur von Schirach in August 1940. Responsible for the 'cleansing operations' programme directed against 'homosexual offences' in the Hitler Youth.

Bormann, Martin

In Hitler's view the 'most loyal' Party comrade. From 1933 Reich Director of the NSDAP, from 1941 (succeeding Rudolf Hess) head of the Party Central Office. Involved in discussion and implementation of the decrees against homosexuals in the NSDAP and SS.

Brustmann, Dr Martin

Psychiatrist at the German Institute for Psychological Research and Psychotherapy in Berlin. From 1940 active as an adviser to the Security Headquarters among others for 'homosexual cases'.

Buch, Walter

SS-Gruppenführer. Involved in 1934 in the arrest of SA leader Röhm. From late 1934 the highest Party judge. At the SS justice department involved *inter alia* in §§175, 175a cases against members of the NSDAP, SS and Police.

Conti, Dr Leonardo

Doctor. Reich Health and Medical Führer, state secretary for health within the Ministry of the Interior, advocate of the 'euthanasia' programme and human experiments on concentration camp prisoners.

Crinis, Professor Dr Max de

Doctor. From 1938 Professor of Neurology and Psychiatry at Berlin University. In late 1944 appointed psychiatric adviser to the Army Medical Inspectorate (succeeding Otto Wuth) and involved in reworking the Wehrmacht's 'Guidelines for the Assessment of Unnatural Sex Acts'.

Ding, Dr Erwin

SS doctor at Buchenwald. From 1942 responsible *inter alia* for compulsory castrations and the typhus fever experiments on homosexual prisoners.

Frank, Professor Dr Hans

Lawyer. From 1933 Reich Führer of the Lawyers' Association, Reich Minister without Portfolio, president of the German Law Academy. Argued for a general tightening of the criminal law against homosexuals and for its extension to lesbians. In 1939 appointed Generalgouverneur of Poland.

Freisler, Dr Roland

Lawyer. From 1942 chairman of the People's Court; known as a hanging judge. From 1935 to 1942 state secretary at the Reich Ministry of Justice, member of the Criminal Law Commission. Centrally involved in implementing the repressive policy against homosexuals.

Gleispach, Professor Dr Wenzeslaus Graf von

Jurist. Professor of Austrian Law. In 1933 special teaching post in criminal law at Berlin University. Member of the Criminal Law Commission. As well as helping to draft a new penal code for the 'Third Reich', he vigorously supported Nazi race legislation, the alignment of Austrian criminal law after the annexation, and tighter wartime legal provisions.

Göring, Professor Dr Matthias Heinrich

Doctor. Relative and favourite of Reichsmarschall Göring. From 1936 director of the German Institute for Psychological Research and Psychotherapy in Berlin. Both there and in his collaboration with the Reich Office for the Combating of Homosexuality and Abortion, investigated the causes and treatment of homosexuality.

Grawitz, Dr Ernst

SS Reich Doctor. President of the German Red Cross. In 1938 put in charge of the 'Lebensborn e.V.' [Spring of Life regd. co.]. Involved in organizing the 'euthanasia' genocide, responsible in 1944 for the experiments of SS Doctor Jensen (alias Værnet) on homosexual prisoners at Buchenwald.

Heydrich, Reinhard

Head of the Security Police and the Security Service. From 1939 director of the Reich Security Headquarters, the terror centre of the SS. Worked very closely with Himmler.

Himmler, Heinrich

Farmer. Reichsführer-SS and Head of the German Police. Architect of the Nazi policy for the prosecution of homosexuals.

Jensen, Dr Carl Peter

Danish doctor. In 1921 changed his name to Carl (Peter) Vaernet. From 1932 carried out endocrinological experiments. In 1944 attached on Himmler's orders to Deutsche Heilmittel GmbH, a cover institution of the SS. In late 1944 experimented with 'reversal of hormonal polarity' on homosexual prisoners at Buchenwald.

Joël, Dr Günther

Jurist. From 1936 chief public prosecutor, assistant head of department at the Reich Ministry of Justice. In 1937 appointed by Justice Minister Gürtner as liaison officer with the Reichsführung SS. From May 1939 the Gestapo's contact man on all matters (including homosexuality) of special interest to the Security Service and the Gestapo.

Keitel, Wilhelm

Field marshal. Chief of the Wehrmacht High Command after Werner von Blomberg's fall in 1938. During war ruthlessly pursued or issued orders for genocide (1941: 'Night and Fog Decree'). In 1943 issued the 'Guidelines for the Handling of Criminal Cases of Unnatural Sex Acts'.

Klare, Dr Rudolf Paul

Jurist. SS-Scharführer. Doctorate in 1937 on 'Homosexuality and the Criminal Law'. Later active as Gestapo agent at the German Cultural Institute in Tokyo and at the press agency of the German Consulate in Shanghai.

Lemke, Dr Rudolf

Doctor. Lecturer at the Clinic for Psychiatric and Nervous Diseases at the University of Jena. Expert witness at §175 and §175a trials. In 1940 post-doctoral *Habilitation* thesis 'On the Causes and Criminal Assessment of

Leading figures in the Nazis' policy
against homosexuals

Professor Dr Karl Astel (upper left)
Reinhard Heydrich (upper right)
Dr Erwin Ding (centre left)
Arthur Axmann (centre right)
Professor Dr Hans Frank (bottom right)

Dr Karl-Heinrich Rodenberg (upper left)
Heinrich Himmler (upper right)
Josef Meisinger (centre left)
Dr Gerhard Schiedlausky (lower right)
Arthur Nebe (bottom left)

Homosexuality'. Argued for compulsory castration and detention of male homosexuals in 'Cure and Care' centres.

Linden, Dr Herbert

Doctor. From 1938 undersecretary in the 'People's Health' department of the Reich Ministry of the Interior; from 1941 Reich representative for Cure and Care centres ('euthanasia programme'), in 1942 director of the 'Heredity and Race Care' subdepartment. Advocated the compulsory castration of homosexual men.

Meisinger, Josef

Member of the SD Headquarters. From 1934 manager of Dept. II 1 H1, the so-called Party and SA department at Gestapo headquarters, which opened a special office for the handling of homosexual cases in the same year. From 1936 to 1940 personally directed both the Reich Office for the Combating of Homosexuality and Abortion at the Reich Criminal Police Bureau and the Gestapo's special office. Responsible for organizing and implementing violent actions against male homosexuals, especially where this involved political cases (e.g. the Röhm putsch, the proceedings against Fritsch in 1938). In 1940 commander of the Security Police and SD in Warsaw. Measures of terror against Jews and Polish intellectuals. Transferred to Tokyo because of his brutal practices.

Nebe, Arthur

Officer in the Criminal Police. In 1933 director of the executive branch of the Gestapo. From 1935 director of the Prussian Crime Bureau, later the Reich Crime Bureau.

Rodenberg, Dr Karl-Heinrich (also Carl-Heinz)

Doctor. From 1937 director of the Heredity and Race Care Department at the Reich Committee for Public Health at the Ministry of the Interior. From 1939 to 1942 worked at the Heredity and Race Care Department of the Reich Health Bureau. From 1942 at the Reich Security Headquarters, where in mid 1943 became consultant on sexual-psychological matters in Bureau V. In 1944 appointed special scientific representative. Particularly concerned with investigating homosexual 'tendencies' (the manuscript of his *Habilitation* thesis on this subject is thought to be lost). Vehement supporter of compulsory castration for offences under §§175, 175a.

Schiedlausky, Dr Gerhard

Doctor. From 1941 to 1943 camp doctor at Ravensbrück, then until April 1945 at Buchenwald. Involved with Dr Jensen's (alias Vaernet's) experiments on homosexual prisoners.

Vaernet, Dr Carl: see Jensen, Carl Peter

Wuth, Professor Dr Otto

Psychiatrist. From 1939 to 1944 director of the Institute for General Psychiatry and Military Psychology of Army Group C at the Academy of Military Medicine, Berlin. As psychiatric adviser to the Army Medical Inspectorate, the highest assessor of homosexual 'cases' in the Wehrmacht.

Preface

The documents presented here make available for the first time source material relating to anti-homosexual policies under National Socialism. In bringing together a large quantity of texts scattered in various central and regional archives, the collection offers an overview of one area of the Nazis' rule that has previously been neglected by researchers and is little known to the public.

The published material is not complete. There are a number of reasons for this, of which we shall mention just the two most important. We have not been able to provide a complete documentary record of the repressive treatment of this group of people. Files are not available from Gestapo headquarters (particularly the special department set up in 1934 to deal with homosexual cases) and from the central Reich Criminal Police Bureau (RKPA) established in 1936 – either because they were consumed by the effects of war or because they were destroyed by members of the SS and police during the last weeks of the war.

Use has been made here for the first time of various archive materials from the former GDR, including documents to which the public did not previously have access. It long remained unclear what had happened to the records of the institution set up on Himmler's secret orders in 1936 within the RKPA, the 'Reich Office for the Combating of Homosexuality and Abortion'. Misleading information from the former State Archive of the GDR forced one to assume that, for whatever reason, relevant files of that office had not been given up to be processed. Research by the editor of this volume between 1985 and 1991 has strengthened previous views that the records themselves were not preserved. It is likely that they were destroyed in bombing raids on the RKPA.

Access to particular files often came about by chance or through well-disposed colleagues working in various archives. In the new *Länder* of the Federal Republic, there was a further complication because the research was done in a period when the *Länder* in question did not yet have their own law concerning archives. This made it difficult to examine the personal files of both the perpetrators and the victims, and the authorization procedure consumed a great deal of time.

The present volume has collected together fragments of records from the Reich Ministry of Justice, the department of the Reichsführer of the SS, the Army Medical Inspectorate, and various regional administrations, courts and police headquarters. It includes the texts of laws, decrees, orders, speeches, minutes and correspondence, which have been selected for the light they throw upon anti-homosexual policies conducted under the National Socialist regime. Use has been made only of those which are typical of a certain form of repression, or which significantly clarify the interests of particular leadership elites (such as the SS, the police or parts of the youth and army commands). The collection as a whole documents the persecution of homosexuals – from the preparatory arrangements to the adoption of more intensive and radical measures during the wartime years.

It is, of course, possible to argue about why this document and not another has been included, and plausible arguments can be given against a particular choice. It was decided not to include documentation relating to the so-called Röhm Putsch in 1934, the 'Cloister Trials' from 1936 to 1939, and the affair of the commander-in-chief of the army, General Werner Freiherr von Fritsch in 1938. Such documents served overwhelmingly apologetic purposes. Also absent are materials which have already been published elsewhere and are thus readily available to the interested reader. This is the case, for example, of Himmler's speech on homosexuality at Bad Tölz in 1937, and the horrific draft law on the treatment of 'social aliens'.

In making his selection the editor had to face two problems. Previous investigations and publications concerning Nazi policy on homosexuals, if they have considered at all the fate of gay men *and* lesbian women, have limited themselves to the observation that intimate relations between women were not as such prosecuted at law. No doubt this distinguished the life situation of homosexual women from that of men. But the lack of penal sanctions for lesbianism did not mean that women known or denounced as lesbians escaped all prosecution. Apart from the fact that an extension of §175 of the Reich Penal Code to women continued to be discussed until the beginning of the war, there is evidence that shortly after the Nazi 'seizure of power' lesbian women were already being carried off to concentration camps, and that from 1936 they became the object of re-education programmes at the Berlin Institute for Psychological Research and Psychotherapy. We are most grateful to Claudia Schoppmann for her special contribution in which she traces the effects of the fascist rulers' image of women in the propaganda media upon the social situation of lesbians. The persistent denial to lesbianism of the right to exist certainly had the result that very little material in the archives gives us any idea of the fate of lesbian women during those years – a fact which is ultimately reflected in the present volume.

The second problem had to do with the arrangement of the material. The obvious course, providing the reader with ease of access, seemed to be to follow a chronological sequence. But in the end the decisive argument for a mainly thematic structure was the need to demonstrate the ramifications in Nazi practice. This does not involve any claim to completeness: historical research still has many gaps to fill in this area. These gaps are particularly sorely felt with regard to the fate of gays and lesbians in the fascist concentration camps – a subject on which very little work has so far been done. Unlike other groups of victims, gays and lesbians have never been the focus of a study of sources in a particular camp – not to mention the many difficulties presented by the sources themselves. For this reason it was decided to limit the material presented here to the camp at Buchenwald.

The documents have all been faithfully reproduced from the originals. In most cases the archive sources are themselves copies, often made on the occasion of being sent to a third party. No changes have been made to the wording of the material – only the spelling and punctuation have been adapted to today's norms. When documents have been reproduced in an abbreviated form, they are preceded by the heading 'Extract'. Explanatory remarks have been given in the footnotes only when this was necessary to identify individuals or to make a connection with certain events.

The editor wishes to thank most warmly for their help and support the directors, archivists, experts and officials in charge of the archives he has consulted – especially the Bundesarchiv in Koblenz, the Military Archive at Freiburg-im-Breisgau, the erstwhile Central State Archive of the German Democratic Republic, the Buchenwald National Memorial, the Institute of Contemporary History in Munich, and the Document Center in Berlin. To Ralf Dose of the Magnus Hirschfeld Society in Berlin, Manfred Herzer of the Gay Museum in Berlin, and Dieter Schiefelbein of the Initiative in Memory of the Persecution of Homosexuals, in Frankfurt-am-Main, I am grateful for much valuable advice, and to Margitta Kressin for the laborious copying of the documents.

Günter Grau

Abbreviations

BAK	Bundesarchiv (Federal Archives) in Koblenz
BA-MA	Bundesarchiv/Militärarchiv (Federal/Military Archive) in Freiburg-im-Breisgau
BA-ZPA	Bundesarchiv/Zentrales Parteiarchiv (Central Archive of the former East German Socialist Unity Party)
BArchP	Bundesarchiv Potsdam (former Central State Archive of the German Democratic Republic)
BArchP-AH	Bundesarchiv Potsdam, Hoppegarten Branch
BDC	Berlin Document Center
BDM	Bund Deutscher Mädel (German Girls League, part of Hitler Youth)
BV	Berufsverbrecher (professional criminal)
DA/BA	Dachau/Bundesarchiv
DAF	Deutsche Arbeitsfront (German Labour Front organization)
GStA	Geheimes Staatsarchiv (Secret State Archives) at Berlin-Dahlem
Gestapo	Geheime Staatspolizei (Secret State Police)
Gestapa	Geheimes Staatspolizeiamt (Gestapo Headquarters)
IfZ	Institut für Zeitgeschichte (Contemporary History Institute) in Munich
KZ	Konzentrationslager (concentration camp)
KPD	Kommunistische Partei Deutschlands (Communist Party of Germany)
LA	Landesarchiv (Regional Archive)
MBliV	Ministerialblatt für die Preussiche innere Verwaltung (Prussian Ministerial Gazette)
NSDAP	Nationalsozialistische Deutsche Arbeiterpartei (National Socialist German Workers' Party)
NSKK	Nationalsozialistisches Kraftfahrerkorps (National Socialist Drivers Corps)
NSV	Nationalsozialistische Volkswohlfahrt (National Socialist People's Welfare)
OKW	Oberkommando der Wehrmacht (Armed Forces High Command)
OuMD	Organisation und Meldedienst der Reichskriminalpolizei (Police Organization and Registration Service)
PVG	Preußisches Polizeiverwaltungsgesetz (Prussian police administrative law)

RF SS	Reichsführer (Reich Leader) of the SS
RGBl	Reichsgesetzblatt (Reich Law Gazette)
RKPA	Reichskriminalpolizeiamt (Reich Criminal Police Bureau)
RJM	Reich Ministry of Justice
RSHA	Reichssicherheitshauptamt (Reich Security Headquarters)
RMBliV	Ministerialblatt des Reichs und Preußischen Ministerium des Innern (Reich and Prussia Interior Ministry Gazette)
RStGB	Reichstrafsgesetzbuch (Reich Penal Code)
SA	Sturmabteilung (Nazi Storm Troopers)
SD	Sicherheitsdienst (Security Service)
SPD	Sozialdemokratische Partei Deutschlands (Social Democratic Party of Germany)
SS	Schutzstaffeln (Guard Detachments – elite Nazi corps)
VO	Verwaltungsordnung (administrative rules)

Günter Grau

Persecution, 'Re-education' or 'Eradication' of Male Homosexuals between 1933 and 1945
Consequences of the Eugenic Concept of Assured Reproduction

The prosecution of people with homosexual feelings took particular forms under the Nazi regime, but it was not a distinctively Nazi phenomenon. Homosexual men were being put on trial long before 1933 – indeed, their criminalization stretches right back to the early Middle Ages. In Germany a nation-wide ordinance had existed since 1871 in the shape of Section 175 of the Reich Penal Code. Also in the 'Second Reich' (to use the Nazi terminology) a police and judicial apparatus had been in place to mount effective operations. The anti-homosexual policy of the National Socialists did not therefore start from scratch. Hitler, Himmler and their 'national comrades' did not have to invent any new laws, nor establish any new apparatus. The National Socialists only had to come to power to carry out what they had preached before the 'seizure of power': that is, the shaping of society in accordance with national [*völkisch*] ideals. Whoever opposed this policy or sought to escape it was threatened with 'eradication' or 're-education'. The campaigns against male homosexuals were one element in this policy. 'Keeping the people's body pure', 'reproduction of the species', 'maintaining the sexual balance' – these were some of the slogans that defined, or were supposed to define, the policy directed against them.

This is not enough, however, to explain why so many people were willing to cooperate in strict and radical implementation of this policy, well beyond the narrow layer of legal experts, doctors and party spokesmen who had been involved since the turn of the century in discussing the solution to the so-called 'homosexual question'. At first sight this preparedness does indeed seem surprising. After all, in the Weimar Republic there had been extremely lively debates about the possible decriminalization of homosexuality, and these had had considerable and lasting effects. Let us mention just two.

1 Homosexual women and men, as well as groups supporting their rights, had made great efforts to achieve some form of social recognition. The most important prerequisite, an end to legal discrimi-

nation, had been called for by a number of weighty figures and groups even outside the medical and legal professions. Moreover, a number of special organizations and societies had come into being. In the big cities, especially Berlin and Hamburg, widespread toleration of a specifically homosexual leisure and contacts culture indicated a liberal interpretation of the relevant penal laws.[1] There was also a significant rise in the activities of the lesbian and gay press and the Scientific-Humanitarian Committee founded by Hirschfeld as early as 1897; in 1919 a Sexual Science Institute had also been created in Berlin. Together with the League for Human Rights, these two institutions spoke out particularly strongly for an end to criminal prosecutions and for the social equality of homosexual men and women.

2 Greater public sympathy for such changes in the criminal law meant that political parties too had been under increasing pressure to take a position. Their different attitudes became apparent in 1929 when the Reichstag Committee on Criminal Law again discussed the draft of a common German Penal Code and recommended, among other things, the deletion of Section 175.[2]

At the same time, various legal experts and doctors had put forward proposals which had been either fully or partly incorporated into the political programmes of influential parties of the Weimar Republic. There were, to be sure, also demands for harsher penal sanctions, for compulsory medical treatment of homosexuals, and for court-ordered castration or sterilization or even preventive detention of homosexual offenders (the latter mainly in relation to offences or crimes falling under §§174 and 176, para. 3 of the Reich Penal Code).

The Nazi Party, joining in these discussions after 1925, had left no room for doubt about its attitude. Thus NSDAP deputy Frick, later to become Minister of the Interior, worked himself up into a fury during the Reichstag debate in 1927 on reform of the criminal law and rounded on the SPD fraction: 'Your Party Congress in Kiel thought it would contribute to the moral renewal of the German people by demanding the deletion of §175 and an end to the

[1] See the exhibition catalogue *Eldorado. Homosexuelle Frauen und Männer in Berlin 1850 bis 1950. Geschichte, Alltag und Kultur*, Berlin 1984; B. Jellonek, *Homosexuelle unter dem Hakenkreuz*, Paderborn 1990, pp. 39ff.; H. Stümke, *Homosexuelle in Deutschland. Eine politische Geschichte*, Munich 1989, pp. 53ff.; R. Plant, *Rosa Winkel, Der Krieg der Nazis gegen die Homosexuellen*, Frankfurt/Main 1991, pp. 31ff.
[2] On the differences in the programmes of the various parties see W. U. Eissler, *Arbeiterparteien und Homosexuellenfrage. Zur Sexualpolitik von SPD und KPD in der Weimarer Republik*, Berlin 1980.

punishment of adultery. Our view, however, is that these §175 people [...] should be prosecuted with all severity, because such vices will lead to the downfall of the German nation.'[3] In August 1930 the *Völkischer Beobachter*, official paper of the NSDAP, informed its readers of what would happen to homosexuals. Since 'all the foul urges of the Jewish soul' come together in homosexuality, 'the law should recognize [them] for what they are – utterly base aberrations of Syrians, extremely serious crimes that should be punished with hanging and deportation.'[4]

Until 1933 no decisions were taken on the matter. A juridical solution of the 'homosexual question' failed to materialize, because it was impossible to reach a compromise supported by decisive forces in society.[5] The sometimes very bitter debates did produce one result: there was broad agreement that practical solutions belonged in the medical field of competence. But although the final decision was tied to scientific clarification of all the related matters, the actual scientific postulates were completely inadequate.

Already before 1933 the medicalization of homosexuality had given rise to overwhelmingly negative and cliché-ridden formulas. Four reasons, in particular, were given for the supposed inferiority and danger attaching to homosexuality:

1 Inability (or refusal) to beget issue. With every homosexual a potential producer of children was lost to the nation.

2 The danger of 'corruption' of young people, and hence the possibility of epidemic spread.

3 The tendency to form cliques. Every homosexual was suspected of being a 'potential oppositionist' and thus regarded as an enemy of respectable society.

4 The endangering of 'public morality'. Sexual relations between people of the same sex were supposed to impair the sense of shame, thereby undermining morality and encouraging the 'decline of the social community'.

This all added up to an important (subjective) prerequisite of Nazi policies: namely, the self-justifying contention on the part of the perpetrators that their victims were an acute and immediate danger

---

[3] Quoted from P. H. Biederich, *§175: Homosexualität*, Regensburg 1951, p. 41.
[4] Quoted from H. Stümke and R. Finkler, *Rosa Listen, Rosa Winkel. Homosexuelle und 'gesundes Volksempfinden' von Auschwitz bis heute*, Reinbek 1981, p. 96.
[5] See B. Mende, 'Die antihomosexuelle Gesetzgebung in der Weimarer Republik', in the exhibition catalogue *Die Geschichte des §175. Strafrecht gegen Homosexuelle*, Berlin 1990, pp. 82–104.

to the rest of the population, and that serious measures therefore had to be taken against them. Further (objective) preconditions were the great vulnerability of minority groups as a result of their social marginalization, and the concentration of power in the hands of the perpetrators.

Once the coup d'état had provided them with a monopoly of power, they were able to subjugate both the courts and their jurisdiction to Nazi ideology – which meant that these could also be used to serve the goals of their anti-homosexual policies.

A major role was played by various eugenic concepts. Seeing male homosexuals as an immediate threat to the growth of the nation, National Socialist ideologues partly blamed them for the lower birth-rates and preached the need to make optimum use of the 'generative power' of the male population. In this way they supplied ideological justification for all the intended, and eventually implemented, forms of persecution. The 'eugenic' aim of putting the 'hereditary flow' in order, by eliminating that which is 'unhealthy' and undesirable and blocking the reproduction of inferior blood, was the basic drift of measures that were designed and eventually put into operation against homosexuals as well as other groups.

The declared aim of the Nazi regime was to eradicate homosexuality. To this end homosexuals were watched, arrested, registered, prosecuted and segregated; they were to be reeducated, castrated and – if this was unsuccessful – exterminated. In the twelve years of the National Socialist dictatorship, the arsenal of repressive measures devised in support of its population policy became ever more extensive. They included:

- the ordering and carrying out of police activities and of measures designed to instil terror;
- the sharpening of penal sanctions;
- the creation of special administrative bodies to carry out prosecutions;
- deportation and isolation in concentration camps;
- extension of the grounds for compulsory castration, and
- the organization of para-medical experiments, up to and including 'reversal of hormonal polarity'.

Prosecutions and other repressive measures began just a few weeks after the Nazi seizure of power. In the following years the pressure on those concerned became more intense and severe, and the various measures used against them escalated with the help of state violence and in the framework of a comprehensive system of manipulation.

In this respect the Nazi period can be roughly divided into three phases. The first, lasting from the 'seizure of power' until 1935, was marked by: (a) the suppression of scientific institutions and associations that had been active in the sexual-political reform movements of the Weimar Republic, especially if they had persistently advocated the decriminalization of homosexuality as part of their propaganda for liberalization; (b) the first campaigns against homosexuals, launched with a great propagandist flurry, which followed the so-called Röhm Putsch in 1934; (c) individual terror and targeted actions by the police and Gestapo against homosexuals, their meeting-places, clubs and associations; and (d) changes to §175 of the Reich Penal Code. These changes in the legal situation marked a crucial break, after which the measures against male homosexuals (the position of lesbians is considered separately) became more intense.

The second phase stretched roughly from 1936 to the beginning of the war. It brought: (a) the establishment of a special administrative body, the 'Reich Office for the Combating of Homosexuality and Abortion'; (b) a drastic qualitative increase in the numbers of those sentenced under §175, as well as a sharpening of penal sanctions; (c) the second anti-homosexual campaign, the so-called Cloister Trials, which in scale and demagogic zeal was the most massive in the history of the 'Third Reich'.

The third phase, which lasted from the beginning of the war until the defeat of fascism, was defined by: (a) the extension of physical terror and the formal legalization of internment in concentration camps; (b) the introduction of the death penalty in 'especially serious cases'; and (c) growing pressure on homosexual men to be 'voluntarily' castrated.

The above periodization might give the impression that we are dealing with a cleverly thought-out long-range strategy on the part of the National Socialists, a kind of overall plan for a final solution to the 'homosexual problem'.

Another view sometimes heard is that the Nazis' loudly trumpeted policy of 'eradicating' homosexuality amounted to a 'homocaust' somehow comparable to the extermination of the Jews.[6] As with the Jews, it is argued, any male homosexual who came to the attention of the Nazi authorities fell victim to their apparatus of

[6] This is argued by, among others, the journalist and Italian gay movement activist Massimo Consoli, in *Homocaust. Il nazismo e la persecuzione degli omosessuali*, Milan 1991.

murder – and the number killed has accordingly been estimated at anywhere from several hundred thousand to one and a half million.[7] However, a mere glance at the crime statistics for this period (and they were maintained with 'Prussian meticulousness') is enough to show that such notions do not stand up to critical scrutiny. Between 1933 and 1945, the relevant number of people sentenced by Nazi judges was roughly fifty thousand. And after sentence had been served, we know from internal documents of the Nazi leadership that some five thousand of that total were deported to concentration camps.

In these speculations about a supposed 'final solution' to the problem of homosexuality, there is clearly a failure to differentiate what was said in Nazi programmes from what was actually carried out. If Himmler's eradication rhetoric is thought to reflect the fate of individual homosexuals, then obviously the Nazis' policy will be seen as a drive to exterminate them all in the literal sense of the term. But things appear in a different light once we distinguish between anti-homosexual propaganda for public consumption and the reality on the ground. Himmler's phraseology did indeed refer to the eradication of homosexuality, which he saw as a (decadent) phenomenon of public life. But his aim was not to wipe out every single gay man who was apprehended for a 'sex offence'. 'If Himmler spoke of the homosexual as the bearer of homosexuality, he nearly always used the singular case. This shows that what he had in his sights was the homosexual type, and obviously not the fate of each individual homosexual man taken into custody by the prosecuting apparatus ... If a homosexual man could convincingly demonstrate under Gestapo questioning that he was not homosexually active, and if proof to the contrary did not fall into the hands of the Gestapo, he would escape prosecution. The crucial point was carefully to prove that the suspect had engaged in homosexual activity, and not just that he had homosexual inclinations. This was a further difference from the practice of anti-Semitic persecution, where it was quite immaterial whether someone observed the rules of their faith in everyday life or had renounced the Jewish religion altogether.'[8]

All the decrees, directives, orders and prohibitions also show that the concept of extermination does not adequately describe Nazi

[7] See, among others, W. Harthauser, 'Der Massenmord an Homosexuellen im Dritten Reich', in W. S. Schlegel, *Das große Tabu. Zeugnisse und Dokumente zum Problem der Homosexualität*, Munich 1967; and J. Boisson, *Le triangle rose. La déportation des homosexuels (1933–1945)*, Paris 1988.
[8] Jellonek, p. 327.

practice in this domain. What we see is a rather differentiated series of punishments and deterrents, whose purpose was to dissuade the 'homosexual minority' from their sexual practice: that is, either to integrate them as 'proper' (heterosexual) men into the 'national community', or to make them abstain from sex in general. The key concern was 're-education'. That was the spirit in which the criminal law was drastically tightened up: re-education through deterrence. And anyone who could not be deterred was sent to a concentration camp: re-education through labour. Psychology was also brought into service: re-education through psychotherapy. And even 'predisposed' homosexuals, for whom the Nazis held out no hope of improvement, could still be exploited as manpower for the 'national community' – provided that they were first castrated.

Although only a fraction of homosexual men were caught in the wheels of the Nazi courts, the everyday life of all homosexuals – whether gays or lesbians – was powerfully shaped by the official policy of repression. Rulers and society were at one in their disapproval of homosexuality and their contempt for homosexuals.

No resistance was to be expected from homosexuals themselves, who were never safe from denunciation by the (heterosexual) world around them. They responded with a high degree of social adaptation. Homosexual men and women got married to make a show of falling into line with the prevailing norms. To some extent at least, trial records indicate what effects the policy of repression had on the way people interacted in sub-cultures that had by no means disappeared. A large number of men showed clear signs of a deeply disturbed personality-image.

The long-term effects are still today largely unknown, especially with regard to the hardening of prejudices after 1945. Nor do we know how the individual gay survivor – and the majority did survive – psychologically worked through the experience of those times, or what consequences they had for his (homo-)sexual identity. At any event they were all victims, whether they were interned in a concentration camp, imprisoned by a court or spared actual persecution. For ultimately the racist Nazi system curtailed the life-opportunities of each and every homosexual man and woman.

Claudia Schoppmann

The Position of Lesbian Women in the Nazi Period

The situation of lesbian women in the 'Third Reich' can only partly be described in terms of clear-cut criteria of persecution. When one looks more closely at the Nazis' policy on homosexuals, it becomes clear that despite a blanket hostility at the ideological level they sharply distinguished in practice between the two sexes. This was due, among other reasons, to the exclusion of women from positions of power in the 'Third Reich', so that female homosexuality was not perceived as 'dangerous to society'. For lesbian women not at risk because of other stigmas, such as Jewish origin or membership of a political party, the most crucial factors in determining their lives were the institutionalized gender hierarchy and the National Socialist policy on women. Apart from seeking to incorporate women and to influence them ideologically, this policy mainly concerned itself with family and population matters and, if necessary, was subordinated to the needs of the war economy or other priorities.

The following remarks will refer above all to 'Aryan' women; it was to them that Nazi policy on women was directed. Nevertheless, this policy must be considered in the context of parallel eugenic measures against people written off as suffering from a 'diseased heredity', as well as the development of a murderous anti-Semitism and racism which denied the right to live to 'inferior' ethnic groups.

The subordination of all women to 'Aryans' of the same sex within the Nazi state went together with a eugenically restricted, supposedly 'natural' destiny within marriage and motherhood and the unpaid reproductive labour associated with them. This was not only of great economic significance; it was also an indispensable condition for the policy of military conquest. Despite the introduction of marriage incentives, despite the intensive propaganda in favour of motherhood and the simultaneous tightening of the ban on abortion, the regime was able to 'notch up' only a slight rise in the number of weddings and births.

After the Nazis came to power, women were driven from the few influential public domains and leadership positions which they had arduously won for themselves in the 1920s, as well as from professions enjoying high social prestige. Even in less highly skilled occupations they were at a considerable disadvantage, particularly in financial terms. And not the least affected were unmarried lesbian women compelled to take up gainful employment. If they admitted their homosexuality at the workplace, they quite often faced the threat of dismissal.

A further major shift in 1933 was the prohibition, or self-dissolution, of the various wings of the so-called bourgeois women's movement. This involved the destruction of a movement whose demands for equal rights called into question the roles traditionally assigned to women. Certainly the National Socialists assumed not only that it was a 'catchment area' for lesbian women but that it was active mainly on their behalf.

The dissolution or *Gleichschaltung* of the women's associations at the beginning of the 'Third Reich', together with the incorporation and ideological influencing of millions of 'Aryan' women by Nazi organizations placed under male leadership bodies, were important reasons why the Nazis did not see female homosexuality as a social and political danger capable of threatening the male-dominated 'national community'.

Gender-specific practices concerning homosexuality were based upon a differential assessment of male and female sexuality in general; for the value differences between the two sexes were especially pronounced in a regime like the National Socialist one with its strong gender hierarchy. The Nazi state assumed a comprehensive 'natural' dependence of women upon men – especially in sexual relations – and sought as far as possible to give this a legal and institutional underpinning. Any self-determining female sexuality, including lesbian forms, was unthinkable within a centuries-old patriarchal tradition that identified passivity as a female sexual characteristic.

The stereotype of the (at most) 'pseudo-homosexual' and therefore 'curable' lesbian woman, which had been reinforced since the turn of the century by medical research projects, had the effect that a majority of Nazi figures specializing in population policy did not see female homosexuality as a threat to 'sound heredity' and the declared aim of raising the number of 'Aryan' births.

Nevertheless, particularly when it came to drafting a new penal code for the 'Third Reich', there were debates about a general criminalization of lesbian women. A number of jurists – Rudolf Klare, for example – demanded the extension of §175 to women out of fear of lesbian 'seduction' of heterosexual women, and dramatized the so-called breakdown in births. The danger was supposed to be especially great from the 'congenital tribadies' who specialized in the seduction of heterosexual women. In September

1934 Senate Chairman Klee, at the 45th session of the Criminal Law Commission within the Reich Ministry of Justice, argued that the state had a major interest in ensuring that 'normal sexual intercourse [...] is at the fore and must not be impaired by other perversities.'[1] Most legal experts and politicians specializing in population policy were apparently of the view, however, that the dangers of 'seduction' were 'not nearly as great' in the case of women as they were in that of men, for 'a woman who is so seduced does not lastingly withdraw from normal sexual intercourse but remains as useful as before in terms of population policy.'[2] During a session at the German Law Academy in March 1936, Assistant Head of Department Schäfer further explained that 'the practice of this vice impairs a woman's psyche far less than it does a man's'.[3] And according to district court chairman Strauss in April 1937, 'women disposed towards lesbianism' nevertheless remained 'capable of reproduction'.[4] The misogynist philosopher Ernst Bergmann even called in 1933 for 'the sex of masculine women' to be 'compulsorily mated in order to cure them', and there was 'no need to fear that they would transmit their degeneracy to their issue'.[5]

The decisive factor at stake in criminal prosecutions was 'the will of the German male to procreate'.[6] Thierack, justice minister from 1942, already anticipated in 1934 a formulation that the Reich Ministry of Justice was using in 1944: that is, the purpose of the 'sex offences' sections in the Penal Code was 'simply to protect fertility. Unlike men, women are always prepared for sex.'[7] This featured too in the reasons given by the Criminal Law Commission within the Reich Ministry of Justice for not extending §175 to women: 'In [homosexual, C.S.] men the reproductive power is wasted and they mostly withdraw from procreation; in women that is not the case, or at least not to the same degree.'[8]

The constant propagation of traditional gender norms – norms called into question by homosexuality as such – was intended to preserve the heterosexist social structure and thereby promote the

[1] Bundesarchiv Koblenz [hereafter BAK] R 22/973, fol. 4.
[2] BAK R 61/127, fol. 198.
[3] Ibid.
[4] BAK R 61/332, fol. 332.
[5] E. Bergmann, *Erkenntnisgeist und Muttergeist. Eine Soziosophie der Geschlechter*, Breslau 1933, p. 404.
[6] Institut für Zeitgeschichte [hereafter IfZ], Munich, MA 624, fol. 4227.
[7] BAK R 22/973, fol. 5.
[8] F. Gürtner, ed., *Das kommende deutsche Strafrecht. Besonderer Teil: Bericht über die Arbeit der amtlichen Strafrechtskommission*, Berlin 1935, p. 125.

stability of the regime. The reproach of 'masculinization' was used as a threat to prevent women from breaking out of the existing order. Many lesbian women in the 'Third Reich' therefore adapted their appearance and clothing to a 'feminine' image; and not a few found themselves obliged to enter into a formal marriage and to lead a psychologically damaging double life.

Himmler too, the especially homophobic head of the SS, several times denounced the 'masculinization' of women and identified the weakening of gender polarity as a cause of homosexuality. What Himmler had to say about homosexuality was no doubt important in itself, but as head of the SS and of the German Police after 1936 he had the backing not only of the central authority, the Reich Office for the Combating of Homosexuality and Abortion, but of all regional and local police forces. As is well known, Himmler aired his views more than once on homosexuality in the course of 1937. In February, in a speech to SS-Gruppenführers (that is, generals) he expressed the fear that a lack of 'feminine charms' might lead to homosexuality in the 'male estate'.

'We must not allow the quality of the male estate and the advantages of male association to turn into defects. In my view we have a much too strong masculinization of our whole life, which goes so far that we militarize impossible things and – if I may here speak openly – see the height of perfection in lining people up and organizing them and getting haversacks packed. It strikes me as a catastrophe when I see girls and women – mainly girls – carrying around a beautifully packed haversack. It's enough to make you feel sick. I regard it as a catastrophe when women's organizations, women's societies, women's associations get involved in a field of activity which destroys all feminine charm, all feminine grace and dignity. I regard it as a catastrophe when we so masculinize women that over time the gender difference or polarity disappears. Then the road to homosexuality is not far off.'[9]

In another speech in June 1937 to the 'Expert Advisory Committee for Population and Race Policy', an important body within the Reich Ministry of the Interior, Himmler saw the greatest danger in the fact that homosexual men were marrying for 'camouflage', driving their wives to adultery (a million according to Himmler's figure), and, even worse, 'blocking' their procreative potential.[10] Moreover, children brought into the world in such 'camouflage'

[9] Himmler, Speech of 18 February 1937 at Bad Tölz, in B. F. Smith and A. F. Peterson, eds., *Heinrich Himmler: Geheimreden 1933–1945 und andere Ansprachen*, Frankfurt/Main 1974, p. 99.
[10] BAK NS 2/41, fol. 57–73.

marriages, having been damaged by the 'tendency' towards homosexuality, were 'eugenically inferior'.

The exclusion of women from the power centres of the 'Third Reich', together with the National Socialists' sexist image of women, were the main reasons why the harsher penal sanctions introduced in June 1935 did not include an extension of §175 to women. It was considered superfluous to criminalize lesbians. In September 1934 at a session of the Criminal Law Commission within the Reich Ministry of Justice, which was responsible for drafting a new penal code, the criminologist E. Mezger suggested that whether female homosexuality should be a punishable offence was 'not a logical question, but a question of weighing up two different evils'.[11] In his view the greater evil would be to go for criminalization: this would involve a flood of legal proceedings, 'since lesbianism is generally widespread among prostitutes'[12] (homosexuality once again being equated with antisocial and criminal behaviour). Besides, the 'naturally' more tender relations among women would give rise to 'unjustified harassment of completely innocent people' – which might 'open up unpleasant prospects'.[13] The advice, then, was to leave female homosexuality unmentioned in the law. Even reports that the 'transgression' was on the rise and that the resulting 'birth deficit' would have fatal consequences for population policy could not outweigh this verdict, which was ultimately dictated by quite pragmatic considerations.

The position taken by the Ministry of Justice remained controversial. There were some jurists who tried to correct it in the course of work on the new penal code. Among the 'hardliners' were Reich Minister Hans Frank and various members of the 'German Law Academy' that he controlled, as well as the already mentioned Rudolf Klare and one Ernst Jenne who worked at the People's Court. They justified their demand for criminalization by pointing to the inherently 'race-corroding', 'race-debasing' and therefore ethnically threatening character of homosexuality. But although such 'arguments' were highly popular in the 'Third Reich' and verifiable evidence did not need to be mustered in their support, they were not capable of winning through in the end. There was also the fact that Hitler delayed the adoption of a new penal code, and with the beginning of the war all work on it was suspended.

The non-criminalization of female homosexuality meant that lesbians were not intensively prosecuted in the same way or to the

[11] BAK R 22/973, fol. 1–5.
[12] Ibid.
[13] Ibid.

same degree as homosexual men. But they did suffer, for example, the same destruction of clubs and other organizations of the homosexual subculture, the banning of its papers and magazines, the closure or surveillance of the bars at which they met. This led to the dispersal of lesbian women and their withdrawal into private circles of friends. Many broke off all contacts for fear of discovery and even changed their place of residence. A collective lesbian life-style and identity, which had begun to take shape since the turn of the century and especially in the years of the Weimar Republic, was destroyed when the Nazis came to power, and the effects would last well beyond the end of the 'Third Reich'.

The exemption of female homosexuality from penal sanctions was one major reason why the registration and prosecution bodies set up within the Gestapo and the Criminal Police in the wake of Röhm's murder in June 1934 mainly concentrated on the male homosexual 'enemy of the state'. The paucity of sources makes it impossible to gauge the extent to which lesbian women were also being compulsorily registered – for example, as a result of denunciation to the authorities. Scattered evidence indicates that reports were collected about lesbians by the police, and also by other organizations such as the Race Policy Bureau of the NSDAP. But the scale of this is not known – nor, above all, are the consequences which followed from it.

In only a few cases can it be demonstrated that women were tried on the pretext of other offences but in reality because of their homosexuality. In one documented instance female homosexuality was cited by the administration of the Ravensbrück concentration camp as the grounds of detention. Thus, on 30 November 1940 the transportation list for this women's camp names the day's eleventh 'admission' as the non-Jewish Elli S., exactly 26 years of age. The term 'lesbian' actually appears in the entry as the reason for detention. Elli S. was apparently put among the political prisoners, but nothing further is known about her fate.[14]

Other cases are known in which lesbians were punished as 'subversive of the military potential'. And where a so-called relation of dependence existed between a superior and a subordinate (as in the 'Reich Labour Service for Female Youth') or between a teacher and a schoolgirl, the provisions of §176 of the penal code could be applied.

It is possible that lesbians also risked prosecution for non-specific

[14] R. Schramm, *Ich will leben [. . .] Bericht über Juden einer deutschen Stadt*, Weissenfels 1990, p. 30 (facsimile of the intake list).

'anti-social' offences. Himmler's decree of December 1937 on the 'Preventive Combating of Crime' authorized the police to take far-reaching measures against 'internal enemies' of the 'national community'. Thus, even people who had not committed a criminal offence but were 'socially maladjusted' and deemed 'anti-social' were now arrested by the police and placed in so-called preventive detention – that is, interned in a concentration camp. The highly flexible label 'anti-social' was applied above all to those who tried to evade the totalitarian demands of the Nazi state. Major emphasis was placed upon work capacity, reproductive behaviour and social need, so that persons of no fixed abode, the unemployed and prostitutes – but also homosexuals and gypsies – were especially hard hit.

Some eugenicists subsumed homosexuality under the concept of 'anti-social behaviour', and the SS or the Race Policy Bureau commonly spoke of homosexuals as the 'anti-social prototype'. The prostitute was regarded as the prototype of female 'anti-social behaviour', and the Nazis drew a special connection between lesbians and prostitutes. However, it is not possible to estimate how often lesbians were jailed as anti-socials or because of ostensible prostitution.

In one such case a lesbian named Else (b. 1917), who worked in Potsdam as a waitress and lived there with her woman-friend, was apparently detained because of her homosexuality and then sent to Ravensbrück. From there, under circumstances that remain unclear, she went to the Flossenbürg camp, which from 1938 was mainly used for the internment of men classified as 'anti-social' or 'criminal'. The camp brothel in Flossenbürg became Else's station of the cross. Presumably she had been forced into prostitution at Ravensbrück, where women were lured with the false promise that they would be released after a 'period of service' in the brothel.

Erich, who had been interned in Flossenbürg for homosexuality – and would spend ten whole years in various camps – came to know Else at the brothel in the autumn of 1943. She worked there for a few months and for Erich was 'the only person with whom I struck up a friendship during the ten years. The Nazis were especially keen on putting lesbian women into brothels. They thought it would get them back on the right path.'[15] This example of friendship and solidarity was not to last long. Else suddenly disappeared from the camp and died, probably before 1945. But it is impossible to be more precise about what happened to her. After the SS's

[15] J. Lemke, *Ganz normal anders. Auskünfte schwuler Männer aus der DDR*, Frankfurt/Main 1989, p. 26.

recommended time of half a year for a camp prostitute had come to an end, she may have been shipped off to Auschwitz and put to death.

For the reasons mentioned above, it is not clear how many women had to undergo the horror of a concentration camp because of their homosexuality; most lesbians were spared that fate if they were prepared to conform. What is certain is that there was no systematic prosecution of lesbian women comparable to that of male homosexuals. Whereas men were often, though not always, detained in connection with a punishable offence under §175, that option was not available in the case of women. The few eyewitness accounts of women wearing pink triangles in the camps probably rest on faulty memory. In the recollections of heterosexual women prisoners, which are often marked by their prejudice, there are many references to the lesbian activity of other prisoners, most of whom are described as 'anti-socials'. But this is not convincing proof that such women had actually been arrested and jailed because of their homosexuality.

Part I
Public Discrimination against Homosexual Men
Particular Actions after 1933

(a) Disputes about Whether Homosexuality Should Be a Criminal Offence

The arguments about homosexuality which had been taking place for years within the medical profession had a decisive influence upon the way in which the Nazis proceeded.

One group of medical people – mainly neurologists and psychiatrists – defined homosexuality as a degeneration of the personality and attempted to trace its causes to morphological changes in the brain, disturbances in the nervous system or hormonal imbalance. All such analyses went together with an expectation that causally effective therapeutic procedures could be developed. Homosexual men and women were thus perceived as being ill: they should no longer be treated as criminals but cured instead, and also prevented from spreading the disease through contagion (= seduction).

On the other side, not a few doctors sought to furnish proof that homosexuality was a particular evolutionary path, a 'natural' predisposition. The central figure of this current was the Berlin sex-doctor Magnus Hirschfeld, whose theory of intermediate stages and natural difference removed all legitimacy from criminal prosecution.

Hirschfeld and other leaders of sexual reform movements in the Weimar Republic were opposed by illustrious experts in the medical profession – above all Karl Bonhoeffer and Emil Kraepelin, the doyen of German psychiatry. Kraepelin firmly rejected the assumption of natural difference in relation to homosexuality, which he regarded as a vice caused by masturbation. Already in 1918 he was calling for measures of 'educational discipline', such as those which were to be introduced after 1933: severe penalties against seduction or 'corruption', applicable not only to homosexual intercourse but more generally to any activity having sexual gratification as its object.

Arguments deployed in this dispute were subsequently taken up by the Nazis. Their political demands for epidemic prevention, for strict punishment of 'corrupters', for expansion of the area of criminality to include any activity deemed homosexual, thereby acquired the appearance of conforming to scientific knowledge. Together with eugenic demands (preached even before 1933) for optimal use of the procreative power of the male population, they not only offered ideological justification but directly legitimated the forms of eventual persecution and often inhumane treatment of this group of people.

[1] Vice, illness or predisposition?

Assessor (senior civil servant) Oyen. Instructions concerning unnatural sexual offences (Extract). Issued by the Reich Ministry of Justice (1934?)

[...] In the last few decades many furious attacks have been launched against §175 of the Penal Code. Nevertheless, there can be no doubt that in the forthcoming penal code of the National Socialist State the threat of punishment will continue to apply to unnatural sexual acts.

It is interesting to start by considering the direction from which the fiercest attacks on §175 have come.

When those who are themselves in the grip of the vice put up a fight against its criminalization, there is no cause for surprise. It must be noted, however, that it is precisely Jewish and Marxist circles which have always worked with special vehemence for the abolition of §175 [...]

But if it has mainly been internationally oriented circles which have represented such tendencies, this is already an a priori reason to suppose that their struggle does not serve any goals which uphold the state and national traditions. This has to be said, even at the risk that such arguments might be described as 'unscientific'.

The opponents of §175 set out a series of grounds for the ending of criminalization.

According to the opponents of §175, homosexuality is not a vice into which one can fall through seduction or addiction; it is based rather upon an inborn disposition, a phenomenon of nature, against which the affected individual is powerless. This 'natural riddle of uranism' (Assessor Ulrich's 'uranism' [*Urning*] is derived from 'Uranos', and he is also fond of the term 'uranist' [*Uranier*] for male homosexuals) is based upon a 'contrary sexual feeling' (Krafft-Ebing, Moll et al.). Just as a person with normal sexual feelings is not likely to become a 'uranist', so a contrasexual is unable to resist his innate drive and to find satisfaction in intercourse with the other sex; indeed, he often feels an insuperable aversion to the other sex, which makes sexual intercourse with it psychologically and physically impossible for him. According to this view of things, it is the duty of everyone with this knowledge – which is the 'result of secure research' (Hirschfeld) – to do all in their power to disseminate it. 'Just as no one in Germany thinks any more of burning a heretic or a witch, so will immortal credit be due to men who have [...] fearlessly worked to ensure that it is the natural right also of uranists to live within their four walls as nature

Guiding Principles
1. Chief among the sexual aberrations are onanism and homosexuality, which exercise a deleterious effect upon population growth.
2. There is not a shred of convincing evidence for the hypothesis that homosexuality is based upon an innate organization of the brain peculiar to it. On the contrary, it has been established that in psychopathological personalities homosexuality develops through the effect of unfavourable sexual experiences upon an immature, early awakened and poorly controlled sex drive.
3. Homosexuality and the closely related bisexuality signify that the sexual development of the psyche remains fixed at one of the various stages through which a healthy sexual life also usually passes.
4. The development of homosexuality is stimulated, first, by displacement of the sexual goal onto one's own sex through onanism in conditions of sexual precociousness and later psychic impotence, next by the linking of vivid premature sex impulses to homosexual relations, and finally by seduction. The influence of alcohol acts as an accessory.
5. The combating of homosexual aberrations will have to be primarily directed against onanism, especially of the mutual kind. This is done by means of educational measures, the hardening or steeling of the will through physical exercises, the holding in check of premature sexual impulses, the prevention of seduction, and timely and prudent instruction. Along with the promotion of companionly relations between the two sexes and the encouragement of early marriage, what most helps to curb homosexuality is the averting of the seduction of young people and the stamping out of male prostitution.
6. The threat of punishment in relation to homosexual intercourse between adults is mostly ineffectual and therefore dispensable. On the other hand, the causing of public offence by such behaviour, or publicity to spread homosexuality by any means and the commercial offering or practising of homosexual intercourse, should be severely punished, as should the abuse of relations of dependence and the use of violence, stupefying drugs or alcohol to achieve homosexual ends.
7. Homosexual dealings by over-age people with male persons under twenty-one years should be severely punished. The threat of punishment should apply not simply to 'intercourse-like' behaviour but to any actions having sexual gratification as their purpose.

E. Kraepelin, 'Geschlechtliche Verirrungen und Volksvermehrung', *Münchener Medizinische Wochenschrift*, 1918, Vol. 65, Nr. 5, pp. 117–20.

commands them to do' (van Erkelens, p. 20). In vain will one seek to compel these uranists – whom nature has made with different drives – not to obey their own nature; and innocent as they are, it would be judicial murder to brand the mark of the criminal on their brow. [. . .] The threat of punishment, moreover, is supposed to be unjust, because only a tiny proportion of punishable actions comes to the notice of the authorities for judgement to be passed upon them. But at the same time court sentences are said for this reason to be ineffectual, the result being simply that unfortunate people with contrary sexual feelings who are otherwise law-abiding spend their whole life on reprieve, subject to the undeserved psychological pressure of the threat of punishment.

It has been further objected that it is not at all clear which right is safeguarded through the threat of penalty; that violence, seduction of young people, etc. may be punished, exactly as they are in heterosexual relations, but there is no justification for the threat of punishment in the case of homosexual intercourse between freely consenting adults.

A final argument against the threat of penalty is that it is especially damaging because it constantly exposes the individuals concerned to the danger of blackmail, and experience shows that the threat of penalty actually breeds blackmailers. In the big cities, blackmail on the basis of the sanctions contained in §175 is a commercial pursuit, whether in the form whereby wealthy homosexuals of high standing in society are forever at its mercy until in desperation they finally put an end to their life, or whether in the form of a partnership in which a 'decoy' leads a uranist to remote parts where, at a given moment, the other partner appears as a morally outraged third party who threatens to inform the police and is prepared to forget about it only after strong pleading and the handing over of an appropriate sum of money. This cancerous evil – so the argument goes – will be conquered only when the threat of punishment is lifted from love between men.

The main case against the penalization of pederasty is therefore based on the idea that it is not a vice but the result of an innate contrary direction of the sex drive. To decide on the legitimacy of this claim is, of course, the business not of jurists but of medical science. If one actually looks at scientific opinion, one cannot help but wonder at the self-assurance with which it is claimed that this opinion is the result of secure research. The conclusion at which one arrives is rather that Hirschfeld's 'results of research' are anything but secure, and that there is no agreement at all among experts in the field. It is probably unnecessary to say any more here

'It is therefore not admissible simply to declare the homosexual
drive-structure as in every case the symptom of a pathological life of
the psyche in general. Nor, however, is it possible to stigmatize it as a
sui generis disease, for there is no uniformity of aetiology,
constitution diagram or general predisposition.'

A. Kronfeld, 'Sexualpsychopathologie', in G. Aschaffenburg, ed., *Handbuch der Psychiatrie (Spez. Teil)*, Part 7, Section 3, Leipzig and Vienna 1923, p. 56.

about the numerous and in part utterly contradictory theories. [...]

The dominant view of medical science is the following. The basis
of homosexuality may be an innate predisposition (contrary sexuality), but it may also be a vice which causes normal sexual feelings
to be lost over time. [...] From this it follows that there are cases
where the psychological and physical possibility exists for both
homosexual and heterosexual intercourse, and where the two
forms of intercourse are actually practised alongside each other.
[...]

The mere possibility that contrary sexuality can be acquired
through external circumstances [...], and not mainly the fact that
homosexual intercourse is pursued purely as a vice, is enough to
show that the demand for an end to all penalization of pederasty is
without foundation. Insofar as the drive is so pathologically strong
in the case of innate, constitutional homosexuality that the free
exercise of the will is excluded in the pursuit of a forbidden practice, the 'poorest of the poor' (van Erkelens) are by no means at the
mercy of a §175 deriving from the 'medieval darkness of jurists'
heads' (Winzer, p. 17); for §51 of the Penal Code protects them
from punishment. The fact that a contrasexual may otherwise be a
highly intellectual person does not contradict the assumption that

'The explanation of homosexuality is made much more difficult by
the fact that agitational purposes have become mixed up with
questions of science. Section 175, which is untenable in its present
version, [...] has given rise to widespread agitation for a change to
this section which at the same time seeks to put an end to the social
proscription of homosexual love and homosexual behaviour. As the
interests of homosexuals here play a role, the realm of scientific fact
is obscured.'

A. Moll, ed., *Handbuch der Sexualwissenschaft*, vol. 2, Leipzig 1926, p. 764.

in the specifically sexual domain he suffers from a pathological disturbance to the activity of the mind. [...]

In the interests of the others, however, for whom the drive is not irresistibly strong, it is not justified to drop the penal sanctions from §175 – even if they feel horror at the female sex and must therefore do completely without sexual satisfaction. One might just as well – although any comparison is inappropriate – call for a man with normal feelings to be left unpunished who commits an act of rape because no woman will give herself to him of her own free will.

What then of the argument that no right is violated by homosexual behaviour, and that the threat of punishment in §175 is therefore unjustified? It should be said that the old theory of Feuerbach, which restricted the concept of crime to direct violations of a right, has long been abandoned. [...] Moreover, it should not be open to doubt that the healthy moral sense of the overwhelming majority of the people would find it completely incomprehensible if the present-day state were, so to speak, to 'recognize' the legitimacy of homosexual behaviour by abolishing the threat of punishment. But the people does have a right to be protected against at least the grossest insults to that moral sense, just as it is expected of the state that it will defend against major insult the people's religious feelings and convictions. In the case of religious offences one could say with much greater justice that they never directly cause harm to anyone – and yet the state punishes them. Besides, today more than ever there should be a return to the belief that the stability of the people's moral thinking is the best guarantee of the stability of the

---

'Homosexuality is no more a disease than a vice; it is a constitutional variant, a middle term between the male–female opposition – one which must exist because nature makes no leaps but everywhere presents fluid transitions. In both psychological and physical respects, homosexuality belongs in the large domain of intersexuality. [...]'

'Let me add a word about the reproach that "my writings caused or encouraged homosexuality", or that homosexuality "is increasing to a terrifying extent under the influence of the Hirschfeld circle". The type of these attacks, and their lack of foundation, I find quite disconcerting. [...]'

'I do not encourage and propagate homosexuality: I only open the eyes of those who are homosexually inclined about themselves, and try to struggle against their social ostracization.'

M. Hirschfeld, 'Ist Homosexualität heilbar?', *Der Nervenarzt*, 1929, Vol. 2, pp. 713–14.

state. Section 175, then, protects a right that deserves to be protected unconditionally.

If it is thought illogical not to make lesbianism subject to penalty, this can at most lead to the demand that it too should be punished [...], but in no way that pederasty should also go unpunished. After what has been said, the other counter-arguments can be dealt with more briefly. It cannot be denied that §175 is often abused for the purposes of blackmail. It has been rightly pointed out, however, that abolition of the threat of penalty would not put an end to the blackmailing of homosexuals; for the fear of social disdain would just as before place a wealthy man at the mercy of blackmailers. Besides, other offences known to a third party are used for the purposes of blackmail, and people do not consider that a reason to call for abolition of the penal code.

'Treatment of homosexuality, in the sense of a promising medical therapy, hardly exists. The gonad transplants performed by Lichtenstern and Mühsam, with and without prior castration, do not appear to yield lasting results [...]. Even in my own cases I have never observed more than a temporary success. Insofar as psychological treatment extends to a transformation of the homosexual drive into a normal one, it too usually ends in failure.'

A. Kronfeld, 'Sexualpsychopathologie', in G. Aschaffenburg, ed., *Handbuch der Psychiatrie (Spez. Teil)*, Part 7, Section 3, Leipzig and Vienna 1923, p. 67.

The same applies to the argument that the sanctions contained in §175 are unjust and ineffectual, as only very few offences under §175 come up for sentence before the courts. With regard to the alleged ineffectuality, there can be no doubt that at least many who are not born homosexuals are held back by the threat of punishment from ever coming into contact with homosexual circles. [...] Nor can it be denied that the state's condemnation, contained in the threat of penalty under §175, makes a strong impact precisely upon young people at the age of puberty with its inner uncertainty and lack of clarity, and influences their own judgement on such matters. Moreover, the demand has never yet been raised to abolish §242 of the Penal Code on the grounds that not all thieves are caught and that it is unfair to punish only those who are.

That not any form of sexual dealings between men is punishable, but only intercourse-like behaviour, has already been established by case law relating to §175 and cannot be in doubt even *de lege*

' "Suprema lex salus populi!"
Service before Self!

It is not necessary that you and I live, but it is necessary that the German people lives. And it can live only if it has the will to struggle – for to live is to struggle. And it can struggle only if it remains virile [*mannbar*]. But it is virile only if it exercises discipline, particularly in sexual matters. Free love is undisciplined and unbridled. That is why we reject it, as we reject everything that is of harm to the people.

'Anyone who aims at male–male or female–female sex is our enemy. We reject everything that emasculates our people and puts it at the mercy of its enemies – for we know that life is struggle, and it is nonsense to think that men will one day lie fraternally in each other's arms. Natural history teaches us otherwise. The stronger are right. And the stronger will always assert themselves against the weaker. Today we are the weaker ones. Let us make sure that we again become the stronger! We can do that only if we exercise discipline [*Zucht*]. We therefore reject any sexual deviation [*Unzucht*], particularly between man and man, because it robs us of the last possibility of freeing our people from the slave-chains in which it is now forced to toil.'

Declaration by the National Leadership of the NSDAP in response to a question on the occasion of the 1928 Reichstag elections. (The wording is attributed to Alfred Rosenberg.) Quoted from R. Klare, *Homosexualität und Strafrecht*, Hamburg 1937, p. 149.

---

ferenda.[1] [...] It does not seem possible to give a more precise legal definition and delimitation of the concept, which would have to be brief and yet cover all punishable behaviour. The text of the New York Penal Code [...] does not encourage one to make such an attempt. Further interpretation may be left to practice and to the sphere of jurisprudence.

[1] The document, which totals 36 pages, is undated. But this sentence allows us to place its composition before June 1935. Probably it was written in connection with the debate about a reform of the penal code which became still more intense in 1934. The amendment of 28 June 1935 to the penal code does not mention such a thing as intercourse-like behaviour but defines a general category of 'sex offence'.

(b) Police Raids, Bans and Arrests: 1933 to 1935

A few days after the Reichstag Fire (27 February 1933), the Prussian Minister of the Interior issued three decrees for the combating of public indecency. The first was directed against prostitution and venereal diseases. The second concerned the closure of bars which 'are misused for the furtherance of public indecency'. Included in this definition were 'public houses solely or mainly frequented by persons who engage in unnatural sex acts', and proceedings were to be immediately started to revoke their licence. The third decree prohibited kiosks and magazine stands, in hire libraries and bookshops, from trading in books or other publications which, 'whether because they include nude illustrations or because of their title or contents, are liable to produce erotic effects in the beholder' – the penalty being a fine, revocation of the hire agreement or withdrawal of the trading licence. Although neither those affected nor the public at large were initially aware of it, these decrees already betokened a policy that would assume a clearer shape over the following months and years: a policy of arbitrary measures designed to deter and to eradicate through terror, and of coercive measures to cure the 'scourge' of homosexuality.

In the next few months, most of the bars known as meeting-places for homosexual men and women were closed down in all the big towns of Germany. The few which escaped for whatever reason would later serve the police and the Gestapo as places where the 'scene', and what was considered as such, could be more easily kept under observation. Public and hire libraries and bookshops were purged of writings that now counted as 'indecent' – in effect, all literary, popular and scientific works published since the turn of the century, and especially since the First World War, which dealt with the theme of homosexuality and 'the love without a name'. Magazines of the homosexual liberation movement – for example, *Blätter für Menschenrecht*, *Die Insel* or *Der Kreis* – had to abandon publication. Publishing houses such as Adolf Brand's (which printed *Der Eigene*, among others) underwent searches and had part of their stock confiscated, so that in the end there remained nothing other than bankruptcy. On 6 May 1933 Magnus Hirschfeld's Sexual Science Institute, renowned well beyond the limits of Berlin, was destroyed, and on 10 May Hirschfeld's writings were publicly burned together with those of Moll, Ellis, Freud and many others. The Scientific-Humanitarian Committee, the political organization which had fought since 1897 to repeal §175 of the Penal Code, was forced to give up its work.

A year later, in February 1934, followed the edicts of the Prussian Minister of the Interior on the preventive detention of 'professional criminals' and the regular surveillance of those still 'running free', as it put it. The concepts of professional criminal and habitual sex offender were arbitrarily defined and then reintroduced into legal terminology.

The ensuing operations especially affected homosexual paedophile men, a category which before 1933 had accounted for the majority of those sentenced under sections 174 to 176 of the Penal Code.

In the second half of 1934, allegedly in connection with the events surrounding the so-called Röhm Putsch, a special section was set up at Gestapo Headquarters to deal with cases involving homosexuality. At the end of the year all Regional Criminal Police Bureaux were asked for lists of persons who had been homosexually active in the past, especial interest being expressed in their membership of Nazi organizations.

It has not so far been possible to ascertain whether and to what extent this registration served as the foundation for nation-wide actions against homosexual men. In Berlin a number of pubs were raided in March 1935. According to a tabular survey drawn up for the Reichsführer-SS, 413 of the 1770 men held in 'preventive detention' were identified in June 1935 as 'homosexuals', 325 of them interned in the infamous concentration camp at Lichtenburg. The brutal proceedings led four gay men to turn for help to Reich Bishop Müller and General Keitel, while remaining anonymous for fear of the consequences.

Parallel to these drastic arbitrary measures devoid of any legal basis, efforts were intensified to develop a new penal code for the 'Third Reich'. In October 1933, on Hitler's orders, Reich Minister of Justice Gürtner hooked the members of an official Criminal Law Commission and made Wenzeslaus Graf von Gleispach, the Viennese conservative theorist of criminal law, responsible for the 'sex offences' rubric. While the Commission discussed how the criminal law should be adapted to the ideology of the Nazi state and whether this required a tightening of §175, a trial at the Weimar Court caused a great stir in April 1935. For the verdict, which sentenced several people to terms of imprisonment for offences under §175, drove a coach and horses through previous interpretation of the law. The judge's opinion warned that in future any homosexual activity would be punished. And the case never got as far as the Reichsgericht [Supreme Court], which should evidently have been brought in at that stage to give a higher ruling.

In late June 1935 the Sixth Amendment to the Penal Code, containing crucial changes in the criminalization of homosexuality, was adopted to widespread surprise.

[2] Closure of public houses
Second Directive of the Prussian Minister of the Interior, 23 February 1933

1 With regard to §2 para. 1/1 and §12 para. 1 of the Public Houses Act of 28.4.1930 (RGBl. [Statute Book] I, p. 146) and of Para. III of the Complement for implementation of this act of 18.6.1930 (GS,

p. 117), the police authorities have let alone some public houses which are being misused for immoral purposes. I am thinking on the one hand of inns known to the police as *dosshouses* or brothellike establishments, and on the other hand of taverns frequented solely or mainly by persons who indulge in *unnatural sexual practices* and of establishments whose whole aspect means that they must be regarded as nothing other than disorderly houses. Such establishments can no longer be tolerated. The rising anew of Germany is ultimately conditioned by a moral renewal of the German people. The spiritual movement initiated in this respect should be supported, as far as possible, by appropriate police measures. Such measures also help the economic recovery of blameless establishments, whose plight has been particularly exacerbated by the competition of low taverns.

2 In order to remedy the existing abuses, I hereby order the following:

(i) Public houses suspected of being among the aforementioned establishments shall be *kept under strict surveillance*.

(ii) If events confirm that the hiring of female employees in an inn or tavern serves mainly to lure customers and to increase business through the provision of hostess services, the proprietor

---

Closure of Night Clubs
Restrictions for Dance Halls and Bars
'A few days ago the chief of police threatened strict measures against inns and taverns which have been the object of complaints concerning morality. On the basis of §22 of the Public Houses Act the following establishments have accordingly been closed with immediate effect: Luisen-Kasino, Alte Jakobstraße 64; Zauberflöte, Kommandantenstraße 72; Dorian Gray, Bülowstraße 57; Kleist-Kasino, Kleiststraße 15; Nürnberger Diele, Nürnberger Straße 6; Internationale Diele, Passauer Straße 27/28; Monokel-Bar, Budapester Straße 14; Geisha, Augsburger Straße 72; Mali und Igel, Lutherstraße 16; Boral, known as Moses, Uhlandstraße 14; Kaffee Hohenzollern, Bülowstraße 101; Silhouette, Gleisbergstraße 14; Mikado, Puttkammerstraße 15 and Hollandais at Bülowstraße 69. In addition, closing time has been brought forward in the case of three further establishments. Major restrictions have also been ordered for dance halls and bars. Hostesses must no longer appear in dancing costumes, or encourage customers to drink with barmaids employed on the premises, or allow themselves to be bought a drink.'

Berliner Tageblatt, 4 March 1933

shall be *forthwith prohibited from hiring female employees*, in accordance with para. III of the Prussian Order for implementation of the Public Houses Act of 18.6.1930 (GS, p. 117). The same shall apply if, in a particular case, access is difficult to the area serving as a public house, or if it is fitted out in such a way that the space or seating is not open to view.

(iii) If events confirm that an inn is being misused for immoral purposes, proceedings shall be immediately initiated for *revocation of its licence*, in accordance with §2 para. 1/1 and §12 of the Public Houses Act. This applies especially in the case of establishments which serve as the haunts of people who indulge in *unnatural sexual practices*, as well as those which are shown to be run solely or mainly as so-called *dosshouses*.

(iv) By 1.5.1933 I expect a first report from chairmen of regional councils about the measures taken on the basis of this directive (the deadline is 10.4.1933 for local police authorities coming under district council chairmen, and 20.4.1933 for district council chairmen and for local police authorities coming directly under regional chairmen).

[3] Banning of indecent publications
Third Directive of the Prussian Minister of the Interior,
24 February 1933

1 In spite of the Directives of 19.6.1931 – If540 (MBliV. p. 657) and 15.12.1932 – IIE.6065 (MBliV. p. 1316) on the combating of indecent displays, there are still kiosks, hire libraries, bookshops and similar businesses which devote a major part of their display to books or other printed matter which, whether because they include nude illustrations or because of their title or contents, are liable to produce erotic effects in the beholder. Some of these are *publications whose sale contravenes §184 para. 1/1 and 1/2 and §184a of the Penal Code or which should be classified as obscene publications* in the sense of the Obscene Publications Youth Protection Act of 18.12.1926 (RGBl. I p. 505).

2 The display of such publications and pictures involves a not insignificant threat to public order, for not only are they liable seriously to endanger the moral development of young people, but to some extent they are also an offence to adults. In the interests of the moral renewal of the German people, such displays can therefore no longer be tolerated. In order to remedy the existing abuses, I hereby order the following:

(i) *Kiosks, magazine stands, hire libraries, bookshops etc.* which show books and publications of the specified kind in their displays *are to be kept under the closest surveillance.*

(ii) If publications, pictures or graphic displays are stocked whose sale contravenes §184 para. 1/1 and 1/2 and §184a of the Penal Code, *the necessary criminal proceedings should be initiated* forthwith. *Until further notice the police authorities are no longer obliged to cooperate with the art committees set up* by the decree of 26.3.1924 (*Reichs- und Preußischer Staatsanzeiger* No. 86).

3 Owners of the kiosks, hire libraries, magazine stands or book-shops, etc. in question must certify, if instructed to do so by the police, that they will avoid *displays* which constitute a threat to public order. If such instructions are not complied with, then in accordance with §55 of the PVG the imposition of a *fine* shall be threatened to the maximum amount applicable for the particular authority. *The fine shall be repeated until the displays fully conform to the requirements of public order.*

4 In the case of kiosks or magazine stands, discussions shall be started at once with the *owner of the space* to urge him *to sever the contractual relationship with the owner of the kiosk.*

5 With regard to *hire libraries*, an amendment to the Reich trading regulations is due to come into force shortly which will make it possible to prohibit the running of a hire library if it stocks publi-cations which are liable to cause offence on moral or religious grounds. The necessary measures should already be prepared, so

---

'The Vatican welcomes the struggle of National Germany against obscene material. The strong measures that Prussia's Minister of the Interior Göring has ordered for the combating of obscene writings and pictures, as well as the directive of the Bavarian Ministry of Education concerning the religious and national attitudes of teaching staff in Bavarian schools, have received serious attention in Vatican circles. It will be recalled that Pius XI, in his recent encyclicals, has repeatedly and vigorously stressed that defensive actions against obscene material are of fundamental importance for the bodily and spiritual health of family and nation, and he most warmly welcomes the type and manner, the resolution and purposefulness with which this struggle has been undertaken in the new Germany.'

Deutsche Allgemeine Zeitung, 6 April 1933

that the continuation of such business can be prohibited without delay after the aforementioned amendment has come into force.

6 In the enforcement of such measures, *close cooperation* is recommended with *organizations existing within the Christian churches for the combating of public immorality.*

7 For the results of measures prompted by this directive, I expect a first report from regional council chairmen by 1.5.1933 (the deadline is 10.4.1933 for local police authorities coming under district council chairmen, and 20.4.1933 for district council chairmen and for local police authorities coming directly under regional chairmen).

[4] How Hirschfeld's Sexual Science Institute was demolished and destroyed (6 May 1933)
Report

A trustworthy eyewitness who, though not himself a member of the Institute, was able accurately to follow the events has kept the following record of the monstrous destruction of this world-famous scientific centre in Berlin for research, education and therapy.

'On the morning of 6 May 1933 the *Berliner Lokalanzeiger* reported that the purging of books with an unGerman spirit from Berlin libraries would take place in the forenoon of that day, and that students at the College of Physical Exercise wished to begin the operation at the Sexual Science Institute. This institute was founded in 1918 by Dr Magnus Hirschfeld at the former home of Prince Hatzfeld and shortly afterwards accepted by the Prussian government as a *charitable foundation.* It enjoyed an international reputation and clientele because of its unique collections and research, its archive and library. Above all, many foreign scholars, doctors and writers came to Berlin to work there.

'When the newspaper announcement appeared, an attempt was made to move some especially valuable private books and manuscripts to a place of safety. This was rendered impossible, however, because the young man with the books was arrested by a guard which had obviously been placed around the institute during the night, and his possessions were thus stolen from him. On 6 May at 9.30 a.m. several vans with roughly a hundred students and a brass band appeared before the institute. They took up a military-style position in front of the house and then forced their way into it to musical accompaniment. As the office was still closed, no one really representing the institute was present – only a few women from the staff and a gentleman sympathetic to the institute. The students tried to gain entry to all the rooms; when these were locked – for example, the ground-floor display rooms and the former and present office of the World League for Sexual Reform – they smashed down the doors. As the downstairs rooms did not have much to offer, they made their way to the first floor and there, in the institute's reception rooms, emptied the inkwells onto various papers and carpets and then set about the private bookcases. They took off what struck them as suspicious, keeping mainly to the so-called 'black list'. But at the same time they pilfered other books, such as a large work on Tutankhamen and many art magazines from the private library of the secretary, Giese. Then they removed from the archive the large boards with representations of inter-sexual cases which had once been prepared for exhibition during the International Medical Congress of 1913 at the Kensington Museum in London. They threw a large number of these boards out of the window to their comrades standing in front of the house.

'They tore most of the other pictures, photographs of important persons, from the walls and played football with them, so that large piles of ruined pictures and broken glass were left behind. When one student objected that the material was of a *medical* nature, another replied that the real point, their real concern, was not to seize a few books and pictures but *to destroy the institute*. During a longer speech a life-size model showing internal secretions was then thrown through the window and shattered. In a consulting room they used a long-handled scrubbing brush to smash a pantostaten used for the treatment of patients. Moving on, they stole a bronze bust of Dr Hirschfeld and took away many works of art. From the institute library they took only a few hundred books for the time being.

'Throughout this time they kept a watch on the staff, and more and more music was played so that inquisitive crowds gathered in front of the house. At 12 o'clock the leader made a long closing speech and the squad pulled out singing a special obscene song plus the Horst Wessel Song.

'The occupiers of the institute assumed that this plunder would be the end of the matter, but at three in the afternoon some more vans appeared with SA people and made it clear that they had to continue with the confiscations, for the morning squad had not had enough time to clear up thoroughly. This second squad then made a further thorough search of all the rooms and carted off with them all the books and manuscripts of any value – a total of two large vanloads. From the swearing it emerged that the students knew the names of many authors represented in the special library. Sigmund Freud, whose picture they removed from the stairwell and carted off, was spoken of as "the dirty Jew Freud"; and Havelock Ellis was referred to as "the swine Havelock Ellis". Of English writers apart from Havelock Ellis, they were looking out especially for the works of Oscar Wilde, Edward Carpenter and Norman Haire; among American writers for the books of the youth magistrate Lindsey, Margaret Sanger and Sylvester Viereck; and among French works for ones by André Gide and Marcel Proust, Pierre Loti, Zola, etc. The books of Van de Velde and the Danish doctor Leunbach also prompted the students to bombard the publishers with swearwords. Whole years of periodicals – particularly the 24 volumes of the *Jahrbücher für sexuelle Zwischenstufen* – were carried away. They also wanted to take completed questionnaires (several thousand) off with them, and only when it was explicitly pointed out that they contained medical histories did the students back off. On the other hand, it was not possible to stop them taking the materials of the World League for Sexual Reform, all the copies of the magazine *Sexus*, and the card index. Numerous manuscripts of Krafft-Ebing, Karl Heinrich Ulrichs and others, many of them hitherto unpublished, fell victim to the intruders.

'They continually asked about Dr Hirschfeld's return. As they put it, they wanted to be "tipped off" when he was due back. Already before the looting of the institute SA men had several times come and asked after Dr Hirschfeld. When they received the answer that he was abroad because of an attack of malaria, they retorted: "*Well, then hopefully he'll snuff it without our doing anything; we won't even need to string him up or beat his brains out.*'

'On 7 May, when the Berlin and other papers reported the operation against the Sexual Science Institute, they included a telegram of protest from the presidium of the World League which pointed out that a lot of the collected material was *the property of foreigners* and that the planned burning should therefore be called off. This dispatch, addressed to the minister of education and the arts, received no attention. Instead, all the writings and pictures were burned three days later on the Opernplatz, along with many works from other sources. The number of volumes destroyed from the institute's special library came to more than ten thousand. The students carried a dummy of Dr Magnus Hirschfeld on the torchlight procession, before throwing it onto the pyre.'

[5] All that was 'aimed only at the ugly excesses of the movement'

Letter from the gay publisher Adolf Brand, 29 November 1933 (Extract)

Adolf Brand Verlag, DER EIGENE
Berlin-Wilhelmshagen
Bismarckstraße 7
29 November 1933

Dear Sirs,

As an honorary member of your society, I feel duty bound to report to you in detail about the complete lack of prospects for the continuation of my life's work in the new National Socialist Germany.

I assume you are sufficiently well informed that, long before the seizure of power, the Reich Chancellor's party spoke out in the sharpest manner against all efforts to obtain the decriminalization of homosexuality and its social equality with sexuality directed towards women.

At that time, when the criminal law committee of the old Reichstag proposed abolition of §175, the Reich Chancellor's party threatened in the *Völkischer Beobachter* – the government organ of the Reich Chancellor Adolf Hitler – to hang all homosexuals from the gallows and to deport all advocates of the repeal of §175, as soon as Hitler came to power. The article in question was targeted especially at the most worthy expert in criminal law Prof. Dr Kahl, who was to be thanked for the satisfactory outcome in the criminal law committee of the Reichstag.

Immediately after the seizure of power, the government of Reich Chancellor Adolf Hitler pressed ahead with all manner of stringent measures for the repression of the homosexual movement. In the main, however, these acts of persecution were aimed only at the ugly excesses of the movement. At that time they were still confined to closure of the places of prostitution which have always greatly damaged the whole movement in the eyes of all upright people, and to the withdrawal of licences from public houses which knew how to make a lucrative business from the seduction of male youth. These were police actions which, in the interests of cleanliness and of the movement's reputation, were nothing but welcome. There were also confiscations of books and publications which really were just obscene or whose irresponsible sensationalism had only saddled the movement with the illest reputation. Here I will just recall Friedrich Radszuweit's terrible piece of kitsch *Männer zu verkaufen!* [Men for Sale], whose completely inane contents were nothing more than a crude speculation on the dumb sensuality and lack of literary taste of plebeian homosexuals – so that the whole movement came to inspire utter contempt and ridicule among all cultured people.

The confiscations aimed at destroying Dr Magnus Hirschfeld's writings had a quite different character. In their case, purely objective factors were not the only decisive ones; in fact the main role was played by anti-Semitic tendencies and prejudices, which affected not so much defenders of homosexuality as homosexual Jews and cast the operation in the martyr's light of the Middle Ages.

You will know that I have also crossed swords with Dr Hirschfeld: not, however, because he is a Jew, but because, contrary to one's better judgement, his whole pseudo-scientific activity stubbornly managed for years on end to deny that bisexuality is a universal tendency and hence desperately distorted the homosexual impulse into something specific to so-called uranists – a course which constituted a catastrophic danger for our whole movement.

His false and laughable theory of uranism, which demoted the most virile men in world history to semi-women and servants, is what we now have to thank for the outraged counter-instincts of all healthy natural-feeling sections of the population – and not least for the current persecutions by the Reich Chancellor's party. (In 1899 Elisar von Kupffer first correctly foresaw these dangers; and in his article 'Die ethisch-politische Bedeutung der Lieblingsminne', published in DER EIGENE, he gave timely public warning of them.) In the interests of Dr Hirschfeld, however, the whole press, and not just its Jewish part, continued to hush up our justified opposition. Now disaster is facing us in the shape of the Hitler movement, which again persistently seeks to undo our work of liberation won with so many sacrifices. This follows logically from the danger we have just mentioned – and from consideration for the broad mass of the population. That Dr Hirschfeld was burned in effigy together with his works on the German students' bonfire was the first materialization of this threat. [...]

On 3 May, shortly before the bonfire business, three detectives from Berlin drove up here quite unexpectedly in their car and confiscated my work on the nude, *Deutsche Rasse*. They seized more than 2000 nude studies and took them away to Berlin. [...]

On 2 September and 4 September the second and third large-scale confiscations took place at my publishing house. On the first occasion, after night had already fallen, uniformed policemen carried off some 3000 of the last year's issues of DER EIGENE, and the second time the criminal police took about 3000 copies of

EROS. In both cases they were issues of my magazines which had appeared long before Hitler's seizure of power and whose public sale the police had not queried in any way.

At the fourth confiscation on 15 November the police seized my most important and valuable books: that is, the volume of novellas *Armer Junge*; Patrick Weston's *Wilderness Dreams* which had first been published in England; and the short philosophical text by Ferdinand Knoll, *Die Liebe der Wenigen*.

At the fifth confiscation on 24 November a few returns of already confiscated numbers of DER EIGENE which had been overlooked on the 2nd of September fell into the hands of the police.

I was completely cleaned out by these five confiscations: I have nothing left to sell and am now ruined from a business point of view. I do not even know what I and my dependants will live on in the future. For my whole life's work is destroyed. Most of my followers do not even have the courage to write me a letter, and certainly not to give any financial support for my work. The loss I have suffered from the numerous confiscations and bans comes to some ten thousand marks.

This situation quite simply means that it is no longer possible to continue my work and to bring out my publications on German soil, and that further publication of my magazine DER EIGENE can only take place in a foreign country where there is the necessary freedom of the press and legal security.

I have remained an individualist, continue to stand on the ground of private property and private initiative, fight for the right to personal liberty, and reject any state-socialist experiment as inimical to freedom and dangerous to the community.

Respectfully yours
Adolf Brand

[6] Radical actions relating to previously convicted men. Preventive detention of 'professional criminals'

Decree of the Prussian Minister of the Interior, 10 February 1934

Prussian Minister of the Interior
C II 22 Nr. 37/34

Berlin
10 February 1934

Express Letter
Re: Application of preventive detention to professional criminals

With my decree of 13.11.33 – IICII.31 Nr. 356/33 – ordering preventive detention of professional criminals, I took the first step to placing in the forefront of police activity the principle of prevention that had previously given way before the idea of prosecution. The strong impact which the introduction of preventive detention has had upon the criminal profession shows that it has had the intended deterrent effect. In further pursuit of my objective of using preventive measures to reduce the number of criminal acts, I now order that in future the following shall come under the provisions of Clause 4 of the aforesaid decree:

(1) Acts whose purpose is the falsification and counterfeiting of metal or paper currency;

(2) Acts whose purpose is the falsification and counterfeiting of checks, bills of exchange, share certificates or passports;

(3) Acts which clearly serve to prepare a fraud involving a deposit, a security, a loan, a job appointment, a check or a bill of exchange;

(4) The founding or running of firms with the object of obtaining by fraud monetary loans or credit on goods (businesses with a short burst of activity). The use of preventive detention should be restricted, however, to persons who, in the founding or running of the firms, act with full awareness of the deceptive machinations.

In cases (2) to (4), a prerequisite for the use of preventive detention is that, apart from a sentence for fraud, the perpetrator shall have been sentenced at least once more for a crime or offence committed in pursuit of gain.

(5) Acts committed by adults (who have completed their 21st year) which morally endanger young persons who have not yet completed their 16th year, if the perpetrator is *proven* to the police as a person who habitually molests young people out of sexual motives. In addition, acts preparatory to a criminal offence liable to prosecution under §183 of the Penal Code which are committed by male persons who habitually cause public offence as exhibitionists.

In both cases, however, a prerequisite for the use of preventive detention is that the perpetrator shall have been sentenced at least once for a sex offence under §§173–183 of the Penal Code.

I hereby raise the number of persons who *may* be taken into preventive detention by regional police forces to 120 for Berlin and 15 for each of the other police authorities – including those already in preventive detention. Greater or lesser requirements may be balanced among the individual police forces where this is requested by the Regional Criminal Police Headquarters. Complaints against a preventive detention order under the decree of 13.11.33 – IICII.31 Nr. 356/33 – and against the present decree are allowed only through official supervisory channels.

[7] Regular surveillance of 'professional criminals' running free
Decree of the Prussian Minister of the Interior, 10 February 1934

Minister of the Interior   Berlin,
C II 22 Nr. 38/34   10 February 1934
                            Express Letter
Re: Regular surveillance of 'professional criminals' running free

(1) In pursuance of the aim of suppressing crime – the aim expressed in the decrees of 13.11.1933 (IICII31 Nr. 356/33) and 10.2.1934 (IICII22 Nr. 37/34) – I hereby order the introduction of *regular* surveillance of professional criminals running free and of habitual sex offenders.

(2) For the implementation of such surveillance I empower regional police forces to impose certain prohibitions and obligations on professional criminals or habitual sex offenders, with the threat of preventive detention in the event of non-compliance. The Regional Criminal Police Bureau shall issue formal administrative guidelines. Such prohibitions and obligations should as far as possible hinder further criminal activity by those in question, but at the same time they should be framed in such a way that they do not bar the way to honest labour or have a detrimental effect upon existing labour relations. This should be thoroughly checked in every instance.

(3) For the time being, authorization to impose prohibitions and obligations should only gradually be made use of, and only to the extent that implementation can be adequately monitored.

(4) I hereby order the following special measures for the surveillance of professional criminals:

(a) A ban on moving residence without police approval. In individual cases such approval may be granted on condition that the person in question reports immediately on arrival to the police authorities covering the new place of residence. The purpose of this ban is to prevent as far as possible the criminal activity of travelling burglars, traders in counterfeit money and other kinds of fraudsters.

(b) A ban on remaining outside the residence notified to the police between the hours of 11.00 p.m. and 5.00 a.m. in summer and 11.00 p.m. and 6.00 a.m. in winter. The person in question may be required to provide the police with keys to his house. The purpose of this ban and obligation is to prevent as far as possible the night-time activity of burglars, especially burglars of shops and cat burglars.

(c) A ban on driving and using motor-cars and motorcycles. This ban should hinder criminals who, for example, use motor-cars and motorcycles to travel for the purposes of theft or trade in counterefeit money, or who seek to evade police surveillance by using such means of transport.

(d) A ban on lingering in certain public places (e.g. railway stations, auction rooms) and on entering racetracks and betting offices. Certain designated places in the vicinity of the main location may also be included in this ban. These measures appear to be effective against receivers, unofficial bookmakers, swindlers and confidence tricksters, as well as robbers such as pickpockets and bicycle thieves.

(e) So-called rent-gangs of male prostitutes may also be eliminated in this way. And a ban on entering certain public parks or woods – especially those with children's play areas – may keep exhibitionists and corrupters of youth away from such places.

(5) These prohibitions and obligations ('a' to 'e') may be imposed only on persons:

(aa) who have already been sentenced to imprisonment or penal servitude at least three times for actions in pursuit of gain, or at least twice in the case of sex offenders convicted under §§173–183 of the Penal Code, and

(bb) who have not spent 5 crime-free years since serving their last sentence or, if the sentence was not served, since their last conviction, and

(cc) who, in the substantiated judgement of the police, should be regarded as professional criminals living solely or mainly on the proceeds of criminal acts or who, in the case of persons sentenced under §§173–183 of the Penal Code, are to be considered dangerous habitual offenders from whom further criminal acts of the same kind can be expected with a high degree of probability.

(6) If the imposed prohibitions and obligations are not respected, the threat of preventive detention shall be brought into force.

(7) Regional police forces must regularly submit a report with brief justifications to the Regional Criminal Police Bureau concerning persons on whom prohibitions and obligations have been imposed, stating the personal details, previous convictions, file references, and the date and type of the prohibition and obligation order. Two photographs and two sets of fingerprints should accompany the report. The Regional Criminal Police Bureau must keep a card index on registered individuals.

(8) The Regional Criminal Police Bureau must arrange for details of every person affected by a prohibition under Sect. 4a and 4c to be entered in the file register, so that police authorities can immediately check whether someone suspected of being outside their locality of residence has contravened a relevant police order. The nature of the prohibitions and obligations, the file references, and the authorities which issued the ban and obligation must be specified in the record.

(9) In individual cases, as soon as a changed life-style on the part of the person concerned makes this seem appropriate, regional police forces may lift the imposed prohibitions and obligations until further notice.

(10) Complaints against prohibition and obligation orders are allowed only through official supervisory channels.[2]

[8] Hitler Youth-Hamburg: 'energetic measures' called for
Complaints about 'conditions' at Hamburg Main Railway Station, October 1934

Minutes
of the meeting held on 5.10.1934 at the Youth Department concerning matters for cooperation between Hitler Youth and the Youth Department.

The following were present under the chairmanship of Director Radusch:

Regierungsrat Dr Niemann	Hamburg Social Security
Senior Inspector Förster	Hamburg Police, Dept. II
Permanent Official Lemke	Youth Department
Mr Gerdts	Hitler Youth
Mr Lüders	Hitler Youth

Director Radusch opened the session. He stated that a report by Mr Lüders about *conditions at Hamburg Main Station* with regard to the dealings of homosexuals and rentboys, which had been forwarded by Mr Lüders to the Hitler Youth and from there to Reich Regional Governor Kaufmann, has given rise to this discussion meeting. The report was not produced at this session and could not therefore be made known verbatim to the participants. In this report Mr Lüders underlined the necessity of Hitler Youth involvement in combating these 'conditions'.

[2] In 1938 the provisions for preventive detention and surveillance were made stricter. See Documents 48 and 49 below (pages 138–47).

Permanent Official Lemke supplemented Director Radusch's account and explained how Mr Lüders – who is a Hitler Youth member and was serving for a short period as a summer replacement at the Station Travellers' Aid Office and the Youth Home – became aware of matters and got the Hitler Youth to take an interest in them.

The Hitler Youth then developed a plan to set up an office of its own at the Main Station, for the support of which the Youth Department should send one member of staff, Mr Lüders. He is paid by the Youth Department, but in practice he comes under Hitler Youth, in the same way that the Hitler Youth office at the Main Station comes under Hitler Youth and is responsible to it alone.

The main purpose of this office is to register and combat homosexuals and rent-boys. It is necessary to work together with the police authorities, the Station Travellers' Aid and the Travellers' Social Security service of the Youth Department, as well as with the Homeless and Travelling Persons Department at Social Security.

Senior Police Inspector Förster then briefly sketched the kind of life led by homosexuals and rentboys as he saw it at the present time in Hamburg. He stressed that not only at the station but *in all parts of the city* and at all times contacts were being made and sexual transactions sought after. Mr Förster outlined the main forms of homosexual activity and explained that time and again older, often dangerous, active homosexuals – most of them intellectuals and influential people – managed to assume leading positions in the youth movement and paramilitary associations so that they could carry on their mischief there undisturbed.

Director Radusch suggested in this connection that before the appointment of Hitler Youth leaders or of persons in charge of any kind of hostel, the Youth Department should be asked, as it was in the past, whether there was anything against the proposed individuals.

Mr Gerdts from Hitler Youth is of the view that this is not practicable in the case of most leaders.

Senior Inspector Förster then drew his remarks to a close. He welcomed the involvement of Hitler Youth and hoped for close collaboration with it, always providing that its office *immediately* sends material on to the police, which then makes all further arrangements.

Mr Lüders from Hitler Youth then drew a very general sketch of conditions at the station and called them intolerable. In the one case he cited – concerning Fischer, who is now an SA man and used to be a steel-helmeter[3] – he observed that homosexuals at the station form a kind of organized gang which communicates by signs when an official is seen as well as on other occasions. Mr Lüders called for energetic measures against these outrageous conditions.

Mr Förster differed with this view of Mr Lüders. Referring to long and wide experience, he again outlined the present situation in the context of female and male-male prostitution. He argued that the situation has greatly improved as a result of energetic police intervention, that the streets in particular have been cleaned up, and that at the present time Hamburg is a shining example in comparison with other towns. Senior Inspector Förster did not believe there was an organization of homosexuals, because this is not at all in their character. His view, rather, is that Mr Lüders, who is still not very familiar with the shape of things, takes as homosexuals and rentboys what are in fact harmless workmen, porters or canvassers for private accommodation and cheap hotels – in short, the kind of people for whom the main station lets drop a few pennies a day. Mr Förster is prepared to put it to the test by organizing a raid at the station with the assistance of Mr Lüders and Mr Gerdts. If conditions at the station really are as Mr Lüders depicts them, they must surely be noticed by the station police and his very active colleagues from the crime watch at the Main Station. Protests by Mr Lüders and Mr Gerdts compelled Mr Förster to go again into the problem of homosexuality, and at the end to request that an objective attitude is maintained in relation to homosexuals and the handling of such difficult matters. Among other things, he pointed out that homosexuality is widespread among all layers of the population, but only a tiny part of them are active, prone to criminal offences and anti-social. Only these should be the target of our struggle. [...]

Hostels of ill repute, where people under age also often stay the night:
Logierhaus von Winzer, Peterstr. 33b
Logierhaus von Kühn, Lincolnstr. 5, Basement
Logierhaus von Staben, Lincolnstr. 10
Home of Sister Bertha Kayser, Rotesoodstr. 8
Logierhaus Klein Concordia, Altona, Finkenstr. 32
Herberge zur Heimat, Altona, Blücherstr. 8/10
Herberge zur Heimat, Wandsbek, Bleicherstr. 66
Herberge zur Heimat, Harburg, Home Mission, Langestr. 15a

---

[3] That is, a member of the right-wing Ex-Servicemen's Association. *Translator's note.*

Zentral Herberge, Bergedorf, Töpfertwiete 8
Herberge zum Rolandsbogen, Bergedorf, Töpfertwiete 4
Herberge Stadt Bremen, Bergedorf, Kuhberg 12.

Known meeting-places of homosexuals:
Minalla, Reeperbahn.
Billardsaal Schmidt ('Monte Carlo'), Reichenstr./Gr. Freiheit 8

*List of names of persons (males) who have been homosexually active in
any way October 1934 (Extract)*

Ser. No.	Surname & Forename	Date & place of birth	Occupation	Address	Remark
	(a) *Persons previously convicted of an offence under §175:*				
1	V., Heinz	9.8.1912 Hagen	Worker	Hagen, Bismarckstr. 32	
2	B., Josef	21.5.1909 Hagen	Printer	Hagen, Friedensstr. 109	H
3	O., Erich	10.5.1909 Milspe	Packer	Hagen, Auf dem Birnbaum, 17	+
4	Sch., Walter	2.6.1900 Wreschen	Bricklayer	Hagen, Boclerstr. 73	
5	K., Heinz	27.4.1899 Hagen	Carter	Hagen, Helmholtzstr. 19	
6	M., Peter	11.9.1897 Buchheim	Tailor	Hagen, Dödterstr. 1	
7	H., Wilhelm	23.9.1895 Hagen	Tradesman	Hagen, Frankfurter Str. 96	
8	R., Karl	1.4.1895 Augustusburg	Furrier	Moved to Leipzig on 9/1/28	
9	K., Franz	26.9.1894 Vorhalle	House-painter	Hagen, Gartenstr. 32	
10	L., Josef	28.4.1881 Mönchen-Gladbach	Not known	Not known	
11	L., Hans	11.5.1877 Cologne	Actor	Moved to Berlin on 7.7.25	
12	K., Karl	8.8.1870 Linden	Pensioner	Vogelsang, Breddestr. 8	

Institut für Zeitgeschichte, Munich, MA 131, fol. 103513

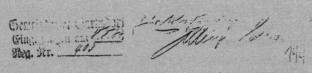

A II/V VO.318.   Chemnitz,am 3.August 1934.

Abschriftlich an die Gemeinderäte und Gen.-Posten

zur Kenntnis und Berichterstattung durch die Gend.-Posten an die
Amtshauptmannschaft bis zum 10.8.34. Es ist Beruf, Vor-und Fami-
lienname, Geburtsdatum, Wohnort und Wohnung anzuzeigen.

Fehlmeldung ist erforderlich.

Die Amtshauptmannschaft.
I.A.
gez.Dr.Becker .

Ausgefertigt:
Chemnitz,am 6.August 1934.

Leyer, VInsp.

Abschrift!

Sächs.Ministerium d.I.   Dresden,.am 30. Juli 1934.
I P A: 26 St.1.

Die NSDAP. Gauleitung Sachsen hat darum nachgesucht,
ihr Personen, die sich in den Reihen der Partei,gleichviel wel-
cher Gliederung,befinden und deren Lebenswandel gegen § 175 StGB.
verstößt, namhaft zu machen.
Die Polizeibehörden werden angewiesen,soweit Personen,
die nach § 175 StGB.bestraft oder homosexueller Betätigung ver-
dächtig sind, als Mitglieder der NSDAP. oder, auch ohne Partei -
zugehörigkeit, als Angehörige der Jugendorganisation bekannt sind,
diese der Gauleitung Sachsen,Dresden-A.1,Grunaerstraße 50,namentlich
lich mitzuteilen.

Ministerium des Innern.
(gez.)Dr.Fritsch.

An pp.

Demand made by the NSDAP Gau Leadership in Saxony on 30 July 1934 for the
reporting of Party members, etc. who have been convicted under §175 or are
suspected of being homosexuals. (*Source*: Kreisarchiv Chemnitz, Rat der Gemeinde
Garmsdorf, No 2.)

A III/V VO.318   Chemnitz, 3 August 1934
   Copies to district councils and gendarmerie offices for information and for
reporting by gendarmerie offices to the Amtshauptmannschaft[4] *by 10.8.34.*
The occupation, forenames and surname, date of birth and place of residence
should all be indicated.
                          Errors must be reported.
                          The Amtshauptmannschaft,
                  p.p. Dr Becker, Chemnitz, 6 August 1934

Copy!
Saxon Ministry of the Interior
I.P.A: 26 St. 1   Dresden, 30 July 1934

   The NSDAP Saxony Gau leadership has called for the naming of persons in
the ranks of the Party, whatever their grade, whose way of life contravenes
§175 of the Penal Code.
   The police authorities are ordered to communicate to the Saxony Gau
Leadership, Dresden-A.1, Grunaerstraße 50, the names of persons who have
been convicted under §175 of the Penal Code or are suspected of homosexual
activity and who are known to be members of the NSDAP or, *without
belonging to the Party,* to be members of the youth *organization.*
                          Ministry of the Interior
                          Signed: Dr Fritsch

[4] *Amtshauptmannschaft*: the district administrative unit in Saxony which persisted until 1939.
Translator's note.

[9] Gestapo has lists drawn up
Telegrams of October 1934

[9a] *Telegram from the Gestapo Berlin, 24 October 1934*

By order of the political police commander, a list of names of all persons who have been homosexually active in any way – perhaps in the form of (or including) a copy of the existing file-sheet – should be submitted by 1.12.1934 to the Secret State Police Bureau Berlin II 1 Special Section. It is especially important that the deadline is respected.

[9b] *Telegram from the Gestapo Berlin, 1 November 1934*

Subsequent to No. 105, 24.10.1934, the following communication is intended to clear up any doubts and to ensure uniform implementation. All persons (males) who have been homosexually active in any way are to be registered according to political organization. As far as possible, the record should then specify: (a) date and place of birth and residence of the person to be registered, (b) occupation, membership of the NSDAP or of a National Socialist organization, and if applicable, since when and at what level of service the person has been in them, (c) whether the person has been convicted by a court of homosexual activity or whether there have only been incidents. Persons who used to live within the area of jurisdiction but have since moved away must also be listed with a reference to this fact. In addition to the criminal police, all state police authorities, political police and state police departments must submit lists by 1.12.1934 if they have any knowledge of homosexual transgressions, especially on the part of political figures.

Copy.

The Reich and Prussian   Berlin NW 40, 28 January 1935
Ministries of Justice   Königsplatz 6.

IV 1111/1079a.

Reg. 28 Jan. 1935.   p. 37

Secret!

To
Secret State Police Bureau
– by the hand of the Prime Minister of Prussia –

Re: Concerted action against homosexuals

According to a report in the *Baseler Zeitung* of 19 December 1934, a purge has been conducted against homosexual elements throughout the Reich on the personal orders of the Führer and Reich Chancellor. The number of people arrested throughout the Reich is said by this source to come to roughly 700.

I consider it imperative for the health of the nation that measures should be taken, both at the level of ideas and materially, to protect other national comrades from this degeneration of the sex drive and to compel those afflicted with this degeneration to refrain from the corresponding solicitation and activity. For this reason I am interested in the report in the *Baseler Zeitung* and request to be notified how many persons have been affected by the action against homosexuals. If more material really is available about this, I would suggest that the Reich Public Health Department should carefully examine the extent to which the spread of this abnormal disposition among our nation can be most effectively resisted. My senior official in charge, Dr Linden, is willing to discuss with the official in charge there how this research might be proceeded with.

p.p. Dr Gutt

Abschrift.

Der Reichs=und Preußische   Berlin NW 40, den 28.Januar 1935.
Minister des Innern   Königsplatz 6.

IV 1111/1079a.

                                   Sing.: 28.Jan.1935.   P.37.

                        Geheim!

     An

das Geheime Staatspolizeiamt
- durch die Hand des Herrn Preußischen Ministerpräsidenten -.

Betrifft: Vorgehen gegen Homosexuelle.

     In der Baseler Zeitung vom 19.Dezember 1934 ist eine
Mitteilung erschienen, nach der auf persönlichen Befehl des
Führers und Reichskanzlers im ganzen Reich eine Reinigungs=
aktion gegen homosexuelle Elemente durchgeführt sein soll.
Die Zahl der im ganzen Reich in Haft genommenen Personen
soll sich - nach dieser Meldung - auf ungefähr 700 belaufen.

     Ich betrachte es vom Standpunkt der Volksgesundheit aus
als dringend notwendig, daß in ideeller und materieller Hin=
sicht Maßnahmen getroffen werden, um weitere Volksgenossen
vor dieser Entartung des Geschlechtstriebes zu bewahren und
die mit dieser Entartung Behafteten dazu zu zwingen, sich
einer entsprechenden Werbung und Betätigung zu enthalten.
Aus diesem Grunde bin ich an der Meldung der Baseler Zeitung
interessiert und bitte um Mitteilung, wieviele Personen von
der Aktion gegen die Homosexuellen betroffen worden sind.
Ich würde, falls wirklich ein größeres Material darüber vor=
liegen sollte, veranlassen, daß vom Reichsgesundheitsamt
der Frage darüber nachgegangen wird, inwieweit der Ausbrei=

                                              tung

Correspondence regarding a report in the *Basler Zeitung* of 28 January 1935
(Geheimes Staatsarchiv Berlin-Dahlem, Rep. 90p. Nr. 65 H Schutzhaft 1934–35/Bd. 3,
pp. 86f.) *Translations are given on pages 47 and 50.*

tung dieser abnormen Veranlagung in unserem Volke
am wirksamsten begegnet werden kann. Mein Sachbearbeiter, Oberregierungsrat Dr.Linden, ist bereit,
mit dem dortigen Sachbearbeiter im einzelnen zu be-
sprechen, wie bei dieser Sammelforschung vorzugehen
wäre.

Im Auftrag
gez. Dr.Gütt.

Abschrift.

Der Reichs-und Preußische   Berlin NW 40, den 9. April 1935.
  Minister des Innern   Königsplatz 6.

IV f 1111 II/1079a.

Eing.: 12.Apr.1935 P.37 II.

Geheim!

An

das Geheime Staatspolizeiamt

durch die Hand des Herrn Preußischen
         Ministerpräsidenten.

Betrifft: Vorgehen gegen Homosexuelle.

Unter Bezugnahme auf mein Schreiben vom
28. Januar 1935 - IV f 1111/1079 a -.

Für eine Mitteilung über den Stand der
nebenbezeichneten Angelegenheit wäre ich
dankbar.

Im Auftrag
gez. Dr.Linden.

Gesehen.

Berlin, den 15. April 1935.
Der Preußische Ministerpräsident.
     Jm Auftrage
     gez. Marotzke.

Copy.

The Reich and Prussian	Berlin NW 40, 9 April 1935
Ministries of Justice	Königsplatz 6.

IV f 1111 III/1079a.

Reg. 12 Apr. 1935.   p. 37 II

Secret!

To
Secret State Police Bureau
– by the hand of the Prime Minister of Prussia –

Re: Concerted action against homosexuals

With reference to my letter of
28 January 1935 – IV f 1111/1079a –.

I should be grateful to hear how things stand with regard to the above matter.

p.p. Dr Linden

Noted.
Berlin, 15 April 1935.
The Prime Minister of Prussia
p.p. Marotzka

---

[10] '... through bad example, seduction!'
*Local Gestapo offices made reponsible for reporting on
homosexual deviations among young people, 8 February 1935*

Secret State Police Bureau	Berlin, 8 February 1935
B.Nr.61 501/35 171 II 1	

To all state police offices in Prussia

Crime has assumed such horrifying proportions among German youth that the Secret State Police feels obliged to propose to the competent authorities new ways of preventing a further rise in the number of youth offenders. Local offices of the state police should help as much as possible in this crucial national-political task by keeping a constant watch and suggesting appropriate remedies. I therefore request you to report on the incidence of youth criminality in your area, to highlight especially striking and symptomatic cases in the reports, and above all to probe into the causes. Especially important are cases which should be regarded as a symptom of the concentration of young people in associations and organizations – for example, sexual aberrations, gang robbery or malicious damage. It is particularly important to mention incidents where it is beyond doubt that youth leaders, through bad example, seduction or the issuing of absurd commands, were the cause of criminal offences by young people under their leadership. It is advised to make contact with the youth prosecution department.

(Long term) signed: Heydrich

[11] Round-up in Berlin

Report by a member of the 'Adolf Hitler' SS Bodyguard, 11 March 1935 (Extract)

On 9.3.35 the storm company under my command provided a detachment of 20 men which was allocated in support of Gestapo agents for the round-up of homosexuals. At 21.15 hours the unit left barracks in two lorries and reported for duty at 22.00 hours to Police Inspector Kanthack.[5] Apart from our unit 10–12 police officers had been assigned for the planned round-up, some of them having already been deployed to ensure that things went according to plan. A few of them came back ahead of our operation. During this time Inspector K. told me what was planned.

At 22.45 hours we left the Gestapo station and went with several vans to the 'Weinmeister Klause' pub in Weinmeisterstraße, where many homosexually inclined people were supposed to be hanging around. As previously discussed, two of our men occupied each of the two exits from the pub with orders to let no one out but to admit anyone wishing to enter. Eight previously assigned men cordoned off the area in front of the bar past the other part of the pub. Two men searched the toilets. Inspector K. and his officers took away from the tables everyone who seemed suspicious. They had to go and stand by the men in front of the bar, and from there they were loaded into the vans and taken by our men under guard to the Gestapo station.

Among those arrested was a woman who was supposed to have had Soviet Russian rabble-rousing leaflets on her. From the Gestapo courtyard the detainees were taken, again under guard, to the corridor of the fourth-floor departments used for such cases. Here our men sorted them in alphabetical order and made them wait under guard with their faces to the wall for questioning; this was begun immediately by most of the previously mentioned officers. After questioning and until it was decided whether they were guilty, these people went to another part of the corridor where they were again kept under guard by some of our men.

[5] Gerhard Kanthack: inspector in the Prussian Regional Police since 1925.

15 November 1934

'Dear Boy,

Your letter arrived yesterday just in the nick of time. As day after day passed without my hearing news of you, a great sense of disappointment spread and gradually took hold of me, so that I became hard and unjust.

But more of that later when I see you.

Now you have given me great joy by saying how much you would like to meet me. In my last letter I already wrote that, for my part, I will go easy on your feelings in future. You need no longer have any worries on that score. But I would be happy if you also took account of how I feel. You know what I think: all or nothing. And since you already have my promise, I would like to believe that you will feel completely joined to me and so give me the joy that I absolutely need. You know I find life hard to bear, because the new times have brought me profound disappointment. So being with you helps me to get over it.

About us meeting, then. Sunday would have been very good, but the late arrival of your letter means that it is no longer on the cards. Now Saturday the 27th of November would be a possibility. If all goes well, we could meet in Fr. at 3.09 and perhaps go over to Mainz. M. is a big town and things aren't really noticed there – or rather, we don't need to be worried about meeting someone we know there. I hope the time will soon come when we can be together again officially.

You will find a card enclosed. Take a postcard and copy it exactly with the typewriter. On Sunday go to Frankfurt on a Sunday ticket and drop it in the post-box. I will then write all the details to you next week. If fate is kind to us, I hope I will also take home warm and happy memories of you, my dear boy. Let us be thinking entirely about each other when we are together. That will also be the case for you – you have my promise. Make sure about the card on Sunday. Of course I will make up the costs of the trip to you.

Warm greetings,

Your paternal friend.'

Bundesarchiv Potsdam-AH/ZBI 830 A 1 fol.17.

After the questioning of the first detainees had begun, Inspector K. continued the round-up with some of his people who were not immediately needed for the interrogation and with the rest of our men. The second place where homosexuals were to be arrested was a beer-pub on the Cottbusser Damm. The cordoning off and searching followed in the way described before. From here nearly two van-loads were taken to the Gestapo station and dealt with in the same way. Immediately afterwards Inspector K. wanted to raid the halls of residence on Landsbergerstraße with six of our men and four detectives. Nothing came out of this, however, because – as he said later – the action against people in there had been delayed by eight days. On the basis of a telephone call, we were supposed to search another pub en route, where mainly SS and SA men with homosexual inclinations hung out. This action also failed to produce results. After we had returned to the Gestapo station, the questioning began with vigour and one of the detectives had to go to police headquarters with details of all those arrested so far in order to check whether any other criminal offences were involved. [...]

Following this the next action began, again with four detectives and roughly eight of our men, who raided the 'Milch Bar' on Augsburgerstraße and another bar on the corner of Kantstraße and Fasanenstraße. Here the haul was one van-load. When we had again taken the people under arrest to the Gestapo station, Inspector K. would have liked to arrest a certain figure whose full name he did not actually know. So he took to the road with two detectives and three of our men plus myself. First we searched a big beer-pub on the Schiffbauerdamm, and after this had proved fruitless we went to Schöneberg and drew up in front of the pub 'Die Insel'. Inspector K. and his officers went in there alone, while we men in uniform occupied the entrance. After this search again proved fruitless, the round-up was brought to an end and the sorting of the people under arrest began at the Gestapo station. On 10.3.35 I conducted the first transport of the guilty to the Columbiahaus, with a guard of eight SS men. After all the questioning was over, those without any proof against them were released. For this our unit formed a line up to the exit and everyone due for release had to pass through it. By around 10.00 hours everyone had been released, except for the ones who were immediately guilty. These we took to the Columbiahaus on our way back to barracks, where we arrived at about 11.15 hours.

[12] Arrest of Hitler Youth members for 'sexual misdemeanours'

Instructions issued by the Gestapo Bureau, 3 May 1935

The Director   Berlin, 3 May 1935
of the Secret State Police Bureau
B.Nr.718/351a

Re: Committal of Hitler Youth members

Further to the instructions of 9 May 1934 for the task force [*Bereitschaftsdienst*], I order the following with immediate effect. A request by the Reich Youth Command or a regional command for the arrest of Hitler Youth members for sexual misdemeanours should in principle be granted without further examination. Only in cases of justifiable doubt is the decision of the chief company commander to be obtained (telephone: C1 Steinplatz 3994). I further make it the duty of task force officers to ensure that they always act in an accommodating manner in relation to Hitler Youth offices.

Signed: Heydrich.

[13] Restructuring at the Gestapo Bureau

Memorandum from Department II of the Gestapo, 22 May 1935, concerning section for the handling of homosexual cases

With immediate effect the section for the handling of homosexual cases, which has hitherto come under II 1 S, is attached as Section 3 to Office II 1 H. It thus carries the designation II 1 H 3, section leader Police Inspector *Kanthack*.

[14] Illusions: 'our glorious Führer [would] punish such acts most severely.'

Anonymous letter from a gay man to the Reich Bishop [Ludwig Müller], June 1935

'Blessed are the merciful; they shall obtain mercy.' '... any man who is angry with his brother must answer for it before the court of justice, and any man who says Raca to his brother must answer for it before the Council; and any man who says to his brother, Thou fool, must answer for it in hell fire.' 'Give to him who asks ...'

Berlin, West, 12 June 1935

Reverend Reich Bishop!

I no longer know what to do and so I am turning my steps directly to you. May God grant that this letter comes directly into your hands! May God grant that you do not close your mind to these lines but that you do everything in your power to put an end to the horror, by protesting at the very top and asking for help in the following matter.

Reich Bishop, before I describe everything I solemnly assure you that I have either myself experienced what follows or that it has been reported to me by trustworthy people who have themselves lived through the terror of it all. It is hard for me to be completely open in describing all these things, with all the hideous words as well – but it has to be, so that you can have a clear picture and take action with all the power of your exalted office.

In the last half-year, in Berlin and throughout the Reich, round-ups have been made of homosexuals or people suspected of being homosexual. They have either been taken from pubs (as half-a-year or so ago) or pursued at home, in the street and so on. These round-ups were arranged by the Secret State Police and carried out by young SS men, mostly Bavarians and other South Germans.

After they have been picked up and kept *standing* for 12 hours and more in the corridors of the Secret State Police, without being given a chance to eat or drink anything at all, they are either released or taken to the so-called 'Kolumbia-Haus' (Tempelhof). Perhaps that does not sound so dreadful, but in reality the poor people under arrest have become so weak they have collapsed in the corridors of the Secret State Police, suffered spasms, fallen faint, and so on. To have to stand for hours with your face to the wall is already a torture, but to do so without once being allowed to answer a call of nature is quite terrible. (Only after 6 hours were the detainees able to use the toilets – under guard!) The way in which the SS guards (members of the Adolf-Hitler Regiment!) treated the detainees was appalling. They kicked people on the shins, screaming and raging as if they had to deal with serious criminals behaving in a stubborn and troublesome manner. (In fact, everyone was so intimidated that they did not utter a word and followed all the guards' orders!) Curses such as : 'You little piece of shit!', 'Pathetic bastard!', 'You bugger, you'll soon get a kick up the arse!', 'What are you squinting like that for, you bit of horseshit!' could be heard all the time. A few complaints by some of the older men were answered with blows. The boss of the operation, one Obersturmführer Meisinger, did not do anything to stop this dreadful treatment; on the contrary, he put in some bellowing of his own from time to time and thus underlined the way his subordinates were behaving.

Such was the way people were treated at the Secret State Police in Prinz-Albert-Straße. But much more dreadful (still today!!) is the treatment of those held in the so-called Kolumbia-Haus, which is already known in Berlin as 'Death Island' and the 'Prussian Siberia'.

The poor people there are tortured for weeks and months on end. (Mentally and physically!) Just a few examples. A very cultured middle-aged gentleman was not allowed to relieve himself, although he continually attracted attention at the door of his cell. They shouted at him from outside but did not let him out. In the end, so as not to dirty his cell, the pitiful man did it *in his mess tin* – which was punished with a long beating. Another prisoner, despite repeated requests, was also not taken to the toilet and did it in his cell; he was then sadistically told under threat to eat his excrement. But he refused and shouted out: 'I won't do it! Beat me to death, rather. I won't do it!' What they then did with him I do not know, but it must have been something quite terrible. [...] Many prisoners have been beaten every day in the Kolumbia-Haus, although they have done absolutely nothing wrong. (I could give you whole pages of examples, but these will surely suffice.)

A very large number of those held in the Kolumbia-Haus are subsequently sent to the Lichtenburg concentration camp. Hardly anyone can describe what they do there to homosexuals and people suspected of being homosexuals. Not only do they use the foulest swearwords with the prisoners; they maltreat them in the most brutal way (allegedly on orders from above, although I simply cannot believe it!) It starts with the so-called 'sport' (physical exercises which are so devised that the strongest men cannot continue, cannot climb any more steps, cannot stand up straight any more, and so on!). For example, knee-bends and stretches forty at a time

(!!), crawling on the elbows in a poorly surfaced yard, etc. etc. If someone cannot keep up or they 'have something' against him, he gets the so-called 'sport special'; that is, tougher and longer 'sport'. No description of that is adequate: it has to be heard from the mouth of someone who has been through it.

For *all inmates* of the concentration camp, the openly held beatings are a terrible experience. Every last man has to fall in, stand still and watch while 50 to 100 blows are rained on a poor creature. (The cries and the sight of flowing blood are terrible experiences for those who have to watch!!) For some trivial matter or other, people have inflicted on them every conceivable punishment in which the sadistic character expresses itself. The darkness down in the so-called 'bunker' is absolutely terrible. A number of people have already gone mad there.

Reverend Reich Bishop! These prisoners are people who have landed there because of some sexual inclination or even simply because they are suspected of it. *But not a single one has appeared before a judge!* (Some are due to be tried for the first time in the next few weeks!) A few hundred have already been released from Lichtenburg. Some of them are broken in body and soul; others have come out white-haired although they are still young in years; others now suffer from persecution mania, wander about lost, and so on. Most of them have lost their job, although no criminal activity could be proved against them. (Suspicion was enough to put them in a bad light with their boss.)

The tortures are continuing. As you read these lines, many hundreds are undergoing the most hideous torments. Reich Bishop, if someone has committed an offence, he should be brought before a judge where he can answer for it! That is the view of all decent Germans. But here people are being tortured and maltreated who, for the most part, have not acknowledged or not committed a single punishable offence.

I beg of you, for our Saviour's love of mankind, please help us! Inform the highest authorities of everything you learn from this letter and from elsewhere! Our Lord will richly reward you for this deed, which will certainly be well-pleasing to him. You are our highest evangelical priest whom we as soldiers especially revere. Please, follow every path you can so that relief comes to us as fast as possible.

People have said that our glorious Führer would punish such acts most severely if they came to his ears. I am of the same view, for Adolf Hitler wishes to see the realization of justice and the most heartfelt love of one's neighbour. But every day here – through these terrible deeds – *new enemies of the state* are being trained. That should not be happening. Please, make your own enquiries as soon as possible, but in such a way that you learn the whole truth! The guilty ones must be brought to account. (4th Company, under a Captain or Sturmführer Bräuning, is especially incriminated!) Obersturmführer Meisinger, Inspector Häuserer and Inspector Kanthack (who are all active in the Secret State Police) and *particularly the director of the Kolumbia-Haus* (!!!) must be examined. There would have to be a thorough *surprise*-inspection in the *Kolumbia-Haus* and at *Lichtenburg concentration camp* and many prisoners would have to be heard *separately*; then the truth would come to light. If it is not done like that, everything will remain as before and many hundred poor souls will continue to be maltreated and thus converted into enemies of the state.

For fear of revenge (I have my grounds!) I cannot tell you my name, Reverend Reich Bishop. Forgive me for not giving my name, but it is not possible otherwise. Our Lord be with you. May he bless you in all you do!

Heil Hitler!
One who suffers greatly in the present state of things.

[15] 'Please, have mercy ...'
*Anonymous letter from three gay men to General Keitel,
June 1935*

Your Excellency!
Most esteemed General!

Once we were also soldiers and now we have to suffer so terribly. We have done nothing wrong. Please, have mercy and make representations in the highest places so that the dreadful tortures cease in the Kolumbia-Haus (Berlin-Tempelhof!) and at Lichtenburg concentration camp. We implore you because every day these tortures are creating new enemies of the state. If you are able to, inform the Führer without delay. The Führer wishes for justice and love of one's neighbour. But here there is the most terrible injustice every hour of the day, and the basest sadistic instincts are out on the loose.

May it please you to gather all the details from the enclosed account that we have sent to the Reich Bishop.

If people have committed an offence they should answer before the lawful judge, but it is not worthy of the state to torture poor helpless prisoners without legal process.

Please excuse us, your Excellency, that we are unable to give our names; we would be afraid of revenge.

With sincere respect three old soldiers greet you with Heil Hitler!

[16] June 1935: 413 homosexual men are taken into 'preventive detention'

Letter from Reinhard Heydrich, 2 July 1935, to the Acting Head of the Prussian State Police, Heinrich Himmler

Secret State Police Bureau   Berlin SW 11, 2 July 1935
B. = Nr.II 1 D   Prinz-Albrecht-Str. 8

To the Acting Head and
Inspector of the Prussian State Police
Internal

Re: Preventive Detention.
Please find enclosed for your attention a numerical table of cases of preventive detention in the period from 11.5 to 10.6.1935. Persons who remained in preventive detention for less than 7 days are not included in the totals.

signed: Heydrich[6]

[17] Special temporary regulations for foreigners during the Olympics

Special decree by Himmler, 20 July 1936

The Reichsführer-SS and   Berlin, 20 July 1936
Head of the German Police

Instruction to the Secret State Police

For the coming weeks I forbid the taking of action, including interrogation or summons, against any foreigners under §175 without my personal approval.

The Reichsführer-SS
signed: H. Himmler

---

[6] The reverse side bears the following remark dated 12 July 1935: 'Returned after noting by Reichsführer-SS. Reichsführer-SS has ordered that the number of people in protective detention coming from the ranks of former KPD-functionaries shall be increased by a thousand in the following month.'

Survey of persons held in preventive detention for more than 7 days in the period from 11.5 to 10.6.19[?]

East Prussia					Branden-burg		Pomer-ania		Posen-West Prussia	Lower Silesia		Upper Silesia	Saxony			Schleswig-Holstein	Hanov[er]		
Königsberg	Tilsit	Allenstein	Marienwerder	Berlin	Potsdam	Frankfurt/Oder	Stettin	Köslin	Schneidemühl	Breslau	Liegnitz	Oppeln	Magdeburg	Halle	Erfurt	Kiel (Altona)	Hanover	Harburg-Wilhelmsburg	Wesermünde
15	11	9	7	247	24	12	8	4	7	104	69	84	20	121	17	48	14	5	–
4	1	–	6	52	10	1	1	1	2	18	8	10	1	19	2	4	3	2	–
2	–	–	–	7	–	–	–	–	–	1	–	1	–	–	4	1	–	1	–
9	10	9	1	188	14	11	7	3	5	85	61	73	19	102	11	43	11	2	–
–	1	–	–	24	3	1	–	–	–	2	–	2	2	15	3	29	4	2	–
6	8	4	–	102	7	8	2	3	4	22	30	56	11	61	6	4	1	–	–
–	–	–	–	18	–	–	–	–	1	2	1	–	2	3	1	2	–	–	–
3	1	5	1	44	4	2	5	–	–	59	30	15	4	23	1	8	6	–	–

| phalia | | Hessen-Nassau | | Rhineland | | | | | | Saarland | Secret State Police Bureau | | | |
Bielefeld	Dortmund	Kassel	Frankfurt/Main	Koblenz	Düsseldorf	Cologne	Trier	Aachen	Sigmaringen	Saarbrücken	Political prisoners	Homosexuals	Total	
3	238	35	52	2	130	29	6	19	1	3	124	513	2177	Total prisoners in previous detention
4	16	4	1	–	12	9	1	3	–	2	13	100	316	Released
.	–	–	1	–	4	–	–	–	–	–	8	–	31	Sentenced by courts
9	222	31	50	2	114	20	5	16	–	1	103	413	1770	Number in previous detention on 10.6.35
														Number of prisoners at
9	73	7	7	1	70	10	–	8	–	–	12	–	322	Esterwegen concentration camp
1	4	14	–	–	10	–	–	–	–	–	14	325	706	Lichtenburg concentration camp
.	1	–	7	–	4					2	4	–	49	Loringen concentration camp
9	144	10	36	1	30	10	5	6	1	1	73	88	693	Various prisons

Part II
Tightening up the Law from September 1935

(a) The National Socialist Revision of Section 175 of the Penal Code

The amendment to the Reich Penal Code was passed on 28 June 1935 and came into force on 1 September. This hasty reworking – as part of the drafting of a new penal code – was tersely motivated by reference to 'bad experiences in the recent period'. By this was evidently meant the so-called 'Röhm Putsch'. It is advisable – stated the legislator's commentary – 'to bring into force beforehand the harsher provisions against homosexual offences between men which have been introduced in anticipation of the general renewal of the criminal law'.

The tougher provisions under §175 of the Penal Code related to two aspects:

1. *The amendment to the old version of §175.*
The concept of 'unnatural sex act' was replaced with the considerably broader one of 'sex offence'. The former had applied only to intercourse-like acts, defined by a ruling of the supreme court [the Reichsgericht] as anal, oral and thigh intercourse; self-gratification in the presence of, against or with another man did not count. Evidence could seldom be produced (since the men were usually dealt with together and they knew the scope for interpretation), so that before 1935 criminal proceedings were initiated in relatively few cases.

In the new version, the existence of an intercourse-like act was no longer required. Nor was it necessary, therefore, to prove that a criminal act had taken place – it became impossible to stop proceedings by means of the law. A 'sex offence' between men now designated not only intercourse-like acts but any kind of self-gratification in the presence of another man. An offence was committed when the member of one male touched the body of another 'with sexual intent', so that even the snuggling together of two naked male bodies came under this definition. Ejaculation was not required to complete a criminal offence.

2. *The introduction of a new §175a.*
Abuse of a relation of dependence based upon service or employment, sex acts with young people under 21 years of age, and homosexual prostitution were considered 'serious sex offences' and punished with up to ten years' penal servitude or not less than three months' imprisonment. According to Clause 2, the person subjected to compulsion or dependence was also liable to punishment – a rule previously unknown in criminal law. In minor cases, according to Paragraph 2, the court might refrain from punishing people who were not yet 21 years of age at the time of the act, but this did not apply to 'intercourse-like acts' committed with other juveniles or persons under age.

In addition to the extension of criminal categories and the raising of sentences, the amendment of 28 June 1935 introduced the fundamental novelty of a so-called analogy section, §2. This read: 'Whoever commits an act which the law defines as an offence, or which deserves punishment according to the basic principle of a criminal law or healthy public feeling, shall be punished. If no definite criminal law is directly applicable to the act, it shall be punished in accordance with the law whose basic principles are most appropriate to it.'

The legal sources which judges now had to use in reaching a verdict were no longer just the written law but equally the 'unwritten source of law', the 'basic principle of a criminal law' and 'healthy public feeling'. The legal maxim 'no punishment without a law' was thereby abandoned and new room created for judges' discretionary decision.

After 1935 there was a huge rise in the number of final judgements under §175, 175a. The court practice of judges followed an extreme interpretation and extension of the new categories.

[18] Section 175
Text of the Reich Penal Code of 1871 and of the 1935 revision

[18a] *The original version taken from the Penal Code of 1871*

§175
An unnatural sex act committed between persons of male sex or by humans with animals is punishable by imprisonment; the loss of civil rights may also be imposed.

[18b] *The new version according to the amendment of 28 June 1935 to the Penal Code, Art 6*

Sex offence between males

(1) §175 of the Penal Code is given the following wording:

§175
A male who commits a sex offence with another male or allows himself to be used by another male for a sex offence shall be punished with imprisonment.
Where a party was not yet twenty-one years of age at the time of the act, the court may in especially minor cases refrain from punishment.

(2) The following rule shall be inserted after §175 of the Penal Code as §175a:

§175a
Penal servitude up to ten years or, where there are mitigating circumstances, imprisonment of not less than three months shall apply
to:

    1 a male who, with violence or the threat of present violence to
body and soul or life, compels another male to commit a sex
offence with him or to allow himself to be abused for a sex
offence;

    2 a male who, by abusing a relation of dependence based upon
service, employment or subordination, induces another male to
commit a sex offence with him or to allow himself to be abused
for a sex offence;

    3 a male over 21 years of age who seduces a male person under
twenty-one years to commit a sex offence with him or to allow
himself to be abused for a sex offence;

    4 a male who publicly commits a sex offence with males or
allows himself to be abused by males for a sex offence or offers
himself for the same.

(3) The former §175 of the Penal Code shall be inserted as
§175b after deletion of the words 'between persons of male sex or'.

[19] Widening of the concept of 'sex offence'
Details of the amendment of 28 June 1935 to the criminal law.
Commentary by Dr Leopold Schäfer, assistant head of department
at the Reich Ministry of Justice (Extract)

[...] 4. Sex offence between males (Article 6).
Bad experiences in the recent period have made it seem advisable to
bring into force beforehand the harsher provisions against homosexual offences between men which have been introduced in anticipation of the general renewal of the criminal law. The essential
defect of the previous Section 175 of the Penal Code lay in the fact
that – at least in former case law – it applied only to intercourse-
like acts, so that public prosecutors and the police could not proceed against evidently homosexual practices unless they were able
to prove such acts. This gap has now been filled, so that any sex
offence between males renders them liable to imprisonment. In
order to prevent this provision from being applied to lesser misdemeanours, which experience shows to occur particularly at a
youthful age, the court is empowered to refrain from punishing
persons under 21 years in especially minor cases. Where persons
under age abase themselves in intercourse-like acts with other

under-age males or even adults, this mitigating factor shall not normally be applicable. In addition to this basic category, other designated cases which carry the threat of penal servitude up to 10 years or, with mitigating circumstances, imprisonment of not less than three months are: The use of violence or of a present threat to life and limb to compel another male to commit a homosexual offence, or the abuse of a relation of dependence based upon service, employment or subordination (e.g., in the Wehrmacht, the police, SA or Hitler Youth) for the purposes of a homosexual offence, or the seduction of a minor by an adult, or male homosexual prostitution.

Cases of bestiality (sexual commerce with animals), which were included in the former Section 175, now appear as Section 175b. [...] (p. 997)

[20] Attacks on morality

Report on the work of the official Criminal Law Commission by Prof. Dr Wenzeslaus Graf von Gleispach (Extract)

The 'sex offences' [*Unzucht*] section covers 'moral offences' [*Sittlichkeitsdelikte*] in the narrow sense and the encouragement of others to commit sex offences, but unlike the current law it does not concern itself with marital offences, which are grouped in a special section together with attacks upon the family. The aim must be a stout defence of sexual morality and of healthier sexual relations, by defining what constitutes an offence as well as the threatened penalties. For morality (again referring to sex life in the sense of this heading) is one of the foundations of a wholesome national life. Many of the offences to be considered here are first of all attacks against individual persons. What is most important in these offences too, however, is the attack upon the moral order of the *Volk*, the danger to its proper moral bearing. This viewpoint justifies the amalgamation of the offences under discussion, and their inclusion in a section which groups together attacks upon the mental and spiritual bearing of the *Volk*.

The current law – not mainly because it was inadequate but because it was not enforced – did but little to check the moral degeneracy which until recently was being brought into the German *Volk* and becoming especially widespread in the big cities. Attempts to dismantle the legal protection of morality certainly produced mountains of brochures and books, but they did not yield any legislative results. The National Socialist Revolution brought about a fundamental change. As a rebirth of the German people, it also helps sound moral conduct to break through, to gain strength and to become more widespread. Within the briefest time of its taking over, and without any fundamental change to the provisions of the criminal law, the new government ended the constant poisoning of the moral atmosphere and cleared pornography and the like from the press, literature, art and public performances. Judicial practice, especially with regard to sentencing, displays understanding of its task. Accordingly, current law may to a considerable extent be incorporated into the draft. It goes without saying that there were loopholes to be filled and many detailed improvements to be made. These will be indicated in connection with the definition of particular offences.

Something more should be said at once, however, about the quite unsatisfactory way in which the section is constructed in existing law. Henceforth it will be based upon the differentiation of five groups. First are attacks on sexual freedom – that is, where someone is violated or is incapable of volition, or where their dependence is exploited. The use of a ruse to pervert someone's will is included here. Group 2: protection of children and young persons. Group 3: unnatural sex acts. Group 4: defence of public morality. Finally group 5: the encouragement of others to commit sex offences.

Concerning terminology, it should be noted that by a sex offence the draft and this report understand intercourse and any other

---

'The political danger from male homosexuals consists:
1. in the reversal of man's nature-given position in relation to woman and the total destruction of all character values;
2. in the elimination of cooperation between the male and female principles and the raising of decadence to the only dominant principle;
3. in the threat it brings of moral and behavioural destruction of national communities and their central institutions;
4. in the attempt to pull homosexuals into their sphere of activity, thereby destroying in accordance with their character ever larger areas of public life;
5. in the support for opponents of our world-view – a danger which, given that there are 1.5 to 2 million homosexuals in Germany, should not be underestimated, as treason, perjury, breach of promise and suchlike are rife among homosexuals.'

R. Klare, 'Die Homosexuellen als politisches Problem'. Part 2: 'Die weibliche Homosexualität', in *Der Hoheitsträger*, vol 3, 1938, p. 17.

sexual activity, unless intercourse and sex offence are specifically distinguished. Thus sex offence without further qualification may denote homosexual relations, both between men and between women. Marital relations can be regarded as a sex offence only under special circumstances (e.g., if they take place in public). The question has been raised whether a more general qualification of the concept of sex offence should not be attempted, whether its compass is not too wide, and whether mere physical contact, for example, might not be harmless under certain circumstances. The question has been answered in the negative. Such attempts are doomed to failure. Rather, it is judicial practice which is called upon to find the proper boundaries, precisely with reference to the circumstances of the individual case and, in particular, to the healthy national attitude of the circles in question.

None of the offences under this heading should be prosecuted without regard for the injured party. But they do not thereby become offences requiring special application or authorization in the sense of current law. Disposal of state penalties can no longer, or not to the same extent as before, be granted to individuals, either in the sense that criminal proceedings are dependent upon a request by the injured party, or in the form of an absolute right of veto by the injured party. In many cases – those which are emphasized below – it is actually forbidden that the public prosecutor should heed the injured party, and at most he should consider any objections raised against prosecution (damage to reputation, reduced chances of marriage, etc.). The public prosecutor will then have to decide whether, *from the standpoint of the national community*, the objections raised by the injured party against prosecution count for more than the interest in securing a conviction. Naturally the public prosecutor will first have to convince himself that such objections are serious, and that they have not been raised as a result, for example, of bribery by the perpetrator. It will be the responsibility of the Criminal Prosecution Service to ensure that this basic standpoint prevails. The point here was only to call attention to it [...] (pp. 116–118).

Sex offence between males

It was agreed without exception that this is indisputably a punishable offence.

It had to be considered, however, whether sexual relations between women should not also be punishable. If they involve the use of violence or threats, abuse of relations of dependence, persons in care or offspring, or if they are committed against children, then they already constitute an offence under this version; further extension might also be considered in the case of corruption (see there). Otherwise the following considerations speak against an extension to women of the offence of non-aggravated homosexual relations. (In the case of men procreative capacity is wasted and reproduction is usually excluded; with women that is not the case, or at least not to the same extent.)

The vice is more widespread among men than women (apart from prostitutes); it more readily escapes observation in the case of women, is less conspicuous and therefore involves less danger of corruption by example. The intimate forms of friendly relations among women would greatly increase the existing difficulties of establishing an offence and the danger of unwarranted proceedings and investigations.

Finally, as it was already stressed in comments on the draft Austrian penal code of 1912, a major reason for the criminalization of homosexual relations is the distortion of public life which occurs when the scourge is not most emphatically opposed. The evaluation of people in public service and economic life and of their individual performance, the occupation of all kinds of office, preventive measures against abuse – all this rests upon the assumption that men think and feel in a male way and are influenced by male motives, and correspondingly in the case of women. Even if a certain tendency cannot be combated by criminal law, its activation can be countered by such means: unrestricted scope for surrendering to it would greatly encourage the spread of the disease and cause its effects to deepen. In the case of women, however, whose relative role in public life is very modest, what has been called the distortion of public life hardly comes into consideration.

The question of whether homosexual relations between men (the only relations considered from this point on) should be explicitly restricted to intercourse-like activity – in accordance with the ruling of the Reichsgericht – has been answered in the affirmative, although it cannot be denied that this covers only one – hardly the most widespread! – activity and creates a difficult problem with regard to evidence. The legislator should, however, strike the right balance in an area where excessive investigations can cause a great deal of harm, and should not include as punishable offences relatively harmless acts which, especially in youth, are in most cases only occasional aberrations due to the impossibility of normal sexual relations.

Abuse of dependence based upon a relationship of service or employment, seduction of a young man under twenty-one years of age (the culprit's own age here being above twenty-one), the committing of an offence for gain or (at an age above twenty-one years) habitually, as well as soliciting, shall be punished as aggravated sex offences with penal servitude or imprisonment of not less than six months, and only the non-aggravated remainder with prison [...] (pp. 125f.).

(b) Discussions Concerning the Prosecution of Lesbians

As a number of well-known German legal experts considered that the political dangers fantasized in relation to lesbianism were far smaller than those involved in sexual relations between men, the official Criminal Law Commission spoke out in summer 1935 against the criminalization of female homosexuality. Nothing changed in this respect until the end of the war. And yet – particularly in discussions on a draft penal code for the 'Third Reich', but also in the legal literature of the time – attempts were continually being made to alter this perception.

Little is known generally of the fate of lesbians in Nazi Germany, and still less of those who came into the sights of the Gestapo or the Kriminalpolizei and, as in the case of the Luftwaffe assistant Helene G , were deported to a concentration camp.

[21] No agreement among the experts

Extracts from discussions among Nazi jurists concerning the prosecution of lesbian relations 1936–1937

[21a] *Academy of German Law. Work preparation subcommittee of the Committee on Population Policy. Extracts from the minutes of discussions held on 2 March 1936*

Measures against sexual relations between persons of the female sex

Professor Spiethoff reported that the director of the Reich Statistical Bureau, Dr Ruttke, had asked him to raise the question of whether female homosexuality (tribadism) – which is apparently rising sharply – should not also be made a punishable offence. It is a striking fact, he argued, that Germany is one of the few countries which lets tribadism go unpunished, whereas most other countries – e.g., Austria – draw no distinction (at least in the penal code) between female and male homosexuality. A distinction should be drawn, he went on, between tribadism caused by circumstances and innate tribadism. The former is scarcely of any harm in terms of population policy, at least in the case of single and widowed women. But innate tribadism carries the danger of seduction, and if this is in reality a major danger – for which there is as yet hardly any accurate evidence – then it should certainly be considered in the context of population policy whether it should not be put on the same footing as male homosexuality.

The *chairman* expressed the view that there are so far no grounds for thinking that this matter is of sufficient importance for population policy to merit the presentation of proposals before the official Criminal Law Commission. But he declared his willingness to allow Director Ruttke the opportunity of presenting his point of view to the committee.

Assistant Secretary Dr Schäfer argued that the Criminal Law Commission should have been guided in its deliberations by the following considerations. The danger of seduction is itself not nearly as great in the case of innate tribadism as it is in that of male homosexuality. For it can generally be assumed that if a woman is seduced she will not for that reason lastingly withdraw from normal sexual relations, but will be useful as before in terms of population policy. Furthermore, the practice of this vice does not by any means do as much damage to a woman's psyche as in the case of a man, and the danger for the state is therefore by no means as great. A further reason to refrain from any penal sanctions lies in the danger of denunciations – one which is especially great because of woman's natural inclination toward effusiveness and caressing.

'The criminal law is first and foremost a law of struggle. Its enemy is anyone who threatens the survival, strength and tranquillity of the *Volk*. The aim is to eradicate not only individuals who disturb the nation's way of life but "bearers of the anti-social principle in general". *Punishment* should not be a reaction to an illegal act, but rather "*a permanent apparatus for self-purification of the national body*". [...]

There is no doubt that *homosexual activity is not a characteristic feature of German womanhood*. Indeed, it is regarded by all as immoral. Tribadism as such is an obstacle to further development of the race values, and it cannot claim to be a protector of the German heritage.

It is not clear, therefore, why female homosexual relations should not be made a punishable offence. [...]'

R. Klare, *Homosexualität und Strafrecht*, Hamburg 1937, p. 122.

It is not therefore proposed to make tribadism in general a punishable offence. But the criminal law will in future offer powerful instruments for the inclusion of cases that really do require punishment. For abuse or violation of the feeble-minded, as well as the making of an appointment depend on consent to illicit sex acts, will in future be made punishable offences.

Whereas 'seduction' through abuse of relations of dependence could previously be committed only by a man upon an unsullied virgin, the criminal law will in future provide more extensive protection by threatening to punish anyone, regardless of sex, who 'induces a person into extramarital intercourse or intercourse-like acts by abusing his or her dependence based upon a relation of service or employment'; such inducement will thus also include the intercourse of a female employer or housewife with an employee or home help. Finally, in addition to the protection of young people up to the age of fourteen, it will also become a punishable offence for anyone 'to induce a person under 18 years of age to commit together an illicit sex act, or allow himself to be used for the purposes of an illicit sex act, by abusing his or her dependence based upon a relation of service or employment'. The question largely remains open whether girls aged between 14 and 16 should be protected from seduction into homosexuality by a general definition along the lines of: 'Whoever seduces a person under 16 years of age into extramarital intercourse or intercourse-like acts, etc.' As a member of the subcommittee set up by the Criminal Law Commission to examine the text passed at the second reading, he would try to push this forward, but he could not say whether the Criminal Law Commission would be in agreement.

[...]

[21b] *Expanded committee on criminal law. Extracts from the minutes of the discussion held on 16 April 1937.*

[...]

Professor Dr Schoetensack:

If the point of view of population policy is placed in the foreground, it does also appear necessary to make so-called lesbianism a punishable offence. It has already been pointed out in earlier discussions that unfortunately this vice is especially prevalent in big cities. I know from legal circles in Basle what disturbances are caused by this vice. Sometimes it is completely devastating.

The question will therefore have to be addressed of whether it is not necessary – precisely from the standpoint of population policy – to introduce a threat of penalty. [...]

Dr Orlowsky:
There is obviously no great readiness to tackle the question of punishing women for homosexuality. It is said that a man who is homosexually active on a permanent basis gradually loses any inner capacity of having intercourse with a woman, but the same cannot be said of women. It is supposed to be of no practical significance whether the woman remains frigid or whether sexual intercourse is a real experience for her. But I would doubt that this is the key factor. One unspoken reason is perhaps that this vice is so widespread that we would have to lock up a huge number of women. [...]

Prof. Mayer:
[...] Now for the specifics! The problem of classification! I basically agree with the reporter on this, and in my book I even maintain that the problems of race, genetic health and sex offences actually form a single whole. But I should like to ask the reporter – who here thinks a little too much in starkly biological terms – to consider whether it is not more accurate to understand sex offences as the protective wall that the *Volk* erects around monogamous marriage. I am convinced that this monogamous order is the only possibility of national survival. Not only must the male and female reproductive organs be kept intact; there are also psychological prerequisites which support the reproductive capacity, and that in my view is the point of monogamous marriage. Sex offences should be understood from this point of view. [...]

And so I come now to the question of §175 and lesbianism. Section 175 is very interesting for the question of how the criminal law is able to function. As is well known, it was at first very narrowly interpreted in practice, so that sentences were meted out

---

'National Socialism has made us aware that the nation's future rests in the lap of women, that death is the nation's inevitable fate if woman denies to it the fertility of her womb. The nationally valuable forces which the creator has placed in the womb and heart of the German woman are highly esteemed and totally established in the life-and-death struggle of our nation. National Socialism has taught us that woman bears a great responsibility for protecting the purity of German blood.'

'The "ideal of beauty" of the recent past, which lifted small-breasted and narrow-breasted little painted dolls onto the throne, is beginning to totter. People are again looking to powerful, blossoming female shapes full of healthy naturalness, to the German female type whose proud physical and mental beauty embodies holy fertility and the will to live of the German *Volk*.'

Der Nationalsozialismus hat uns zum Bewußtsein gebracht, daß im Schoße des Weibes die Zukunft des Volkes ruht, daß der Volkstod unser unabwendbares Schicksal ist, wenn das Weib dem Volke die Fruchtbarkeit seines Schoßes verweigert. Die völkisch wertvollen Kräfte, die der Schöpfer in Schoß und Herz der deutschen Frau gelegt hat, werden im Existenzkampf unseres Volkes hoch gewertet und restlos eingesetzt. Der Nationalsozialismus hat uns gelehrt, daß das Weib als Hüterin der Reinheit des deutschen Blutes eine große Verantwortung trägt.

Die Wende in der Mädchenerziehung

Ein Beitrag aus der Praxis der dorfeigenen Schule

Von Franz Rade

Das „Schönheitsideal" der jüngsten Vergangenheit, welches das schmalhüftige und engbrüstige angemalte Püppchen auf den Thron hob, ist im Wanken. Man beginnt wieder aufzuschauen zu kraftvollen, blühenden Frauengestalten voll gesunder Natürlichkeit, zu dem deutschen Frauentypus, der in stolzer leiblicher und seelischer Schönheit eine heilige Fruchtbarkeit und den Lebenswillen des deutschen Volkes verkörpert.

1 9 3 7

Druck und Verlag von W. Crüwell, Dortmund-Breslau

The title page of *Die Wende in der Mädchenerziehung* [The Turn in Girls' Education] by Frank Kade, published in 1937 in Dortmund and Breslau
(Translation on opposite page)

only in very few cases. So long as there was not a really major homosexual trend, this restricted sentencing actually sufficed to maintain society's condemnation of homosexuality. But that no longer worked once it became known, through the activity of Magnus Hirschfeld and others, that a few precautions allowed one to escape punishment. Now we have sentencing which in my view has gone way beyond measure. At the conference of criminal law experts, I heard that the Münster police have even set up a special department for the prosecution of such offences. We need to be clear that mutual onanism and things reminiscent of lesbianism are simply widespread phenomena in adolescence which are certainly unwelcome, but which from the point of view of population policy it is not at all desirable to combat by means of the criminal law. One wonders whether the lesbian factor does not play such a great role that we are incapable of distinguishing these so-called impurities among young people from serious violations of the biological norm, whereas we are able to do so in the case of male homosexuality. Of course, they cease to be impurities among young people as soon as a certain age difference is present. It is very hard to establish how prevalent such bad habits are among young people. [...]

District court chairman Strauss:
[...] As regards lesbianism, it is certainly true that women with lesbian inclinations nevertheless remain capable of reproduction. Much more important, however, is the question of whether women with lesbian inclinations still summon up any will for natural intercourse. Normally this must be denied, and so it seems to me absolutely necessary to punish lesbianism as well. In my view, the reasons which have previously spoken against this have more to do with the fact that it is usually very hard to come up with evidence. But I would point out that to prove pederasty we have always had to rely on some not very pretty methods, and that we should therefore accept that the process of establishing proof will also not exactly be clean in lesbian prosecutions. It is obvious that occasional aberrations in adolescence should not be grounds for criminal proceedings. Here the establishment of the criminal proceedings committee, on the basis of the principle of expediency, ought to improve things considerably. [...]

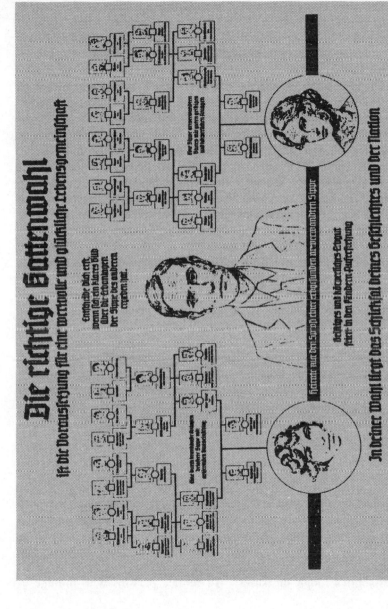

'The right choice of mate is the precondition for a worthy and happy symbiotic relationship.'
A table prepared as a teaching aid by the Reich Committee for the Health of the Nation

[22] Should §175 of the Penal Code be extended to women?
Article by People's Court Justice Ernst Jenne

I have already once answered 'yes' to this question, in the *Reichs-wart* of 22 October 1927,[1] and can only do the same again in opposition to the negative reply given by the official Criminal Law Committee in the publication 'Das kommende Strafrecht, beson-derer Teil'. [...][2]

The reasons presented there are not at all convincing. Although on the face of it women have been less important in the public life of the National Socialist state, this is not true of their more profound significance. Indeed, this has grown through the operation of the race concept, with special emphasis on heredity and eugenic considerations. Thus men and women are of equal value and importance, if women are not more important as bearers and protectors of the life of the *Volk*. Women as well as men must therefore have a healthy orientation of the sex drive, and deviations involving homosexual intercourse must be made a punishable offence. Difficulties in establishing the facts of a case, or the danger of unfounded testimony and investigations, cannot outweigh this necessity; both are also possible in the prosecution of men.

The changed times in no way undermine the argument with which the 1909 outline of an all-German penal code justified the extension of penalties to women: 'The reasons for punishing un-natural sex acts between men point logically to the punishment of unnatural sex acts between women, even if these are not so frequent or not quite so much in the public eye. The danger for family life and young people is the same. There is reliable evidence that such cases have been on the rise in recent times. It is therefore in the interests of morality and of the general welfare that women should also be made liable to punishment.'

It was only by chance that §175 was not extended to women at that time. For in the discussions of the draft, two members of parliament stated that they simply could not imagine what was meant. The extension was therefore not carried, although it would not have been anything novel or isolated in the legislation of various nations. In both past and present there have been numerous cases where male and female homosexuality have been equally threatened with punishment. Special emphasis should be given to Mussolini's tough measures: 'All female persons who indulge in

---

[1] *Reichswart*, Vol. 8, No. 43, 22 October 1927.

[2] There follows here the argument from the report on the work of the official Criminal Law Commission. See Document 20 above.

this abominable and disgustingly sordid vice are liable to punishment only if they attract attention to themselves. Then they shall be vigorously and most energetically compelled in a place of confinement to perform hard labour of use to the community.'

Concerning the storm of protest which German feminists directed at the extension of §175 in the 1909 draft, Dr E. S. W. Eberhard points out in his profound book *Feminismus und Kulturuntergang* (2nd edn., 1927) the close connection between tribadism and women's emancipation and mentions as a further significant fact 'that in nearly all so-called "female states" male but not female homosexuality is punished. Usually the punishability of tribadism has been ended with the growing influence of emancipated women.' May it suffice here, finally, to mention Dr Eberhard's view that sex research which he regards as objective refutes a differential evaluation of male and female homosexuality, including in terms of the criminal law.

In his emphasis on the dangers of tribadism Dr Eberhard fully concurs with Franz Scott, the author of a book that also appeared in the *Systemzeit*[3]: *Das lesbische Weib* (Pergamon-Verlag, Berlin). The wealth of material presented there shows perhaps even more clearly that it is right to oppose the justificatory argument mentioned at the beginning, according to which the vice is more widespread among men than women. In fact, there is good reason to believe, especially from observations in the big cities, that the author's remarks at a later point are valid: 'The problem of tribadism is beginning to come more and more into view, having worked for two whole years by festering beneath the surface. That was due partly to the connections set out at the beginning, and partly to deep fear of the eradication announced by the Führer. Those tensions have disappeared, for it is men and men alone who have been caught by what has happened.'

Nevertheless, the question of extending §175 cannot be considered to have been settled with the negative response of the official Criminal Law Committee. Is tribadism at least as harmful and dangerous as pederasty? Must both be prosecuted with equal severity, without considering in either case whether many or few cases can be included? The National Socialist state can and must not spare an area which is closed to public knowledge if it constitutes an indisputable danger. Legal safeguards against it should meet with full understanding especially from the world of German

---

[3] *Systemzeit*: the Nazi term used to refer to the Weimar Republic, highlighting the supposed centrality of a formal legal and political system. *Translator's note.*

women, which should make the matter its very own and demand that the criminal law should provide protection against sexual degeneracy regardless of gender. Here too the public interest must count as the supreme law standing higher than the fate of individuals, even if they deserve purely human sympathy.

People's Court Justice Ernst Jenne

[23] 'Heidi W. (or something similar), known as "blonde Heidi", and Frau K.'

Informer's report from the Sicherheitsdienst to the State Police Offices, Frankfurt-am-Main, 9 January 1936

According to a report received here, the above-named Frau K. is in a relationship of homosexual (lesbian) dependence upon 'blonde Heidi'. Frau K. is the divorced wife of an SS-man and appears to have been the guilty party, as she is not in receipt of any alimony. For two years she was employed as an office-worker at the H. and B. company; it has not yet been possible to establish where she lives. 'Blonde Heidi', aged 22 to 23, is the very elegant daughter of an innkeeper W., or something similar, from Langen in Hessen. He owns the largest business there but is thinking of giving up his concern in Langen and taking over a pub in Frankfurt. W. is said to have formerly played a major role in the SPD and, as an SPD big shot, to have been chief of police (or some such position) in Krefeld. In 1933 he is said to have spent a year in a concentration camp. From here it has not yet been possible to establish to what extent these claims correspond to reality.

The daughter, 'blonde Heidi', has a permanent two-room flat in Bettinastraße in Frankfurt-am-Main. Gatherings of people often take place there, and according to statements made by 'blonde Heidi' to Frau K. their composition appears highly suspicious. By all appearances what is involved here is a circle of drawing-room bolsheviks. Among other things Frau K. said the following to our contact: 'If all communists were like "blonde Heidi" everything would be all right; she is an ideal communist!' Many artists (?) and other intellectuals (sic!) are said to visit the flat regularly, and from a hint given by K. there is often 'plenty going on' there. In particular, sex orgies are often supposed to be held there.

K. is completely dependent on 'blonde Heidi'. In these circumstances it is only with the greatest skill that something could be got out of K.

'Blonde Heidi' goes a lot to the Kaffee Bettina in Bettinastraße, where she is often to be seen with elegant young girls. She also frequents the *Bauernschänke* near the 'Iron Bridge' over the Main, which is said to be a meeting place for homosexuals. All these details are based on reports by our contact, and so far it has not been possible to check their accuracy. We shall make enquiries about this matter and, if applicable, send the results there.

If something more definite can be established there, he will be asked to come and make a statement.

'Sufficient material is now available about the scale and spread of homosexuality. To be able also to combat female homosexuality (lesbianism), we urgently require information about observations made by our colleagues themselves, or reports given to our colleagues from elsewhere. For this purpose, addresses of individuals known as lesbians should be provided whenever possible. The reports should be forwarded to: Rassenpolitisches Amt – Reichsleitung – Rechtsstelle Berlin W8, Wilhelmstr. 63.'

Intelligence Service. Race Policy Bureau of the NSDAP. National Leadership, 20 June 1938, No. 49, BAK NSD 17/12.

---

[24] 'Headmistress has lesbian tendencies.'
Communication of 25 April 1938 from the Secret State Police in Munich to the NSDAP

Secret State Police   Munich, 25 April 1938
Munich Region State   Briennerstr. 50
Police Headquarters
B. Nr. 29563/38 II B b.

To the NSDAP
Bureau for Teachers
– National Socialist Teachers' League –

München
Gabelsbergstr. 26

Subject: Political assessment of schoolmistresses L. and W., both formerly at the ... school in Sch.
File: letter of 3/3/38 R/K. Personnel office.

The State Ministry for Education and Culture ordered the following on 22/1/38 No. IV 2334:
'There can be no question of readmitting the teachers Johanna L.

and Luise W. at Sch. into the public elementary school service, now that the Munich/Upper Bavaria district leadership has denied them both credentials of political reliability.'

Owing to the public prosecution of the headmistress of ... school for perjury, injurious perjury and immoral conduct, of which she has also been convicted, the ... school was closed down on 3/6/37.

L. and W. are not themselves involved in the criminal proceedings. But the whole spirit of ... school has no place at all in our times, and schoolmistresses who voluntarily took up a post at the ... school cannot be teachers in the Third Reich.

The headmistress of the ... school has lesbian tendencies and has approached individual teachers in that way. The ... school itself is a division of the Anthroposophical Society. The Anthroposophical Society was dissolved and prohibited by the order of 1/11/35 – II 1 B 2 – 69121/66/L. 35 of the Secret State Police Bureau, Berlin. The grounds were that in its historical development the Anthroposophical Society has been internationally inclined, and that still today it maintains close relations with foreign freemasons, Jews and pacifists. The educational methods based on the pedagogy of its founder Steiner, which are applied in anthroposophical schools still in existence abroad, follow an individualist mode of teaching geared to separate persons which has nothing in common with National Socialist educational principles. Because of its opposition to the *Volk* thought upheld by National Socialism, there is a danger that the interests of the National Socialist state might be endangered by further activity of the Anthroposophical Society.

[25] Luftwaffe assistant deported to a concentration camp for subversion of the military potential
A report

'My friend Helene G. from G. in Schleswig-Holstein was a Luftwaffe assistant in Oslo between 1943 and 1945. She worked as a telex operator and came under the secrecy regulations. She had telex contact with, among others, the German Embassy in Stockholm regarding espionage and agent communications. In the Luftwaffe quarters she lived in intimate companionship with another female Luftwaffe assistant who had the bad luck to please a lieutenant in the air signals corps. When she rejected his advances, the two lesbians came into the line of fire of National Socialist conventions of war. The two women were arrested by the secret military police and separated from each other. Helene G. was

brought before a court-martial for subversion of the military potential, discharged from the Wehrmacht and sent to the Bützow concentration camp in Mecklenburg. There she was put in a special
block with six other lesbians. Bützow had originally been a punishment camp for war prisoners. One block was occupied by women.
The lesbians went to a completely empty block and were guarded
by male *kapos*. When they handed them over, the SS guards said to
the war prisoners: 'These ones are the lowest form of life. We
wouldn't even fuck them with a sofa leg. If you run them through
properly, you'll each get a bottle of schnapps.' It should be known
that in the Nazi period intimate relations between German women
and foreigners were a criminal offence. The SS guards first set
Russian and French war prisoners on the imprisoned lesbians, to
'fuck them up good and proper'. The lesbians, strictly separated
from other women, were taken to work under SS guard and given
the usual concentration camp food (watery soup with rotting cab-
bage leaves and no meat or fat, and so on).

Two women died there of starvation. My friend survived the first
post-war year and then died from tuberculosis.'[4]

[26] No prosecution of lesbians
Letter from the Reich Minister of Justice, 18 June 1942

The Reich Minister of Justice   Berlin, 18 June 1942
917C Norweg./2–IIIa² 1263/42

To:
The Reichskommissar for the occupied Norwegian territories
in Oslo

Subject: Unnatural acts between women
Re the letter of 27 May 1942
– I R Just 5 Tgb. Nr. 7812 –

The results so far of the discussions of the official Commission on
Reich Criminal Law do not envisage making unnatural acts be-
tween women punishable.
The main reasons for this are as follows.

---

[4] Claudia Schoppmann has pointed out two inconsistencies in this report. (1) Bützow was
supposed to be a regular camp for prisoners of war containing only men. (2) Punishment
camps for POWs came under the Wehrmacht Supreme Command rather than the SS. 'As no
documents appear to exist about the Bützow camp, it is not possible to throw any light on
these inconsistencies. Possibly they are connected with symptoms of disintegration in the final
months of the war.' C. Schoppmann, *Nationalsozialistische Sexualpolitik und weibliche
Homosexualität*, Pfaffenweiler 1991, p. 232.

Homosexual activity between women, apart from prostitutes, is not so widespread as it is among men and, given the more intense manners of social intercourse between women, it more readily escapes public notice. The greater resulting difficulty of establishing such behaviour would involve the danger of unfounded testimony and investigations. One major reason for punishing sex offences between men – namely, the distortion of public life by the development of personal ties of dependence – does not apply in the case of women because of their lesser position in state and public employment. Finally, women who indulge in unnatural sexual relations are not lost for ever as procreative factors in the same way that homosexual men are, for experience shows that they later often resume normal relations.

p.p. Dr Schäfer

'Female homosexuality should essentially be regarded as punishable behaviour, for it is likely to undermine blood values and to draw women away from their duties to the *Volk*. However, the special circumstances of the present time – above all, the great loss of men in the world war which has reduced women's prospects of marriage – do not make it seem appropriate that lesbianism should be prosecuted under the criminal law. The definition of such an offence must be postponed because female homosexuality in its full extent is no longer simply substitute behaviour but an inner lack of stability.'

R. Klare, 'Die Homosexuellen als politisches Problem', Part Two, op. cit., p. 17.

Part III
The Stepping up of Prosecutions from 1936

(a) Nation-wide Registration of Homosexual Men

Tougher provisions in the criminal law were the most important prerequisite for the stepping up of actions against homosexual men. At the same time, Himmler's reorganization of the Criminal Police in 1936 was designed to create the administrative base for more efficient legal proceedings. Thus a central police authority was established for the whole German Reich: the Reich Criminal Police Bureau (RKPA), coming out of the Prussian Land Criminal Police Bureau (PLKA). This was reproduced, with some minor differences, by a criminal police headquarters in each of the larger non-Prussian *Länder* and of the various provinces of Prussia itself. As a rule this simply involved a renaming of the former Land criminal police bureaux. Each of the fourteen newly formed criminal police headquarters took charge of between two and six criminal police authorities, of which there were a total of fifty-five. The area covered by one of these police authorities coincided with a unit of Land government or an equivalent regional administration.

The formation of a centrally directed police force would have a lasting effect. Investigation and prosecution departments could now be deployed in unison in accordance with the conditions deemed politically necessary by the Nazi rulers. Reinhard Heydrich, as head of the Kriminalpolizei, the Security Service and the Gestapo, frankly acknowledged that 'instead of multiple fragmentation' there must emerge 'a tightly knit organization free of theoretically motivated restrictions which will firmly unite in one hand all the forces down to the last man. Any order issued by the supreme command must be immediately binding on the most junior officer, without being watered down or held up by intermediate bodies. Only this will guarantee the instantaneous deployment of the police which is essential for the struggle against enemies of the people.'[1]

The end result of this restructuring was that legal investigative authorities, the 'normal' police apparatus, were brought under the deeply anti-humanist and truly criminal conceptions of the Nazi rulers. Not only did this involve tougher action against social reprobates (such as drug addicts or prostitutes) and various lawbreakers (thieves, burglars, swindlers, violent criminals); it also meant that well-trained police forces, with their expertise and their technical-organizational apparatus, were marshalled for the investigation and isolation of people declared to be 'criminals against the German *Volk*'.

[1] *Organisation und Meldedienst der Reichskriminalpolizei*, with a preface by the head of the security police SS-Gruppenführer Reinhard Heydrich, edited by SS Police Generalmajor Nebe and SS-Obersturmbannführer, senior government and crime adviser Werner, published by the Reich Criminal Police Bureau, Berlin 1941, p. 9.

A veneer of legitimacy for action against homosexuals branded as 'national pests' [*Volksschädlinge*] was provided by Himmler's secret directive of October 1936 on the 'combating of homosexuality and abortion', which laid down a series of uniform national guidelines. These essentially gave local police authorities the power to prosecute relevant offences. A report had to be presented on special forms to the Reich Office for the Combating of Homosexuality and Abortion, newly established within the Reich Criminal Police Bureau. All local police authorities had to report not only any legal proceedings but even suspected violations of: Section 174 of the Reich Penal Code ('sex offences with dependants'), Section 176 ('coercion of children etc. to commit a sex offence'), Section 253 ('blackmail on grounds of homosexuality'), Section 175 ('sex offences between men') and Section 175a (so-called 'aggravated cases' of §175).

In the last two areas a report was only required if the persons in question: (a) were members of the NSDAP or one of its sub-divisions; (b) occupied any position of leadership; (c) belonged to the armed forces; (d) were members of a religious order; (e) belonged to the (very broadly defined) category of civil servants; (f) were Jews; or (g) held a leading position before the Nazi takeover.

In such cases the report had to be made on form B, and a (light-green) IS index card had to be filled in. This also applied to so-called rentboys, who were supposed to be completely 'eradicated' in the sense used by the Nazis. There was also a special obligation to report cases involving young people (under twenty-five) and those doing military service.

The regime's aim of compiling the fullest possible register of homosexual men opened the flood-gates for an unprecedented wave of public denunciations and for arbitrary actions on the part of the Criminal Police and the Gestapo. From the stipulations accompanying Himmler's secret directive it would appear that officers were required to make use of suitable informers. Male suspects were fingerprinted and photographed, and they remained subject to further discriminatory measures even if the suspicions were not corroborated.

All this targeting of homosexual men was coordinated and implemented by an institution set up under the terms of Himmler's secret directive: the Reich Office for the Combating of Homosexuality and Abortion.

[27] Himmler's secret directive on the combating of homosexuality and abortion
10 October 1936

The Reichsführer-SS and Head   Berlin, 10 October 1936
of the German Police at the Reich
Ministry of the Interior

SV 1 24/36g   Secret!
                                            Not to be printed in the RMBliV

To:
the Secret State Police Bureau Berlin
the Prussian Land Criminal Police Bureau, Berlin,
all regional and local headquarters of the State Police in the Reich
all regional and local headquarters of the Criminal Police in the
Reich

Subject: The combating of homosexuality and abortion

The serious danger to population policy and public health represented by the still relatively high number of abortions which are a
major violation of the fundamental National Socialist world-view,
as well as the homosexual activity of a not inconsiderable layer of
the population which poses one of the greatest dangers to the
youth, requires more than before the effective combating of these
public scourges.

1 The handling of the abovementioned offences is essentially the
responsibility of the local police.

2 In order to ensure uniform guidelines for central registration and
for effective combating of these offences, I hereby establish within
the Prussian Land Criminal Police Bureau a:
    Reich Office for the Combating of Homosexuality and Abortion.

3 Where it becomes necessary for the state police to take certain
measures, the Secret State Police Bureau should be informed and
the necessary measures set in motion there. A special department II
S is being created at the Secret State Police Bureau to deal with this
area.

4 In order to ensure swift cooperation, the special department II S
at the Secret State Police Bureau and the Reich Office for the Combating of Homosexuality and Abortion attached to the Prussian
Land Criminal Police Bureau shall be directed by the same officers.

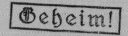

Der Reichsführer SS und Chef
der Deutschen Polizei im
Reichsministerium des Innern

Berlin, den 10. Oktober 1936

S V 1 24/36 g

Geheim!

Geheim!

Kein Abdruck im RMBliV.

Betr.: Bekämpfung der Homosexualität und der Abtreibung.

Die erhebliche Gefährdung der Bevölkerungspolitik und
Volksgesundheit durch die auch heute noch verhältnismäßig
hohe Zahl von Abtreibungen, die einen schweren Verstoß gegen
die weltanschaulichen Grundsätze des Nationalsozialismus
darstellen sowie die homosexuelle Betätigung einer nicht un-
erheblichen Schicht der Bevölkerung, in der eine der größten
Gefahren für die Jugend liegt, erfordert mehr als bisher eine
wirksame Bekämpfung dieser Volksseuchen.

1.

Die Bearbeitung der obenangeführten Delikte liegt
grundsätzlich der örtlich zuständigen Kriminalpolizei ob.

2.

Um eine zentrale Erfassung und eine wirksame Bekämpfung
dieser Vergehen nach einheitlichen Richtlinien sicherzustel-
len, errichte ich beim Preußischen Landeskriminalpolizeiamt
eine

Reichszentrale zur Bekämpfung der Homosexualität und
der Abtreibung.

An

das Geheime Staatspolizeiamt, Berlin,
das Preußische Landeskriminalpolizeiamt, Berlin,
alle Staatspolizeileitstellen und Staatspolizeistellen im Reiche,
alle Kriminalpolizeileitstellen und Kriminalpolizeistellen im Reiche.

Cover page of Himmler's secret directive of 10 October 1936 setting up the Reich
Office for the Combating of Homosexuality and Abortion.

5 From 15 October 1936 a report should be sent to the Reich Office for the Combating of Homosexuality and Abortion:

(A) in cases coming under §218 of the Penal Code,
    (a) immediately after the initiation of proceedings, if the offence was not committed by the pregnant woman alone,
        on the enclosed form A a,
    (b) for all convictions under §218
        on the enclosed form A b,
    (c) for all acquittals on the charge of abortion
        on the enclosed form A b.

(B) in criminal cases coming under §§174, 176 and 253, where they are based on homosexuality, and under §§175, 175a immediately after the initiation of proceedings
        on the enclosed form B,
    (a) if the offender is a member of the NSDAP or one of its subdivisions or occupies a position of leadership,
    (b) if the offender belongs to the armed forces,
    (c) if the offender is a member of a religious order,
    (d) if the offender is a civil servant,
    (e) if the offender is a Jew,
    (f) if persons are involved who held a leading position in the period before the taking of power.

In reports per A a and B it should be indicated whether and on what grounds it appears necessary for the state police to take certain measures. State police measures shall be ordered by special department II S within the Secret State Police Bureau upon application by the Reich Office for the Combating of Homosexuality and Abortion.

6 The Reich Office for the Combating of Homosexuality and Abortion shall maintain a national file on abortionists and rentboys. A report on individuals already known in this connection should be sent on the enclosed form I P to the Reich Office for the Combating of Homosexuality and Abortion, indicating precise personal particulars and, where possible, enclosing a photograph. Any change of address of such persons should also be notified at once.

7 Reports under paragraph 5 above to the Reich Office for the Combating of Homosexuality and Abortion do *not* relieve the local police authorities of their duty immediately to take all measures necessary to counter the offence. The Reich Office for the Combating of Homosexuality and Abortion is authorized, in agreement

with special department II S, to issue instructions on the conduct of investigations or to continue them itself.

On behalf of:
signed Heydrich

'[...] When we took power in 1933 we also discovered the homosexual associations. Their registered membership was over two million; cautious estimates by officers dealing with the matter range from two to four million homosexuals in Germany. I myself do not put the figure so high, because I do not believe that everyone in these associations was personally a homosexual in the real sense. On the other hand, of course, I am convinced that not all homosexuals were registered in the associations. My guess is between one and two million. But one million really is the minimum we can assume, the very lowest and weakest estimate permissible in this area.

Please think what that means. According to the most recent population figures, we have 67 to 68 million people in Germany – that is, taking raw figures, roughly 34 million males. So there are approximately 20 million sexually capable men (males above the age of sixteen). Perhaps this is wrong by a million, but that is of no significance.

Assuming one to two million homosexuals, the result is that roughly 7–8% of men in Germany are homosexual. If that is how things remain, our nation will fall to pieces because of that plague. A nation will not for long bear such a destruction of its sexual economy and equilibrium. [...]' (p. 93)

Heinrich Himmler, speaking on 18 February 1937 to SS-Gruppenführers at Bad Tölz, quoted from B. F. Smith and A. F. Peterson, eds., *Heinrich Himmler: Geheimreden 1933–1945 und andere Ansprachen*, Frankfurt/Main 1974, pp. 93–104.

[28]　Registration bureaucratized
Various registration forms

[28a] *Form B, used for the registration of crimes and offences under §§174, 175, 175a and 176 of the Reich Penal Code*

Meldung über Verbrechen und Vergehen
nach §§ 174, 175, 175a und 176 RStGB.

Am _____　ist bei _____

durch

Anzeige wegen Sittlichkeitsverbrechens und Vergehens nach §§ 174, 175, 175a, 176 und 253 RStGB.

Verdacht des Sittlichkeitsverbrechens und Vergehens nach §§ 174, 175, 175a, 176 und 253 RStGB. zur Kenntnis gekommen.

I. Angaben über die Person des Beschuldigten:

　1. Name und Vorname: _____

　2. Beruf: _____

　3. Wohnort und Wohnung: _____

　4. Geburtstag und Geburtsort. _____

　5. Religion (auch frühere): _____

　6. Rasse: _____

　7. Familienstand: _____

　8. Staatsangehörigkeit: _____

　9. Mittäter: _____

II. Einschlägig vorbestraft: _____

　1. als Jugendverführer bereits bekannt geworden: _____

　2. als Strichjunge bereits bekannt geworden _____

　3. als Erpresser auf homosexueller Grundlage bereits in Erscheinung getreten: _____

　4. Der Täter ist angehöriger: _____

　　(vgl. vorstehenden Erlaß B a bis f, möglichst genaue Bezeichnung).

B

Bei Verbrechen nach §§ 174, 176 und 253, soweit sie auf homosexueller Grundlage beruhen, und in den Fällen der §§ 175, 175a sofort nach Eingang einer Anzeige nach dem Vordruck B,

　　a) wenn der Täter der NSDAP oder einer ihrer Gliederungen angehört oder eine führende Stellung einnimmt,

　　b) wenn der Täter der Wehrmacht angehört,

　　c) wenn der Täter Mitglied einer Ordensgemeinschaft ist,

　　d) wenn der Täter im Beamtenverhältnis steht,

　　e) wenn der Täter ein Jude ist,

　　f) wenn es sich um Personen handelt, die in der Zeit vor der Machtübernahme eine führende Stellung innehatten.

　　In den Meldungen nach A a und B ist anzugeben, ob und aus welchem Grunde staatspolizeiliche Maßnahmen erforderlich erscheinen.

[28b] *Form IS, used for the reporting of homosexual offences among persons on military service*

[28c] *Form HJ. FR2 used for the reporting of homosexual offences involving juveniles*

A n l a g e 1
zum Meldeblatt Nr. 37 vom 24.5.1938 -Ziff.2-.

....	Meldung über homosexuelle Straftaten	An die
....	Jugendlicher !	Reichsjugendführung
	(aufzuführen sind alle Beteiligten	Personalamt
....	des Vorgangs, auch strafunmündige	-Überwachung-
Bezeichnung der	Jugendliche).	in B e r l i n NW 4
Behörde)		Kronprinzenufer 15.

Datum	Aktenzeichen:	Verfahren gegen (Hauptbeschuldigter):	Ist die Straftat durch die HJ oder den HJ-Streifendienst zur Anzeige gebracht ja – nein

Personenverzeichnis:

Nr.	Name,Vorname,Beruf. Wohnort,Straße. Geboren am, in. Glaubensbekenntnis	Haupttäter (H) Mittäter (M) Verführter (V)	HJ-Formation (Gefolgschaft/ Bann) Dienstrang	Bemerkungen.
1				
2				
3				
4				
5				
6				
7				
8				

Kurze Schilderung des Sachverhalts auf der Rückseite.

Vordruck
J. 2.

[29] Practical implementation of the secret directive
Guidelines of the Kassel Police Authority, 11 May 1937
(Extract)

State Criminal Police   11 May 1937

Kassel Criminal Police Headquarters
K 8422   Confidential

To the
Council Chairman in Eschwege

Subject: The combating of homosexuality and abortion

The enclosed guidelines of 11/5/1937 for the combating of homosexuality and abortion are being sent for perusal, with the request
that they are strictly adhered to.

Further copies of the guidelines are enclosed for the local police
authorities and the district gendarmerie.

It is requested that all efforts are made to ensure that the local
police authorities and gendarmerie officers pursue the struggle
against homosexuality and abortions with all permissible means
and in the closest contact with the criminal police office.

Special emphasis is laid on the confidentiality of the guidelines.

Enc.

State Criminal Police   11 May 1937

Kassel Criminal Police Headquarters
K 8422   Confidential

Guidelines for the combating of homosexuality and abortion

I. General
The directive of the Reichsführer-SS and Head of the German
Police within the Reich Ministry of the Interior dated 10/10/1936 –
S.V.1.24/36g – and the complementary orders of 19/12/1936[2] [...]
and 9/2/1937[3] [...] enjoin a ruthless and far-reaching struggle
against male homosexuality and abortion, on state-political
grounds and in the interests of maintaining German national
strength. [...]

---

[2] The first order on the implementation of the secret directive, dated 19/12/1936, cannot be
found. Clearly the most important repressive measures are listed in the guidelines of the Kassel
criminal police, under *II. Combating Homosexuality.*
[3] See Document 30 below.

The Head of the German Police wishes from now on to have presented to him at quarterly intervals the reported cases of homosexuality and abortion and the resulting lists of actual arrests. Officers who do not follow his guidelines in handling such cases shall be called to account.

Especially concerning homosexuality

1. Homosexual men
Homosexual men are enemies of the state and should be treated as such. What is at stake is the recovery of the German national body, the preservation and boosting of the strength of the German *Volk*. [...]

Especially dangerous are homosexuals who feel attracted to the youth. By their arts of seduction they are constantly winning over and contaminating young people. The homosexual sadist does not even shrink from murderous deeds. Experience teaches us that the victims of such a criminal are always terrifyingly high. Someone who is known as a corrupter of youth is to be mercilessly removed from human society. It should not be thought that he has done it only once. And the likelihood of a subsequent offence is so great that, in the interests of the state, it appears necessary to put him for a long time in a place of confinement.

2. Rentboys
Especially dangerous are 'rentboys' who, just like female prostitutes, support themselves from the proceeds of commercial sex. Only some of them are homosexually inclined. Men with quite normal sexual inclinations are to be found among them. They behave as pederasts in relation to homosexual men and it is purely out of self-interest that they offer themselves for immoral purposes. Male 'whores' who are homosexually inclined or think of themselves as homosexuals often have pimps, just like female prostitutes. [...] These pimps of men are especially dangerous, because they lead their dependent rentboys into theft and blackmail or themselves try to blackmail their clients. Even if there are no sections of the criminal law directed against male pimps, the police has a great interest in eradicating precisely such depraved characters. They should be recorded as participants, accomplices, aiders and abettors, or blackmailers, and steps should be taken for them to be put in a concentration camp with the help of the state police. [...]

'[. . .] We must be clear that if we continue to have this vice in Germany without being able to combat it, then it is all up with Germany and the Germanic world. Unfortunately it is not as easy for us as it was for our forebears. In their time there were a few isolated cases of an abnormal kind. The homosexual, whom they called a uranist, was lowered into the marshes. Professors who find such corpses today in the marshes are obviously not aware that in ninety per cent of cases they are dealing with a homosexual who was lowered down with his clothes and all. This was not a punishment but simply the snuffing out of an abnormal life. It had to be removed, much as we pull up nettles, put them in a heap and set fire to them. [. . .]' (p. 97)

Heinrich Himmler, speaking on 18 February 1937 to SS-Gruppenführers at Bad Tölz, quoted from B. F. Smith and A. F. Peterson, eds., *Heinrich Himmler: Geheimreden 1933–1945 und andere Ansprachen*, Frankfurt/Main 1974, pp. 93–104.

II. Combating homosexuality

1. The fight is to be waged against:

(a) homosexual men who cause offence or make a nuisance of themselves in public, especially rentboys and their hangers-on. They should be convicted through constant surveillance of roads open to traffic, railway stations, parks, public conveniences, employment exchanges, public houses, etc., if necessary with the assistance of confidential agents. The aim is to eradicate rentboys completely, by removing the opportunities for their services.

(b) homosexual men who are particularly careful and operate more secretly by taking victims to their room, to hotels and tourist accommodation or by approaching them on walks and rambles. They draw attention by, among other things, avoiding association with women and appearing almost exclusively in male company, often arm in arm. Hotel doormen, station porters, taxicab drivers, toilet attendants, hairdressers (especially at stations and hotels) and bath attendants are well suited to provide information for the apprehension of such homosexuals.

(c) homosexual men who do their mischief when in charge of young people in schools, youth organizations, military institutions and monasteries. Occasional remarks by young people and inmates of such institutions about strange behaviour on the part of their teachers or fellow-inmates will provide the basis for a summons.

By order of the chief of police, Leipzig, Department II
9 April 1935
By reason of public order and as a measure of public protection of
juveniles exposed to seduction and abuse, W. is hereby *forbidden* in
the urban area of Leipzig, under penalty of 14 days' imprisonment
for each contravention:
to enter the entire Promenade Ring and the public conveniences
located there, the parks attached to the main railway station, its
entrance halls, cross-platforms and conveniences, as well as
conveniences open to the public in department stores, automats and
fixed-price stores, city woodlands, green spaces and parks, *in order
to establish contact* with male persons for immoral purposes.
    Appeal may be made against this order to the district captain
within a period of fourteen days.
    The present order has been notified to W. on 9 April 1935 and
delivered to him in one copy.

[signed: Signature]

'Strichverbot' from Leipzig chief of police, Leipzig. Staatsarchiv Leipzig PP-S 6213.

2. It is necessary:
(a) to keep a constant check on hotel and pension guests – homo-
     sexuals like taking double rooms.
(b) to monitor the advertising section of daily newspapers for sus-
     picious offers etc. likely to have been inserted by homosexuals.
(c) to register all male persons suspected of having homosexual
     inclinations.
(d) that a police officer who wishes to combat homosexuality effec-
     tively should have contact with all layers of the population. He
     must have sharp ears and check up in appropriate ways on
     suspicious remarks made by national comrades about osten-
     sibly abnormal men. It is also often advisable to make use of
     reliable and trustworthy intermediate agents. In this way he
     must get to know directly every individual in his local area who
     is regarded as sexually abnormal.
(e) to maintain careful files or lists which must show clearly the
     homosexual's name and address, and the nature and date of his
     offence. Rentboys, blackmailers, corrupters of youth must be
     specifically identified as such.
(f) to cooperate closely with the criminal police and public health
     authorities. In all important, difficult and large-scale cases, or
     where there is a lack of suitable collaborators, a request should
     immediately be made for the expert cooperation of special

officers of the Kassel Criminal Police, who may, if applicable, make contact with the relevant offices of the state police.

3. Action against homosexuals:

(a) Offences committed by homosexuals shall be punished under Sections 174, 175, 175a, 176 para. 3, 183, 253 and 361 paras. 6 a–c.

(b) All known homosexual men are to be detained for police purposes, photographed and fingerprinted. If they are suspected of having committed punishable offences, they should be brought before a judge.

In such cases it should always be assumed that there is a danger of suppression of evidence. If a punishable offence cannot be proven, they should on no account be immediately released. After photographing and fingerprinting, they should be thoroughly searched for letters from like-minded people and friends, and their accommodation should also be closely inspected. If these searches do not yield any incriminating material, so that no further action can be taken, the suspects should be given a detailed warning, kept under observation and checked up on again and again. If they again arouse suspicions, a special report should be sent to the Kassel Criminal Police so that it can take the required measures.

(c) It must be ensured that the processing of homosexuals takes place without any disturbance. It is not permissible to conduct the interrogations and other official procedures in the presence of third parties who have no light to shed on the case.

(d) It is absolutely necessary that the officer in charge of the case should perform his duties with tact and, in particular, that he should treat with the required sensitivity wayward youths under the age of twenty-one, who in minor cases may be let off by the court. It would be most reprehensible if he were to let himself be tempted to ask unnecessarily embarrassing questions and to dig around in 'erotic matters'. He will do his duty only if a man seduced into homosexuality or a victim of blackmail gains the impression that the police want not only to inflict the deserved punishment but also to help him become a respectable person again. Someone being blackmailed must lose his inhibitions about making a statement to the police. He must be convinced that without their help he will never be rid of his 'tormentor', and that the police will treat his statements with understanding and the greatest discretion. Reference should be made to Section 154b of the State Police Regulations.

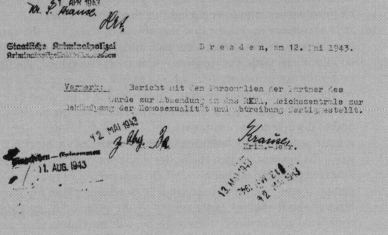

Reichskriminalpolizeiamt
Reichszentrale zur Bekämpfung
der Homosexualität und Abtreibung

Nr. _____ 194 3 /B3d

Berlin C2, den _17. 4. 194 3
Werderscher Markt 5/6

An die
Staatliche Kriminalpolizei
Kriminalpolizei-leit-stelle

in   D r e s d e n

2 APR 1943

Betrifft: Erich ....b.2 .6.1?14
wegen widernatürlicher Unzucht

Bezug: ...T.13 von 4. 4. 1?43 -...b...r.T.T.III 3o?55/43 -

Ich bitte um Mitteilung der Personalien der Partner, mit denen der Obenbezeichnete
sich homosexuell betätigt hat, und um kurzen Tatbericht.

I. A.

Do.

(a) A letter from the Reich Office for the Combating of Homosexuality and Abortion to
the Dresden Criminal Police Headquarters, requesting personal details about the
partner of a homosexual man, Erich ...

(b) Notification that such a report has been prepared

(e) If necessary, special care measures should be taken in the case of juveniles.

4. Compulsory registration on form

[...]⁴

[30] Second order for the implementation of Himmler's secret directive

(Extract)

Head of the Security Police   Berlin, 9 February 1937
Daybook No. S-PP (II H) 2 86 1/37

To:
the Secret State Police Bureau Berlin
the Prussian Land Criminal Police Bureau Berlin,
all regional and local headquarters of the State Police in the Reich
all regional and local headquarters of the Criminal Police in the Reich

Subject: Combating homosexuality and abortion. Second order for the implementation of the directive of the Reichsführer-SS and Head of the German Police, Reich Ministry of the Interior, 10 October 1936 – SV 1 24/36g

Reports so far received and various queries give reason to clarify the provisions of the directive as follows:

On Clause 1. Insofar as the matter has not yet been dealt with by the state police and there are no political aspects in evidence, it is the responsibility of the criminal police with jurisdiction in the area – i.e., of the local police authorities competent both geographically and in terms of substance – to handle the above-mentioned offences.

However, the importance of the matter, as well as experience so far, make it more necessary than before that there should be collaboration of a more informed nature between special officers of the state and the criminal police. In order to ensure this, I request that so far as possible special officers should be more widely employed on all major cases.

On Clause 3. Measures should be taken by the state police if the offender's behaviour represents (in nature or scale) a threat to population policy or public health, a serious violation of the funda-

---

⁴ There follow instructions for compulsory registration and completion of the forms. Cf. Document 28.

mental principles of the National Socialist world-view, or a danger to the youth. Preventive detention is to be included among state-police measures.

This is authorized particularly if public security and order is directly threatened by the nature or scale of the offender's behaviour.

In especially urgent cases, an application for preventive detention may be made to the relevant state police authority, with reference to this directive.

The state police authority shall then proceed in accordance with the existing provisions.

On Clauses 5 and 6. The provisions of the directive apply *mutatis mutandis* to state police authorities.

In every case it should be indicated on forms Aa and B whether and when the offender has been arrested (type of custody) and in which institution he is at that time.

The facts of the case should then be briefly outlined, including any previous legal proceedings against the offender (with the references of the prosecutor's office). A delay should not occur on this account to reports under points 5 and 6 [...].

The Reich Criminal Police Bureau in Berlin (Werderscher Markt). Also the location of the Reich Office for the Combating of Homosexuality and Abortion.

[31] 'I expect the Secret State Police and the Criminal Police to collaborate in the closest way …'

Reinhard Heydrich in a directive dated 4 March 1937

Head of the Security Police   Berlin, 4 March 1937
S-Kr. 1 No. 245/37

To:
the Secret State Police Bureau
the Prussian Land Criminal Police Bureau
all regional and local headquarters of the Criminal Police
all regional and local headquarters of the State Police

Since the reorganization the Security Police comprises the Secret State Police *and* the Criminal Police. They both come under a single leader. It is of no significance, therefore, whether their jurisdictions are today already as clearly delimited as it would appear desirable for them to be. There will always be situations where the jurisdictions cut across each other (fires, explosions, suspected sabotage, §175, §218). I expect that the Secret State Police and the Criminal Police will collaborate in the closest way, and I shall have no sympathy if, as so often in the past, friction and misunderstandings occur. I request mutual support, mutual reporting and involvement in every case, and – once the other's jurisdiction is established – the handing over of cases accordingly. I have heard that things will not be done in accordance with this order, and so I reserve the strongest measures against the officers in question.

signed: Heydrich

(b) The Reich Office for the Combating of Homosexuality and Abortion – an Instrument of Practical Implementation

The Reich Office for the Combating of Homosexuality and Abortion belonged to a system of fifteen central registration offices which were either taken over from departments existing before 1933 in the Prussian Land Criminal Police Bureau (LKPA), or else founded in 1936 in the course of the reorganization of the Criminal Police. Their basis was provided by already existing police records departments. These Reich Offices were locked into the Reich Criminal Police Bureau (RKPA). After the beginning of the war, the Criminal Police department at the Headquarters of the Security Police was merged with the RKPA in the Reich Security Headquarters (Reichssicherheitshauptamt – RSHA), the terror centre of the SS. From then on, the various Reich Offices belonged to Bureau V for the Combating of Crime (the original RKPA).

At Bureau V the Reich Office for the Combating of Homosexuality and Abortion came under Task Group B, Department 3: Immorality. This department included four other Reich Offices, dealing respectively with the combating of obscene materials, the international white slave trade, drug offences and vice.

The tasks of the Reich Offices were essentially to compile records on criminals and people declared to be criminals or anti-social elements, which would be available on file to the Criminal Police and Gestapo so that they could act as quickly as possible against people denounced as 'habitual criminals', 'social pests', 'enemies of the people' or 'sex fiends'.

The same was basically true of people and case areas which came under the Reich Office for the Combating of Homosexuality and Abortion. Its activity ranged from the recording of all manifestations of homosexuality, through the registration of transvestites and so-called waged abortionists, to the monitoring of the production and sale of abortifacients and contraceptives.

The most important task of the Reich Office was to quantify, index and compare relevant data, with the aim of recording as many incriminated individuals as possible. In 1940, four years after it was set up, its data bank stored personal details of 41,000 men convicted or suspected of being homosexuals. (Once a file had been opened on an individual about whom there was a complaint, the Reich Office was authorized to request personal details about his sexual partners.)

Special card indexes were compiled on so-called rentboys and corrupters of the youth. As the regime considered them 'incorrigible' and 'especially dangerous', they had to face particularly severe measures. Thus, in its annual report for 1939 the Reich Office stated: 'During the war rentboys and corrupters of the youth have repeatedly used the blackout for their own purposes. Hopefully a number of recent deterrent sentences will not fail to have their effect. In numerous cases, of course, preventive detention [in a concentration camp – G.G.] has also been imposed.'[5] A year later followed Himmler's decree formally legalizing internment in a concentration camp for those groups of people.[6] In the few cases where we know the fate of men convicted as corrupters of the youth (under §§174 and 176) or more than once as rentboys under §175, they were sent after serving their sentence to a concentration camp and castrated.

The central data bank also put the Reich Office in a position to initiate

[5] [A. Nebe], *Jahrbuch Amt V (Reichskriminalpolizeiamt) des Reichssicherheitshauptamtes der SS 1939/1940*, [Berlin?], p. 17.
[6] See Document 89.

and/or coordinate measures for the arrest and prosecution of people suspected of relevant offences, and special powers were conferred upon it for this purpose. In certain cases it could order the deployment of mobile units with full powers of arrest. And its records were used to supply institutions as well as selected individuals doing official research into the supposed prevention and cure of the 'scourge' of homosexuality. Examples of such investigations are known at the Institute for General Psychiatry and Military Psychology of Miliary Group C at the Academy of Military Medicine in Berlin (director: Prof. Otto Wuth), the German Institute for Psychological Research and Psychotherapy, Berlin (director: Prof. Mathias Heinrich Göring), and the Teaching and Research School for Human Heredity and Race Policy at the University of Jena (director: Prof. Karl Astel). There was also close collaboration with the forensic-biological investigation and data-gathering centres attached to penal institutions, especially on matters concerning the supposedly hereditary determination of homosexuality and the effects of castration.

Although the decree setting up the Reich Office stated that all relevant offences would come under local police jurisdiction, close links were established with the Gestapo. It had to be called in if, according to Nazi thinking, the offender's behaviour represented a threat to population policy or public health, a serious violation of the fundamental principles of the National Socialist world-view, or a danger to the youth. On these grounds the special department set up within the Secret State Police Bureau in 1934 remained in existence until the outbreak of war; and the direction of the Gestapo department and the Reich Office were placed in the hands of a single person. Both answered to the SS and Crime Officer Josef Meisinger, a brutal man widely feared (even in the SS) because of his unscrupulous behaviour.[7] In 1940 a change took place when Meisinger was posted to Warsaw and his place was taken by Erich Jakob (who since 1935 had been director of the abortion department of the Berlin police). In 1943 he had at his disposal a staff of roughly seventeen, and in June SS-Sturmbannführer Dr Carl-Heinz Rodenberg became its scientific director. As a neurologist and psychiatrist he had been an adviser to the High Court of Hereditary Health in Berlin, and he had the reputation of consistently advocating an extension of the grounds for compulsory castration of male homosexuals.[8]

From 1936 the Reich Office was the crucial body in the Nazis' programme against homosexual men. Although even today little is

[7] On Meisinger see S. Aronson, *Reinhard Heydrich und die Frühgeschichte von Gestapo und SS*, Stuttgart 1971, p. 232; and B. Jellonek, *Homosexuelle unter dem Hakenkreuz*, Paderborn 1990, pp. 102ff.

[8] On Jakob and Rodenberg see C. Schoppmann, *Nationalsozialistische Sexualpolitik und weibliche Homosexualität*, op. cit., pp. 194ff, esp. 198f.

known about the individual fate of men listed in its records, there can be no doubting the fact that they were dehumanized in the bureaucratic abstraction of figures and columns. The columns of homosexual men in the concentration camps exist first of all as columns of figures in the records of the Reich Office. In other words, acts of bureaucratic registration preceded acts of criminal prosecution.

[32] Nation-wide activity
The tasks of the Reich Offices (Extract)

The Reich Offices – including the Reich Office for the Combating of Homosexuality and Abortion set up by the Decree of 10/10/ 1936, RF SS and ChdDtPol., S.V. 1 24/36g – carry out their activity for the whole area of the Reich. They collect reports received from Criminal Police authorities or elsewhere and analyse them in an appropriate manner. They maintain card indexes of punishable offences and lawbreakers [...]. The corresponding index material located at the Criminal Police Headquarters Berlin and the former Prussian Intelligence Office should be handed over to the Reich Offices.

[33] The staff of the special homosexuality and abortion department at the Secret State Police Bureau
From the Gestapo Bureau's planned division of responsibilities, 1 July 1939 (Extract)

Section II
[...]

Department II S: The Combating of Homosexuality and Abortions

Head of Department: SS-Obersturmbannführer, Undersec. Meisinger
Deputy: SS-Sturmbannführer, Undersec. Stage

Area II S 1: Combating of homosexuality
Director: Police commissioner Schiele
Deputy: Police inspector Fehling

Area II S 2: Combating of abortion
Director: Police commissioner Kaintzik
Deputy: SS-Untersturmbannführer, Police commissioner Georg Müller

[34] A list of the Reich Offices
Their structure after the formation of the Reich Security Headquarters (Overview)

[...] Group B handles the executive side of the Reich Criminal Police Bureau. The Reich Offices are amalgamated in the following departments:

Dept. B 1: Serious Crime
(a) Reich Office for the Combating of Serious Crime (homicide, manslaughter, robbery and robbery by blackmail, brutal crimes and poaching)
(b) Reich Office for the Combating of Serious Crime (arson and explosions, road accidents and industrial accidents)
(c) Reich Office for Missing Persons and Unidentified Corpses
(d) Reich Office for the Combating of International and Interregional Pickpockets
(e) Reich Office for the Combating of Itinerant and Professional Burglars

Dept. B 2: Deception
(a) Reich Office for the Combating of Itinerant and Professional Swindlers and Forgers (general deception)
    Reich Office for the Combating of Fake Works of Art
(b) Reich Office for the Combating of Itinerant and Professional Swindlers and Forgers (business fraud)
(c) Reich Office for the Combating of Deception (corruption of and among public officials)
(d) Reich Office for the Combating of Gambling and Cheating
(e) Reich Office for the Combating of Swindles Involving Money, Securities and Postage Stamps

Dept. B 3: Immorality
(a) Reich Office for the Combating of Obscene Pictures, Writings and Advertisements
(b) Reich Office for the Combating of the International White Slave Trade
(c) Reich Office for the Combating of Drug Offences
(d) Reich Office for the Combating of Homosexuality and Abortion
(e) Reich Office for the Combating of Immorality and Sex Offences [...] (p. 60)

[35] Areas of work within the Reich Office for the Combating of Homosexuality and Abortion

From the RSHA division of labour plan (Extract)

Group	Dept.	Section	Area	Involvement	
				Bureau V	Other bureaux
B*	3*	d	*Reich Office for the Combating of Homosexuality and Abortion* All manifestations of homosexuality Transvestites Abortion Registration of all waged abortionists Monitoring of population movements Monitoring of production and sale of abortifacients and contraceptives Monitoring of activity of foreign abortionists consulted by German women Combating of all enemies of positive population growth	IV	IV, VI

* Group B: Task group; Department 3: Immorality

[36] Staff of the Reich Office for the Combating of Homosexuality and Abortion
From the RSHA division of labour plan (Extract)

Consultant (deputy)	Section leader	Specialists	
Assistant consultant			
KR* Jakob	KR* Jakob	KOS†	Nelbe
		KOS	Grünning
		KOS	Klemp
			Saeftel
		KS‡	Seiler
			Mutke
		KS	Sonnabend
		KS	Hunger
		KS	Müller
		KS	Bornhöfer
		KS	Schubert
		KS	Bleser
		KS	Bock
		KS	Schubbeske
		KS	Runge
		KS	Schwanz
		KOA§	Glemmann

Approximate civil-service grade equivalents: * Kriminalrat = Undersecretary, Criminal Police; † Kriminalobersekretär = Secretary, Criminal Police; ‡ Kriminalsekretär = Junior Secretary, Criminal Police; § Kriminaloberaufseher = Superintendent, Criminal Police. *Translator's note.*

[37] Registration of homosexual men
The Criminal Police Registration Office (Extract)

[...] The Criminal Police Registration Office for homosexuals and abortionists is governed by the provisions of the unpublished directive of 10 October 1936 (see *Ausf. Erl.* 11a, p. 64).

These regulations make it perfectly clear that reports on homosexuals and abortionists should be provided not on the RKP forms 13 and 14 but on the specially designed forms IS, Aa, Ab and B. [...]

These forms should be used, however, only in the case of punishable offences by male persons. Punishable offences committed by female persons (immorality etc.) should be reported only on forms RKP 13 and 14, because they involve category VII sect. A or C [...] offences. The police authorities compiling the report must also distinguish between category VII sect. B 1 and 2 offences (homosexuality and abortions), for which the Reich Office for the Combating of Homosexuality and Abortion is responsible, and those falling under category VII sect. A and C (immorality and sex offences of every kind), which belong to the work area of the Reich Office for the Combating of Immorality and Sex Offences.

If members of Hitler Youth organizations are involved as chief culprits or accomplices or seduced parties in cases concerning homosexual offences, the Reich Youth Leadership should also be directly notified on form HJ.FR. 2 [...]. (p. 101)

[38] 'The combating of homosexuality and abortion as a political task'

Lecture by Josef Meisinger [head of the Reich Office], delivered at the assembly of medical heads of department and experts on 5/6 April 1937 in Berlin (Extract)

Homosexuality and abortion appear at first sight to be two quite different offences. But in reality they have much in common, particularly in their effects. First of all, from the point of view of the criminal law, they differ from all other offences in the Penal Code by the fact that there is no victim, at least not in the narrow sense of the term, who has any interest in prosecuting the breach of the law. With both homosexuality and abortion, everyone involved has an equal interest in maintaining secrecy.

Whereas the incidence of non-political crimes has undoubtedly shown a considerable decline since the taking of power, this cannot be said of the offences of homosexuality and abortion. There can be no doubt that of all crimes and offences those under §§175 and 218 are the most widely and most frequently committed, but unfortunately also the ones which most affect the living marrow of a nation. That is why, more than any criminal behaviour which has attracted a more or less high punishment, homosexuality and abortion have throughout history been a fundamental problem of politics.

First, then, on homosexuality. Homosexuality has not appeared in recent times but has been known in all nations and in all periods. One thing is certain and that is that the centre from which homosexuality has spread so widely is to be sought in Asia. From there it found its way among the Greeks and Romans and finally the Teutons as well. It can already be seen from this path of radiation that homosexuality is alien in kind to the Nordic race. [...]

In the period before the war, homosexuality stayed at a moderate level in Germany. After the war, however, it became so widespread in Germany that people in England and France called it the

'German disease'. This description, by the way, would seem to be completely inappropriate. With no less right one could call it the 'French or English disease'. But in the end homosexuality rose so much in Germany that immediately after the Marxist revolution, homosexuals used the unbridled freedom of the time to form clubs and associations that would represent their interests. [...]

During the taking of power, or after the taking of power, it was a terrifying fact – which we should not try to hush up here – that the number of legal proceedings initiated under §175 increased enormously over 1932. Of course, it would be quite wrong to conclude from this alone, or from the number of people convicted, that homosexuality was itself increasing. We must naturally also take into account the greater public readiness to report as a result of National Socialist education, as well as the more intensive police activity and the clearer judicial practice. But it was precisely the more intensive policing which showed to a frightening degree just how widely homosexuality had spread. [...]

This is probably most striking in the Berlin police figures on sex crimes – or, to be more precise, sex offences on boys under 14 years of age. There were 56 cases in 1920, 70 in 1921, 89 in 1922, 104 in 1924, 281 in 1933 and 297 in 1934. The statistics have not yet been finalized for 1935 and 1936. It is obvious that this rise in crimes is not due simply to a greater willingness to report. The growth is mainly due to the fact that, because of the way in which young people are present in large numbers today, a sex offender is able to approach several at any one time. If a homosexual manages to win over a juvenile from a group or a crowd, then experience shows that his friends will also be abused by the seducer in question. It is not unusual for homosexuals to say frankly, under questioning or in a confession, that they have done their filthy homosexual business with fifty boys or more. There used to be roughly two child seductions per sex offender, but that figure is now many times higher. To go into details would take us too far for the time available here. But I would like to mention some major cases we have dealt with recently, as examples of crimes against young people. The Jew Obermayer, who had 800 cases attributed to him in which all the victims were under sixteen, was only sentenced a few weeks ago in Würzburg to 10 years' penal servitude, 10 years' loss of civil rights and detention in perpetuity.[9] One of the oldest Gymnasia – an institution which can look back on a four-hundred-year history

---

[9] On the shocking fate of the gay Jew Leopold Obermayer, see the study by E. Fröhlich, 'Ein Volksschädling', in M. Broszat and E. Fröhlich, eds, *Bayern in der NS-Zeit*, Munich 1983, pp. 76–114.

– had to be closed down because it emerged from investigations that only twenty of its pupils had not been seduced by their teachers. It is the Schulpforta near Naumburg. The sex crimes of one Lippold, who was also sentenced a short time ago to 8 years' penal servitude, also run into the hundreds. But there is another case which, perhaps because the man involved had committed still greater crimes, has not featured all that prominently in this group. This is the Seefeld case. Not only did Seefeld commit the 20 or so murders to which he eventually confessed; his sex crimes also run into the hundreds and hundreds. Seefeld himself admitted that not a week went by in which he did not homosexually assault some boy or other.

Gentlemen! It is impossible to speak of homosexuality and the corruption of young people without mentioning the institutions which for centuries raised this national scourge behind their walls and·which, with all their hypocrisy, have found nothing abhorrent in such crimes over the last few centuries. Whereas cases of pederasty were virtually unknown among the Teutons before they came into contact with Rome and Christianity, such cases increased with the missions advancing into Germanic provinces. In the oldest Germanic laws no special punishment is laid down for homosexuality. This vice attracted the death penalty or proscription under customary law. During the missionary age the prosecution of pederasty and sodomy was assigned to the Church, which at that time already had to take frequent action against missionary monks, as may also be seen by the many orders of synods and councils. In this connection may I remind you of Emperor Justinian, who had 55 bishops executed in Rome for the defilement of boys. At that time the Church also recognized the death penalty for homosexuality. Later, however, under Pope Sixtus IV in the fifteenth century, pederasty was permitted against the payment of a tax. May I briefly mention that this same pope had a yearly income of 20,000 gold ducats which in the end came from the earnings of houses of ill-repute. The pope was himself very active in this area: he made his 17-year-old friend a cardinal, thus raising him to the highest honour after that of pope.

I think I can speak openly here. Monastic life and homosexuality have for centuries been inseparable from each other. Homosexuality is a method the Church used to build the monastic settlements, the monastic communities. So long as inmates of monasteries – who as such are lost to the state – do their business only among themselves, the state may not have all that great an interest in uncovering and prosecuting such offences. But what if monasteries claim to give young people quite special protection from moral dangers, while in reality they abuse boys put in their care by trusting parents or sick people assigned to them by the state, in the way that investigations in recent months have shown to be the case in monasteries? Well, then the state has not only the right but a damned duty to ensure that our most valuable asset is not placed in the hands of criminals.

Believe me, gentlemen, it is impossible to describe in words the hideous things that came to light in the investigations of recent months in various monasteries. It was impossible to publish anything like that in the papers, starting with the intercourse during confession, at the altar and so on. But I would stress one thing: this was not just a special case of a badly run order; the fact is that such crimes happened wherever the investigations were carried out, regardless of whether those involved were hospitallers, Franciscans or others. For anyone who saw the weeping parents, the weak, helpless and feeble-minded pupils, for anyone who was able to follow the common criminal types communicating with their lawyers in the courtroom, the impression will not fade away for the rest of their life. It would take us too far to speak in this context of sex offences and the Church. One thing must be stressed, however: in nearly every case the authorities in charge of the monastery were aware of the monks' transgressions. This was also true of the case you probably read about in Saturday's papers – the sex murder on Good Friday in Lüttich. Here again you see what we are continually seeing in the Rhineland and everywhere we go – a scourge that has been practised for decades without it ever having been possible to do anything serious against it. Nor can the things that have sometimes happened in the Rhineland be explained away in terms of over-subtlety on the part of the Secret State Police; it is just that here for once energetic action was taken. It had been known of for a long time. There were files on it in every possible police authority and in a number of prosecution departments.

Since, as we know, homosexuals are useless for normal sexual intercourse, homosexuality also has an effect on young blood and will inevitably lead to a drop in the birth-rate. The result is a general weakening of the nation's strength, of the kind that threatens not least a nation's military capacity. In the end, however, homosexuality is a permanent threat to order in the life of the state. Apart from being itself a punishable violation of that order, it is especially dangerous because it is often the starting-point for a series of further crimes. Very often it comes as a preliminary to treason, and in numerous cases it lays the basis for blackmail. A blackmailer knows that his silence is of great value to a homosexual, and so he tries to make capital out of that fact. It is well known that blackmailers are utterly ruthless with their victims, so that when the money has finally run out they urge them to find more by committing new crimes, especially ones of fraud and embezzlement.

'A Reich Office for the Combating of Homosexuality and Abortion has been created within the Reich Criminal Police Bureau. The technical director of this office is SS-Obersturmbannführer Dr Rodenberg, its criminal director SS-Sturmbannführer Undersecretary Jakob. In accordance with the basic principles contained in the order of the SS Justice Headquarters regarding cooperation between sections of the Security Police on criminal cases (*Anordnungsblatt* 1943, Sect. 47), the SS and police courts should, whenever necessary, use the support of this Reich Office in relevant criminal proceedings. The additional involvement of Bureau IV of the Reich Security Headquarters, as prescribed in Sect. 71 of the *Anordnungsblatt* 1943, is no longer applicable.'

Sammelerlasse. Der Reichsführer-SS. Hauptamt SS-Gericht, 15 April 1944. Personal file of Karl-Heinrich (Carl-Heinz) Rodenberg. Berlin Document Center.

It is particularly common for rentboys to go in for blackmail. They are mostly work-shy and degenerate young people who, whatever their sexual orientation, prostitute themselves to homosexuals and then often use the opportunity for blackmail. How far blackmail can go was shown by a recently detected case in which a single man, over a period of not quite three years – he came from highly respected circles – made a total of 120,000 marks in cash by blackmailing a number of individuals. But a real fight against blackmail presupposes a similar one against homosexuality.

If one is really to appreciate the hidden danger of homosexuality, it is no longer enough to consider it as before from a narrowly criminal viewpoint. Because it is now so enormously widespread, it has actually developed into a phenomenon of the most far-reaching consequence for the survival of the nation and state. For this reason, however, homosexuality can no longer be regarded simply from the point of view of criminal investigation; it has become a problem with political importance. This being so, it cannot be the task of the police to investigate homosexuality scientifically. At the most it can take account of scientific conclusions in its work. Their task is to ascertain homosexual trends and their damaging effects, so as to avert the danger that this phenomenon represents for nation and state. No one says to the police: you shouldn't arrest this thief because he might have acquired kleptomania. Similarly, once we have recognized that a homosexual is an enemy of the state, we shan't ask the police – and much less the Political Police – whether he has acquired his vice or whether he was born with it. I should mention here that experience has shown beyond doubt that only a vanishingly small number of homosexuals have a truly homosexual inclination, that most of them by far have been quite normally active at one time or another and then turned to this area simply because they were sated with life's pleasures or for various other reasons such as fear of venereal diseases. I should also say that, with firm education and order and regulated labour, a great number of homosexuals who have come to the attention of the authorities have been taught to become useful members of the national community.

In connection with the combating of homosexuals, may I here briefly dwell on a problem that has often arisen in the recent period: namely, the combating of lesbianism. In our view the danger to the nation's survival is here not at all as great as in the case of homosexual men. Quite different presuppositions are involved. First, it should not be forgotten that in Germany we have always had more females than males; second, we lost two million men in the war; and third, that of the available men several more million do not count because they are homosexuals. The fact that a sizeable part of the female sex is in a state of sexual crisis cannot be denied. To the best of our knowledge, however – insofar as it has been at all possible to carry out reliable and discreet investigations – most girls who are active as lesbians are far from being abnormally inclined. If such girls later have the opportunity to assume the purpose given them by nature, they will certainly not decline. Many other factors are involved in lesbian activity: e.g., a lack of male acquaintances, a stern upbringing, and so on. If we are really to speak of lesbian activity, it is crucially important to ask what was the object of mental images when sexual behaviour was taking place. There is reason to suppose that for an overwhelming majority the imagination was directed to normal intercourse. Proof of this is the onanistic devices often found among women, not least the ever popular candle.

Abortion is no less dangerous than homosexuality to the state. As a phenomenon of national life, abortion is not the aberration of just one period. Like homosexuality it has accompanied the life of nations since the earliest times. [. . .]

[39] Charging of 28,882 men in 1938
From the Reich Office report for 1938

[...] In 1938 the Reich Office for the Combating of Homosexuality and Abortion was able to chalk up some major successes in improving registration. Good progress was also made in developing cooperation with other authorities and departments. [...]

The statistics for 1938 show the following picture:

(A) Abortion: total: 28,366 cases handled
     Of which established as
     1. Self-abortions: 5017
     2. Abortions by third parties: 9947
     3. Fatalities due to abortion: 288
(B) Homosexuality: total: 28,882 persons charged
     Of which,
     1. Corrupters of young people: 7472
     2. Rentboys: 587

Assessment of the material received by the Reich Office made it necessary, even in the year coming to an end, to set up so-called special commissions in certain areas of the Reich. These units have operated with great success [...][10] (pp. 20f.).

[40] 'Profitable cooperation' with various departments and institutions
From the Reich Office reports for 1939 and 1940

[1939]:
The Reich Office for the Combating of Homosexuality and Abortion, which was initially allocated to the Secret State Police Bureau, has again belonged since October 1939 to the Reich Criminal Police Bureau.

With regard to the combating of abortion, in addition to the card-indexing and assessment of reported abortionists, a large number of investigations were directly ordered in various parts of the Reich [...].

Up to the present time some 8000 wage-abortionists have been put on card indexes; this figure includes 1020 doctors, 495 midwives and 355 healers, as well as approximately 4090 female and 2040 male non-professionals.

---

[10] Various details follow about 'special operations' against doctors and midwives, but not about operations directed against homosexual men.

In general, all the signs are that abortion crimes have further [...] decreased in the course of 1939.

At present 33,000 individuals are recorded at the Reich Office as pederasts. This figure includes 7800 corrupters of young people and seducers involved in a number of serious cases, as well as 3800 rentboys.

It should be borne in mind that not all admitted homosexual activity is recorded on card indexes. The above figures reflect the still quite widespread nature of this scourge, which should be treated all the more seriously in that many homosexuals can scarcely be regarded as reformable offenders. Thus, the compilation of central records has laid the greatest stress upon special observation of the last-named group of people. During the war rentboys and corrupters of the youth have repeatedly used the blackout for their own purposes. Hopefully a number of recent deterrent sentences will not fail to have their effect. In numerous cases, of course, preventive detention has also been imposed.

To leave no stone unturned in trying to contain the scourge, tests were made of various people's ideas for the deepening of scientific knowledge about the problem of homosexuality. Finally, there has been profitable cooperation with various departments and institutions, and an exchange of material on the protection of German youth and German military capacity [...] (pp. 15ff.).

[1940]:

In the course of the year a total of 2553 new offenders were recorded in the main card index. This now holds approximately 42,000 cards. Nearly a half of the 1940 registered offenders are corrupters of young people. Still greater attention has therefore been paid to the fight against this category of people, and an order was issued that homosexuals who have corrupted more than one person are to be taken into preventive detention.[11] This measure will certainly help to improve the situation.

As in the past, knowledge of the causes – which are still unclear – is of crucial importance for the successful combating of homosexuality. For this purpose the Reich Office is closely cooperating with a number of scientific institutes, including a department of the Wehrmacht. Material is regularly sent to the Wehrmacht and one of the institutes, while practical cases of treatment are carried through with another institute. The Wehrmacht's purposes are also served by a special index on homosexual servicemen, which at present holds roughly 5000 cards.[12]

[11] See Document 89. [12] See Documents 42 and 43.

The office also examined a number of cases of transvestitism, although a satisfactory solution did not follow on the part of the competent authorities.

Officers of the Reich Office were deployed out of area on six occasions, resulting in the conviction of sixteen offenders [...] (p. 61).

[41] The Thuringia Bureau for Race Affairs
Investigation into homosexuality

[41a] *Letter dated 14 June 1937 from the chairman, Prof. Karl Astel, to the Reichsführer-SS and Head of the German Police, Heinrich Himmler*

Chairman Prof. Karl Astel   Weimar, 14 June 1937
                                                                     Marienstr. 13
                                                                   Telephone 1753

To the
Reichsführer-SS
H. Himmler
Berlin SW 11
Prinz-Albrecht-Str. 8

Reichsführer!
Your thorough inspection of the Thuringia Bureau for Race Affairs has left behind a deep impression in Thuringia. Once again I also thank you most sincerely on behalf of the Reich Governor and State Secretary and of all my colleagues.

Reichsführer, you have thereby performed a crucial service to the work of preserving and elevating our race, not least because you have personally given us all a further powerful impetus. We shall try to show our thanks by our loyalty and performance.

Perhaps you are not fully aware to what extent the decent and upright members of our *Volk* see in you the guarantor of the best manly virtues, for whose everlasting existence, nay domination, we have struggled for so many years and continue to devote our energies.

We consider it a great blessing, moreover, that the Head of the German Police is by nature a born cultivator of men [*eine geborene Züchternatur*] who rejects the delusions about the surrounding world that are constantly resurfacing even in the ranks of the NSDAP, who opposes to them sure knowledge of events occurring in conformity with natural law – for example, the essentially hereditary determination both of pernicious criminals and of splendid exemplars of manhood – and who goes on to draw conclusions about the annihilation of the one, or at least their exclusion from reproduction, and the eugenic [*züchterische*] multiplication of the other.

On the incorruptibility of our will, on the conscientiousness and circumspection of the measures we take, depends the happiness of our children and further descendants – nay, the fulfilment of our whole life's meaning. For our mission is ceaselessly to promote a nobler, sounder, healthier life in conformity with the species.

Apart from my everyday work and the completion of already far advanced scientific investigations, I intend soon to carry out three major projects which in different ways are of significance to you as Head of the Police, insofar as you, Reichsführer, make the necessary means available.

1 The first of these projects you have already described as most welcome. It concerns the investigation of homosexuality – that is, its determination or joint determination by hereditary factors, its possible deposit in the tribe of homosexuals, its widespread occurrence together with certain physical and mental qualities and characteristics, etc.

For this work I need from you the addresses of at least a hundred classified homosexuals from Thuringia and I would ask you to send them in the near future.

2 I am planning an exhaustive project on the constitution of both progenitors of all live-births out of wedlock in Thuringia during the year 1936 or perhaps 1937 – something like 3000 in the year.

By means of this project, discussion of the illegitimacy question – a benchmark for assessment and delimitation of the exceptional cases we desire – could be accurately and unassailably accomplished in the foreseeable future.

3 I would also like to tackle a major project on criminals. That is, I want to establish the incidence of a certain degree of criminality in the set of criminals, to work out the yardstick for the inclusion of criminals in the law on the prevention of hereditarily diseased offspring with a view to sterilization – extremely necessary! – something stronger than the present yardstick for the castration of sex criminals, which needs to be changed because it is a slap in the face for any healthy sensibility to discover that, as things stand, some sex criminal who defiles our children must be a recidivist before he can be castrated, before he can be freed of his diseased instincts and his fellow-men of appalling misery and distress. So I would like to

take on such a major project, which also provides a further yardstick for the use of preventive detention and perhaps for the annihilation – that is, the killing – of criminals even if they themselves have not yet murdered anyone.

For this I would like to have at my disposal some 4000 criminals who have been imprisoned in Thuringia and are on the records of the Thuringia Bureau for Race Affairs complete with photographs and valuable notes on their relatives.

May I take this opportunity to point out that I cannot see eye to eye with the former centres of criminal biology – neither Vierstein's nor Fetscher's nor the one soon planned by the Reich Minister of Justice – for none of them focuses sufficiently on the heart of the matter, which is the possibility of eugenic intervention.

For this work all I require from you is enough extra money for additions to the labour force and perhaps the purchase of office material, postage and so on. I would, if you wish, publish the work on your behalf and myself write up the text.
[...]

I have told the Reich Governor and Gauleiter of your wish that he should of his own accord ask the Führer to inspect the Thuringia Organization of Race Affairs. Perhaps you would do this for your part at the same time. My Reichsführer, please be so kind as to give me a few more signs of the Führer's visit.
[...]

Heil Hitler! Loyally yours

Signed: Karl Astel
SS-Sturmbannführer

[41b] *Himmler's reply of 22 June 1937*

Berlin, 22 June 1937

Dear Comrade Astel,
Thank you very much indeed for your letter of 14/6 [...]
As to the substance, on (1) I shall arrange for you to receive the names of at least a hundred classified homosexuals in Thuringia from the Secret State Police.
I much appreciate your clarification of the questions raised under (2) and (3). Would you please list for me the expenditures necessary for these projects; we can very well publish it as a joint work of the Reichsführer SS and Head of the German Police and of your own bureau.

Heil Hitler!
Yours
Signed: H. Himmler

[41c] *Communication from Gestapo Headquarters, 4 September 1937*

Berlin, 4 September 1937

Dear Comrade Astel!
I have received your letter of 24/8 and would like to briefly reply to it.
The Reichsführer-SS has received your letter from Borkum and is having your proposals attended to at the moment. You will receive the list of homosexuals directly from the person dealing with these matters, SS-Obersturmbannführer Meisinger, Berlin SW 11, Prinz-Albrecht-Str. 8, to whom you are kindly requested to address any queries in this area [...]

Heil Hitler!
Signed: [illegible]

Kriminaliſtik

Monatshefte für die geſamte kriminaliſtiſche Wiſſenſchaft und Praxis

Heft 12   14. Jahrgang   RM 1.10
Berlin, Dezember 1940

Amtliche Zeitſchrift des Reichskriminalpolizeiamtes

Im Auftrage des Reichsführers-SS und Chefs der Deutschen Polizei
herausgegeben vom Chef der Sicherheitspolizei SS Gruppenführer Reinhard Heydrich
Präsident der Internationalen Kriminalpolizeilichen Kommission.

KRIMINALWISSENSCHAFT UND PRAXIS-VERLAG

BERLIN·N·54   Schwedterstr.263

Publications of the Reich Criminal Police Bureau: a monthly magazine, *Kriminalistik*
[Criminology]; the *Jahrbuch* [Annual] of the Bureau; and the first in a series of
brochures published by the Bureau, *Organisation und Meldedienst der
Reichskriminalpolizei* [Organization and Records Department of the Reich Criminal
Police], Berlin 1941.

JAHRBUCH

AMT V

(REICHSKRIMINALPOLIZEIAMT)

DES

REICHSSICHERHEITSHAUPTAMTES

SS

1939 / 1940

Hergestellt in der Druckerei des Reichskriminalpolizeiamtes.
Lichtdruck: Atelier des Reichskriminalpolizeiamtes (Lichtbildabteilung)

Schriftenreihe
des Reichskriminalpolizeiamtes Berlin.
Nr. 1.

Organisation und Meldedienst der Reichskriminalpolizei.

Mit einem Geleitwort des Chefs der Sicherheitspolizei
SS Gruppenführer Reinhard Heydrich.

Bearbeitet und ergänzt von
SS-Brigadeführer Generalmajor der Polizei N e b e
und
SS-Obersturmbannführer
Oberregierungs- und -kriminalrat W e r n e r

Herausgegeben vom
Reichskriminalpolizeiamt, Berlin.

Kriminal-Wissenschaft und -Praxis Verlag Elise Jaedicke
Berlin 1941

[42] Special units for 'corrupters of youth' and 'rentboys' doing military service

A study by the Military Academy, Berlin 1938

[42a] *Questionnaire for homosexual servicemen*
Instruction from Heydrich to Gestapo Headquarters,
24 December 1937

The Head of the Security Police   Berlin, 24 December 1937
-S-PP(II S1)No. 8003/37

To:
(a) the Secret State Police Bureau
(b) Regional and local headquarters of the State Police
(c) the Reich Criminal Police Bureau
(d) Regional and local headquarters of the Criminal Police

Subject: Questionnaire on homosexual servicemen
Enc.: Questionnaire

Investigations are being conducted by Medical Corps Colonel Prof. *Wuth* at the Reich Ministry of War to clarify the nature of homosexuality. In support of this research I request that a questionnaire be completed on the enclosed form about each homosexual serviceman and sent to the Reich Criminal Police Bureau, Reich Office for the Combating of Homosexuality and Abortion. The questionnaires should be completed in respect of each newly emerging homosexual serviceman.

The questionnaire will be forwarded to the Reich Ministry of War by the Reich Office for the Combating of Homosexuality and Abortion attached to the Reich Criminal Police Bureau.

Signed: Heydrich   [Enc.]

Questionnaire for homosexuals

1 Surname:
2 First name:
3 Date and place of birth:
4 Born out of wedlock:
5 Military district unit:
6 Religious denomination:
7 Number of siblings: how many dead:
8 How many brothers, how many sisters:
9 Which number child in the family:
10 Youngest child:

11 Only child:
12 Education:
13 Institutional care: *
14 Workhouse: *
15 Concentration camp: *
16 Sentences (for crimes or offences against Reich laws, not
    misdemeanours):
17 Nature of the last sentence:
18 Degree of sentence:
19 Grounds of sentence:
20 Criminal record in the family:
21 Mental subnormals in the family:
22 Personal impression:

Physique
23 Weakly (asthenic): *
24 Slim (leptosome): *
25 Stocky (athletic, pyknic): *
26 Plump (pyknic): *
27 Strong, muscular (athletic): *
28 Alcohol abuse: *
29 Nicotine abuse: *
30 Drug abuse: *
31 Rentboy: *
32 Corrupter of youth: *
33 Habitual homosexual: *
34 Special remarks:
35 Twin:

* Underline if applicable

[42b] *Letter from Med. Colonel Prof. Wuth, 12 April 1938*

Med. Colonel Prof. O. Wuth   Berlin NW 7
No. 1421/38   12 April 1938

To the:
Army Health Inspectorate
Berlin W 35

I enclose herewith two lists of homosexuals reported to me by the
Reich Office for the Combating of Homosexuality and Abortion.

   After consultation with the Army Health Inspectorate I have
listed only rentboys and corrupters of youth from the total number
of cases reported to me.

Of these, moreover, only those have been reported who at the time of the report had no previous conviction for sex offences, since in such a case they would by virtue of the previous conviction be known as homosexuals to the military district unit and would thus have to complete their service in special sections. The number of servicemen with a previous conviction for sex offences presently comes to a total of 50. The number of servicemen who are habitual homosexuals but have not been identified as rentboys or corrupters of youth, and who have not therefore been reported, amounts to 132.

Only servicemen born in the years 1914–1921 are included, and the reports received here cover the period from 5/2/1938 to 7/4/1938. Further reports will follow.[13]

[Additional observation:
Two lists are enclosed

Corrupters of youth (25 persons)
Surname, first name, date of birth, military district unit, special remarks

Rentboys (42 persons)
Surname, first name, place of birth, date, military district unit, special remarks]

[42c] *Refusal by the Army High Command. Letter of 5 September to the Army Health Inspectorate*

Army Supreme Command
Az 12 i 10.42 AHA/Abt. E (1a)   Berlin, 5 September 1938

Subject: List of names of servicemen who are rentboys or homosexual corrupters of youth
Your ref.: 816/38g VI v. 14.8.38

To:
Army Health Inspectorate (VI)

Reference file is returned with enclosures after perusal.
Forwarding of the lists of names of rentboys and homosexuals to

---

[13] On 21 June 1938 Wuth sent two further lists. He commented on them: 'The number of servicemen with a previous conviction for sex offences presently comes to: 50 + 166 = 216. The number of servicemen who are habitual homosexuals but have not been identified as rentboys or corrupters of youth, and who have not therefore been reported, amounts to: 132 + 149 = 281. The reports received here cover the period from 8/4/1938–21/6/1938. Further reports will follow' (Bundesarchiv/Militärarchiv, Freiburg im Breisgau, BA-MA H 20/479).

the appropriate military recruitment agencies is not considered necessary for the following reasons.

(1) As is apparent from the list, the age-group is in part made up of young people who, though liable by law for military service, are not yet registered by the police in accordance with the levying and medical examination ordinance. These young men do not therefore present to the military recruitment agencies any of the required items such as a registration card, a nominal roll, and so on. It would therefore serve no purpose for the recruitment agencies to have such young men on record [i.e., as homosexuals – *trans.*], because the recruitment agencies receive no notice of any change in their permanent address. But the list fails in its purpose if it cannot be kept constantly up to date.

(2) So long as these young men have not been convicted, the district commanding officer does not have the means – under D 3/1, directive 11 of the Wehrmacht recruitment regulations – to draw them off into a special section. In this respect too, then, there is no value in having them on record.

(3) If records were nevertheless to be opened, they would also have to figure in some form in the recruitment agency files. But then the young man would be branded *throughout his life* for a *youthful transgression* often brought about through seduction, without ever having been convicted of it *by a court.*

(4) If the lists were to be kept up to date, the registration would itself mean an extra burden of work for the recruitment agencies, and given that the recruitment agencies have more important tasks to perform, the end would in no way square with the labour-time put into it.

Order of the Head of Bureau V [RSHA] dated 6 November 1944

Head of Bureau V   Berlin, 6 November 1944

Order

As part of the reorganization of Bureau V I order the following:

I. SS-Obersturmbannführer Undersecretary Dr Rodenberg, a specialist in neurology and psychiatry, is directly answerable to the Head of Bureau V as the special scientific representative in Bureau V.

II. He is responsible for the following tasks.

(A) General

1 Adviser to the Head of Bureau on special medical-scientific matters of criminology.
2 Adviser to all offices of Bureau V on the same special matters.
3 Neurological-psychiatric advice in special cases involving Bureau V.

(B) Scientific collaboration on wider issues

1 Assessment of material arising in criminal practice that might throw further light on the problem of emasculation
(a) in respect of the category of persons
    (homosexuals, other sex offenders, pyromaniacs, habitual criminals);
(b) with a view to establishing the necessary measures of a legislative and legal-administrative kind
    (emasculation of homosexuals among others)
(c) with regard to the solution of still open questions
    (psycho-therapeutic follow-up treatment of emasculated men)
2 Collaboration in organizing the way in which the security police deals with sexual degenerates (transvestites, fetishists and others)
3 Assessment of material arising in criminal practice that might help to solve the problem of female homosexuality

(C) Scientific collaboration on individual criminal cases

1 Evaluation in legal proceedings for homosexual offences.
2 Expert reports in other practical areas concerning criminals (release of emasculated persons in preventive detention, etc.).
3 Involvement as adviser in police investigations and deliberations on exceptional cases.
4 Advisory reports on current or planned psycho-therapeutic treatment of individual sex offenders.

III. SS-Sturmbannführer Dr Rodenberg will hold the personal rank of a group leader.

Signed: Panzinger

BAK R 58, fol 232

[43] Curative treatment

Investigations at the German Institute for Psychological Research and Psychotherapy in Berlin

[43a] *Subject: The combating of homosexuality in Germany. Extract from a manuscript by Felix Boehm of the German Institute, dated 28 February 1938*

[...] We cannot settle whether there is such a thing as innate homosexuality because such homosexuals, if they exist, effectively never submit to treatment and so do not possess any will to be cured. We have observed a large number of cases where, apart from the homosexual activity, definite features of inferior heredity were to be found. Accordingly, the homosexual activity might in such cases be a symptom of inferior heredity. Detailed study in the course of our thorough treatments has shown that in no homosexuals who have come into treatment has there not been proof of early, albeit submerged, heterosexual tendencies, and that the factors which might suggest an inherited predisposition were distributed in varying strength – for example, in the external environment or in the early emergence of strong conscious homosexual inclinations or activities. It may be regarded as almost certain that parents' qualities which favour the development of homosexuality might be inherited – e.g., a weak character of the father on the son. Scientific work on the question of whether there is a truly innate homosexuality has not yet led to a conclusive verdict. [...]

8 In all divisions of the Party, especially the Hitler Youth, the German Girls League and the Young Folk, as well as the Young Girls, the position of confidential doctor should be created – someone with whom those in danger can find things out and say what is on their mind. This confidential doctor should be bound to absolute secrecy, but should also be in touch with our institute. This arrangement is to be temporarily introduced on a trial basis in the area of Greater Berlin. By the way, the danger of female homosexuality should not be underestimated, in the sense of alienation from the later tasks of woman and mother.

9 To implement these measures our institute needs to be attached to a Reich authority and sufficient resources must be put at its disposal for these important tasks.

10 The health insurance schemes should be informed of the great dangers threatening our nation from the further growth of homosexuality, and they must be urged also to make funds available for

the treatment of homosexuals by members of our institute – all the more so as the experience of our institute shows that homosexuality often goes hand in hand with neurotic illnesses.

Signed: Boehm
Secretary of the Institute

[43b] *Circular issued by the German Institute for Psychological Research and Psychotherapy, Berlin W 62, Budapester Straße 29*

6 December 1939

Dear colleagues!

In order to assist scientific understanding of the problem of homosexuality you sent us a report on the treatments you are conducting. The research department of our institute, under the direction of Dr von Hattingberg, has given me the job of further examining and scientifically evaluating the experience of all members of our institute in this field.[14] I would therefore ask you to kindly give me more precise details about the treatments you are conducting, and especially to inform me of everything you have gathered by way of experience in this field. This may involve fundamental knowledge you have gained – e.g., in identifying genetic causes to be taken into account in either male or female homosexuality; or it may be a detailed account of a treatment that especially interests you or has afforded you especially important insights. But it may also involve exceptionally important knowledge from one particular treatment or a particularly characteristic phase in a treatment; also perhaps striking and characteristic behaviour on the part of one patient undergoing the treatment. We are also interested in any characteristic dreams or lapsuses, or unique and very pithy expressions used by homosexuals; perhaps also especially interesting childhood experiences – in short, everything which may have struck or especially interested you in your treatments, or which you think may be of value for a thorough compilation project on this question in our research department. It goes without saying that we will send you a copy of my compilation paper. [...]

Thanking you in advance,
Heil Hitler!
Yours   Signed: Boehm

P.S. What are your views about so-called 'innate homosexuality'?

[14] Cf. G. Cocks, *Psychotherapy in the Third Reich*, New York/Oxford 1985, pp. 202ff., and C. Schoppmann, *Nationalsozialistische Sexualpolitik und weibliche Homosexualität*, op. cit., pp. 143ff.

(c) The Consequences

With the support of new legal definitions of crime, a tightly knit national police and security apparatus, and a public opinion manipulated by propaganda and demagogy, the rate of prosecutions greatly increased after 1936. Whereas just a thousand people were convicted in 1934, there were already 5310 in 1936. Two years later, the statistics referred to 8562 legally valid convictions. The police and prosecution departments, in the words of a regular commentary on crime figures, acted 'with ever growing vigour' against 'these moral aberrations which are so harmful to the strength of the *Volk*'.[15] And Prosecutor-General Wagner stressed what one could not have expected to be otherwise after all the investment in propaganda and police searches: 'the public, through its increased level of reporting, also [supports ...] the fight against these offences. Broadly speaking, no more homosexual acts were committed [...] than before, but they were recorded and prosecuted on a much larger scale than before.'[16] Whereas between 1931 and 1933 a total of 2319 persons were put on trial and found guilty of offences under §175 of the Penal Code, this figure rose nearly tenfold in the first three years after the tougher redefinition of offences. In the years from 1936 to 1938 the number convicted came to 22,143. No reliable data are available for the war years after 1943, so that the total number of convictions for homosexuality in the 'Third Reich' can only be estimated – roughly 50,000 men according to Wuttke. But the Gestapo or the Reich Offfice had considerably more on record as suspects or as presumed partners. Between 1937 and 1940 there were more than 90,000 men and youths.[17]

Alongside this numerical increase there was also a qualitative toughening of prosecution policy. After 1933 the number of acquittals continually declined and by 1936 was down to a mere quarter of the figure for 1918 (the year with the most verdicts of 'not guilty'). The same trend is apparent in the fines handed down by courts, in comparison with which there was a marked increase in sentences of imprisonment or penal servitude. Men with previous convictions were treated with particular severity – above all so-called corrupters of youth, but also young men considered to be 'rentboys'.[18]

At the instigation of the Reich Offfice special mobile units of the Gestapo carried out operations in a number of towns. The reasons could be quite varied: from the eradication of 'centres of the epidemic' in day or boarding schools to denunciations with a real or alleged political

---

[15] 'Entwicklung der Kriminalität', *Deutsche Justiz* 100, 1938/24, p. 934.

[16] 'Die strafrechtliche Fortbildungswoche für Staatsanwälte und Strafrichter', in ibid., p. 1639.

[17] W. Wuttke, *Homosexuelle im Nationalsozialismus*, exhibition catalogue, Ulm 1987, p. 29.

[18] A. Hurst, 'Die Homosexualität, ihre Behandlung und Bestrafung vor und nach der Strafrechtsnovelle vom 28. Juni 1935', legal dissertation, Freiburg 1949, pp. 101ff.

background. There is no evidence of a sudden nation-wide 'clampdown' comparable to the attacks on Jews in the pogrom night of 1938. But the offensive was certainly coordinated in a number of ways. This was particularly true of actions with a clear political motivation: e.g., the arrests of thousands of priests, religious brothers and lay persons during the staged 'cloister trials' against the Catholic Church;[19] or the targeting of the activities of the Bund Youth that had already been banned in 1934, where especial prominence was given to the trial of the Nerother Wandervogel in 1936.[20]

The ultimately arbitrary nature of the Nazis' practice, especially that of Heinrich Himmler as architect of their anti-homosexual policy, is illustrated by the special regulation approved in October 1937 for actors and artists.

Under the pretext of 'Reichization' – that is, of applying uniform norms throughout the Reich – the rules on preventive detention and police supervision that had been issued three years before were made tougher still at the end of 1937. Now anyone who fitted the completely arbitrary criteria for an 'experienced' or 'habitual' male homosexual had to reckon that, after serving his term of imprisonment or penal servitude, he would be deported for 're-education' in a concentration camp.

[44] Raids by special Gestapo units

A 'cleansing operation' against homosexuals in Hamburg.
Report from the Essen National-Zeitung, *28 August 1936*

Berlin, 28 August. A special unit of the Secret State Police has started work on a large-scale cleansing operation against homosexual practices.

The rise in this type of offence due to the loosening of morals after the world war meant that energetic action had to be taken in the summer of 1934, soon after the National Socialists took power. The tougher sanctions which the law of 28 June 1935 introduced for this type of offence, together with vigorous action by the police, led to a sharp decline in such abuses. A special unit of the Secret State Police was established for cleansing operations in Berlin and many other towns. This unit has now also begun activity in Hamburg, and in the shortest time a large number of so-called 'traffic

---

[19] See H. G. Hockerts, *Die Sittlichkeitsprozesse gegen katholische Angehörige und Priester 1936–1937*, Mainz 1971.
[20] See K.-P. Meeth, 'Die Söhne der Windrose. Der Nerother Wandervogel, Teil I 1890–1933', in *Kreis Daun Vulkaneifel. Heimatjahrbuch 1986*, pp. 242–252; and idem, 'Teil II: Der Nerother Wandervogel zwischen Anpassung und "Resistenz"', in *Kreis Daun Vulkaneifel. Heimatjahrbuch 1987*, pp. 205–219. Also A. Klönne, *Jugend im Dritten Reich*, Munich 1990, pp. 198ff.

pubs' [*Verkehrslokale*] have been raided. Several hundred people were arrested. And further arrests are imminent.[21]

Those arrested so far come from nearly every occupational group and layer of the population – which proves how wrong is the widespread idea that this scourge is mainly an offence committed by so-called intellectuals. The wide haul from the Secret State Police searches demands rapid sentencing of the guilty. In Hamburg a special department was set up to bring the charges before the Express Jury Court. The accused were sentenced to terms ranging from one year to a year and eight months.

According to the judicial press agency in Bonn, 69 charges of homosexual offences and crimes are pending with the Bonn prosecution office against people from Bonn and the surrounding area. Here too proceedings are being taken against people from all sections of the population. Some 30 individuals have already been dealt with by the Bonn District Court, which passed jail sentences of between a year and eighteen months.

Secret State Police   Halle am Saale, 23 December 1937
Halle a.S. State Police Headquarters   Dreyhauptstr. 2
Reg. No. II S 5487/37

Subject: Crime among German youth; on the allegedly wayward situation at the Catholic children's home in Bad Liebenwerda

Ref.: your letter of 6/12/37, Pr.S. 27

The investigations at the Catholic children's home in Liebenwerda have not yet been completed because a large-scale operation against homosexuals is currently taking place in Halle/S and my special officers have all their worktime and more taken up with this. After the operation in Halle is over, the Liebenwerda investigations will be completed. I shall then immediately report on the conclusions.

p.p.
Signed: Hildemann

To:
the chairman of the regional council
in Merseburg

Landeshauptarchiv Sachsen-Anhalt, Magdeburg Rep. C. 48 Ie Nr. 1122

---

[21] On the persecution in Hamburg see H. Chr. Lassen, 'Der Kampf gegen Homosexualität und "Rassenschande". Sexualdelikte vor Gericht in Hamburg 1933–1939', in *'Für Führer, Volk und Vaterland . . .' Hamburger Justiz im Nationalsozialismus*, published by the Hamburg Justice Department, Hamburg 1992, pp. 216–289.

[45] Getting tough with political opponents. Dissipating the 'spirit of false romanticism'

Informer's report on the trial of leaders of the Nerother Wandervogel

To the   Koblenz, 20 September 1936
Security Service RF-SS/SD
Koblenz Division

Subject: Main hearing in Düsseldorf of the case against former Nerother Robert Oelbermann and others

The main hearing in Düsseldorf on 18 and 19 September 1936 of the case against 9 members or supporters of the former Nerother Bund or the 'Rheinische Jugendburg' Bund (Jugendburg Association) resulted in the following sentences:

1 Zimmermann, Düsseldorf, 6 months, §175, old, case abandoned on one count (§176, 3),

2 Wüstenfeld, Wiesbaden, 5 months, §175, new, offence of December 1935,

3 Nissen, Düsseldorf, 14 months, §175, new, §176, 3 (corruption of a young person under fourteen),

4 Oelbermann, R., Waldeck, 18 months, §175, old, new (in one case onanism, in the other thigh intercourse),

5 Reichow, Koblenz, 12 months, §176, 3. Corruption of Kohl, then not yet fourteen, D'dorf,

6 Mahlmann, Düsseldorf, 6 months, §175, new, M. had an amorous relationship with a named individual under seven years of age,

7 Hannappel, Düsseldorf, 12 months, §175, new, three counts,

8 Schnelle, Düsseldorf, acquitted for lack of proof,

9 Boeckels, Düsseldorf, acquitted for lack of proof
[. . .]

2. The summing up by public prosecutor Kettner, Düsseldorf. Prosecutor Kettner explained that there were a number of offences and crimes under §§175, old and new versions, and §176, 3, which were all to be laid at the door of the 'Nerother Bund'. In the 'Bund Youth' there had been abuses and signs of degeneracy against which the state had felt compelled to act. The sick attitude of some of these youth leaders, especially Robert Oelbermann, had en-

dangered the work of educating the German youth. The state could not tolerate such elements.

Such things had had a destructive effect inside the Bund, not only morally but also politically. Because of the shortage of leaders in the Hitler Youth, the Nerother had penetrated it and infected the state youth in both a medical and political sense.

[...]

The Röhm revolt showed that sick people of this kind stick together through thick and thin, and this has again been shown in the trial in progress. [...]

3. Lessons of the trial of the former Nerother

One thing was to be learnt from the main hearing of the case against the nine accused, from the questioning, the defence speeches, etc., and this deserves to be emphasized.

The judgement of all cases in the town where the accused live will work against the general interest aroused by the question of the 'Nerother Bund'.

One idea would be, as in the sex trial of monastery inmates, to create a central office to handle and resolve all the questions connected with the whole 'Bund Youth Case'. It would then have been easy for the press, and especially educational workers, to use the results to dissipate the Bund spirit of false romanticism that still lingers in thousands of young people, by listing the offences and crimes of Bund members who live in that romantic atmosphere.

Signed: Fuchs
SS-Oberscharführer

[46] The Catholic Church. Using the 'cloister trials' for propaganda
Memorandum from Gestapo Headquarters, 8 April 1937 (Extract)

G II 113   Berlin, 8/4/1937
81
HT/See

Memorandum
Subject: Discussion with Undersecretary Meisinger apropos of the cloister sex trials

The following points were to be decided:

1 Should all the trials be completed at one stroke within one to two weeks, or should the trials be spread out over a longer period?

2 Should each trial be reported separately in the press, or should there be just one synthetic account?

3 Should the Führer's order be understood in such a way that only clergymen and monks already in custody – or those already under investigation – are to be put on trial, or should it be taken to mean that fresh enquiries are to be opened?

Undersecretary Meisinger had been instructed by the Gruppen-führer to listen to the views of Regierungsrat Haselbacher and SS-Obersturmbannführer Hartl on this matter and had invited them to a discussion at 19.30 on 7/4.

For the propaganda it would be necessary to give as concrete details as possible about each individual trial, because it is these which make the greatest impression on the people. Mixed in with them, scientifically based synthetic articles with a propagandistic slant would have to be published again and again. The Führer's order might be tacitly understood in such a way that fresh investigations can also be started. [...]

Gehe hin und hüte meine –

– Lämmerl

The priestly chief 'shepherd' is surrounded by pigs labelled 'rape, sadistic orgies in monasteries', 'unnatural acts in places of worship' and 'abuse of children and mental defectives'. The ironic biblical reference at top and bottom reads: 'Go forth and watch over my – lambs!' From the SS paper *Das Schwarze Korps*, 6 May 1937

Arrest of actors in 1938 at the Karl May Games in Rathen an der
Elbe
Memorandum of the Dresden Criminal Police, 8 September

State Criminal Police   Dresden, 8 September 1938
Dresden Criminal Police Headquarters
Superintendent's Department III
Pol.Az Kr P VIII 1804/38

[...] But arrest cannot be carried out without approval of
Reichsführer-SS – because actor. If action were still taken against
Sch. then it would certainly have to be taken against O. But then it
should be remembered that the 'Karl May Games' are still going on.
An arrest [...] would call the games into question, and apart from
the harm this would do to the town of Rathen there would also be
unnecessary gossip. [...] Winkler, the mayor of Rathen, also asked
me to do nothing yet so that the 'Karl May Games' could continue
undisturbed.

Signed: Grebedünkel
Chief Assistant

Radio telegram, dated 9 September 1938, from Dresden Criminal
Police Headquarters, Superintendent's Department III, to
Reichsführer-SS and Head of German Police

With reference to the order of the Head of Security Police II S
Nr..6958/37 of 29.10.1937 I request approval to arrest actor S.
performing at 'Karl May Festival Games' in spa town of Rathen, first
name: Charles, b. 1.4.14 Cleveland, Ohio, USA, American citizen,
currently resident in Rathen a. Elbe
Sch., first names: Hermann, Siegfried, b. 5.1.07 Vienna, resident in
Rathen
H., first names: Hans Max, b. 21.3.17 Colmar i. Els., currently
resident in Gera, Wilhelmstr. 28.

Staatsarchiv Dresden, Polizeipräsidium Dresden Nr. 705

[47] Special regulation for actors and artists
Himmler's decree of 29 October 1937

Head of the German Police   Berlin, 29 October 1937
B Nr.PP II S.Nr. 6958/37

To:
(a) the Secret State Police Bureau
(b) regional and local headquarters of the State Police

(c) the Reich Criminal Police Bureau
(d) regional and local headquarters of the Criminal Police

Subject: Arrest of actors and artists for unnatural sexual acts

The Reichsführer-SS and Head of the German Police at the Reich Ministry of the Interior has ordered that any detention of an actor or artist for unnatural sex acts requires his prior approval, unless one of the above is actually caught in the act. I therefore request that in any cases which occur a report should be made in good time, together with a detailed motivation, to the Secret State Police – Department II S. The Secret State Police will then make the further arrangements for the approval of the Reichsführer-SS to be obtained.

RKPA 15[77]/6.1937
Reports on preventive detention orders should be passed on to Department V-A2, before any other detention to V-B3 of the RSHA (no longer to II S)

[48] Tougher provisions throughout the Reich for preventive detention and supervision

Decree of the Prussian Minister of the Interior, 14 December 1937, 'Preventive Combating of Crime by the Police' (Extracts)

Reich and Prussian   Berlin, 14 December 1937
Minister of the Interior

Pol.-S.K. 3 Nr. 1682/37 – 2098   Not published

To
the Land governments (except Prussia)
the Reich Governor for the Saarland

for Prussia:
premier ministers
provincial leaders and regional council chairmen
police chiefs in Berlin
all state criminal police forces
[...]

Preventive Combating of Crime by the Police

The reorganization of the Criminal Police on the territory of the Reich also requires uniform regulation of preventive police measures. The regular supervision carried out with success in

Prussia and most other *Länder* should be continued. In line with evaluations of previous experience and knowledge acquired through forensic-biological research, preventive police detention should be used on a wider scale. The following special provisions do not cancel the obligation, in accordance with National Socialist conceptions, to fulfil the task of the police in general, and hence also of the criminal police, to take the necessary measures to protect the community from any loathsome creature.

On the basis of §1 of the Reich President's order for the protection of the nation and state, dated 28 February 1933 (*RGBl.* I, p. 83), I hereby order that with immediate effect the preventive combating of crime by the police throughout the Reich shall be uniformly conducted in accordance with the following principles:

So-called 'sex criminals' charged within the jurisdiction of Leipzig police headquarters, grouped according to Leipzig Police categories for sex crimes and offences (Sections 174, 175a, 175b, 176, 253 of the Penal Code), for the years 1937 to 1944

Period	Total no.	of which: corrupters of youth	rentboys	arrested	released	preventive detention	detention order	convicted	proceedings abandoned	acquitted
1	2	3	4	5	6	7	8	9	10	11
1937[1]	458	137	12	143	25	–	118	55	9	1
1938	440	68	6	180	46	–	134	104	9	5
1939	359	47	2	135	23	–	112	93	10	9
1940	367	47	–	116	30	–	86	118	3	2
1941	386	72	–	117	19	12	98	96	12	2
1942	443	48	1	60[2]	5	14	55	60	–	1[2]
1943	230	37	–			no details				
1944	170	26	–			no details				
1937–44	2853	482	11	691[2]	143	26	548	366	43	19[2]

[1] According to Klare, the following number of people were reported for 'unnatural sex acts' in the years from 1933 to 1936 in the area of Leipzig police headquarters: 1933 108; 1934 296; 1935 301; 1936 351

[2] Figures for columns 5–11 were available only up to 30.6.1942. The records were simplified by order of the RSHA on 22 June 1942, so that only the accused's membership of the NSDAP, SS, SA etc. was still noted.

The figures include offences under §§174 and 176 not relating to homosexuality. Under §253 (blackmail), however, only offences relating to homosexuality are included.

Staatsarchiv Leipzig PP – V 4952

(A) Requirements for regular police supervision and preventive detention

I. *Regular police supervision*
1 (1) The following may be placed under regular supervision:
  (a) anyone who has made crime his profession and lives or has lived in whole or in part on the proceeds of his wrongdoing (professional criminal), if, owing to criminal offences committed in pursuit of gain, he has been duly sentenced at least three times to either imprisonment or penal servitude for at least three months,
  (b) anyone who, out of criminal instincts or inclinations, has repeatedly committed a criminal offence in the same or a similar manner (habitual criminal), if, because of such offences, he has been duly sentenced at least three times to either imprisonment or penal servitude for at least three months [...]

II. *Preventive police detention*
1 The following may be taken into preventive police detention:
  (a) a professional or habitual criminal – see I 1 (1) a and b – who has culpably violated the conditions imposed upon him when placed under regular police supervision or who has committed a criminal offence during the period of such supervision,
  (b) a professional criminal if, owing to criminal offences committed in pursuit of gain, he has been duly sentenced at least three times to either imprisonment or penal servitude for at least six months,
  (c) a habitual criminal if, because of offences committed out of criminal instincts or inclinations, he has been duly sentenced at least three times to either imprisonment or penal servitude for at least six months,
  (d) anyone who, by reason of a serious offence he has committed and in view of the possibility of a repetition, constitutes so great a danger to the community that it would be irresponsible to release him, or who, through actions which do not yet fulfil the requirements of a definite breach of the criminal law, displays the intention of committing a serious offence,
  (e) anyone who, without being a professional or habitual criminal, endangers the community by his anti-social behaviour,
  (f) anyone who gives no details or evidently false details about his person and arouses the suspicion that he wishes to conceal previous criminal offences or intends to commit new criminal offences under a false name.

2 Preventive police detention should be ordered for professional and habitual criminals only if it is thought that they will also commit criminal offences in the future, and if the effect on them of regular police supervision promises no success. [...]

So-called 'sex criminals' charged within the jurisdiction of Leipzig police headquarters, grouped by membership of organizations, occupation, etc. according to Leipzig Police reports on sex crimes and offences (Sections 174, 175a, 175b, 176, 253 of the Penal Code), for the years 1937 to 1944

Period	NSDAP	SS	SA	NSKK	Hitler Youth	Nazi Students' League	Armed Forces	Labour Service	Priests & religious orders	Civil servants	Actors, musicians, singers	Jews
1	2	3	4	5	6	7	8	9	10	11	12	13
1937	14	2	8	1	8	–	2	–	–	11	–	1
1938	24	2	–	–	11	1	8	–	–	5	3	3
1939	9	–	2	1	13	–	2	1	–	2	1	1
1940	3	–	–	–	2	–	3	–	–	2	–	–
1941	10	–	–	2	24	–	11	–	1	2	–	–
1942	9	–	1	1	17	–	1	1	–	1	–	–
1943	7	–	–	1	6	–	13	1	1	–	–	–
1944	3	–	–	–	6	–	8	1	–	–	–	–
1937–44	79	4	11	6	87	1	48	4	2	23	4	5

The figures contain cases of double counting. If an accused person belonged to more than one of the listed organizations, he was placed in each of the relevant columns. For example, if a civil servant was a member of both the NSDAP and the SA, he appears in three columns.

Staatsarchiv Leipzig PP – V 4952

(B) Implementation of regular police supervision and preventive detention

I. *Regular police supervision*
1 (1) To implement regular police supervision the following conditions may be imposed:
  (a) A ban on leaving the place of permanent or temporary residence without prior permission from the police,
  (b) A ban on staying at night outside the residence registered with the police and an obligation to deposit one key to the house,
  (c) A ban on staying at certain times of the day outside the residence registered with the police,

State Criminal Police
Hamburg Criminal Police Headquarters
Nr. Vb 780/1937   Hamburg, 23.11.1937

Notification proceedings
K., first names: Werner, Richard, b. 18.11.1912 in Hamburg,
resident in Quickborn, Kantine Glückauf bei Willbrand.

According to the police record, after he had been verbally informed
of the meaning of preventive police detention of professional
criminals and dangerous sex criminals, and of the use of regular
supervision as an intermediate preventive measure, the following
declaration was made to him:
By reason of offences committed by you and resulting sentences, you
are to be declared a sex criminal. You are accordingly placed under
regular supervision, by virtue of the decree of 1.4.1937 of the Reich
Governor in Hamburg – Senate.
The following conditions are imposed on you:
1. To report once a week to the competent police authorities in your
   area of residence;
2. Not to leave your area of residence without police approval;
3. To report any change of address within twenty-four hours;
4. Not to leave your address at night-time – that is, between 23.00
   and 5.00 in summer, or between 23.00 and 6.00 in winter;
5. Not to enter children's play areas, not to linger in the vicinity of
   schools, not to linger in public houses with homosexual company
   or in public conveniences and their nearby area – nor in the
   entrance halls and public conveniences of railway stations or their
   nearby area – for the purpose of initiating illicit sexual relations;
6. Not to take accommodation with people where children and
   youths are present.
   In the event of a violation of the obligations hereby served on you,
   you will run the risk of immediate enforcement of preventive
   police detention.

K. stated the following in this connection:
I declare that I am prepared to observe conscientiously the
obligations imposed upon me. I acknowledge receipt of a copy of the
notification proceedings.

Read, accepted and signed   Witnessed and authenticated
Signed: K.   Signed: Müller

K. was first sentenced to five months' imprisonment in 1935 on suspicion of being a
practising 'rentboy' and subsequently 'kept in safekeeping' for three months in the
'protective custody camp' at Fuhlsbüttel. In 1940 he was again taken into preventive
detention as an anti-social element and pederast by the Leipzig Gestapo and on
10.9.1941 transported to Buchenwald concentration camp.

Staatsarchiv Leipzig PP-S 1425

(d) An obligation to inform the local police within twenty-four hours of any change of permanent or temporary residence – regardless of general rules for registration with the police – and of any change in employment,

(e) An obligation to report to the local police at specified times,

(f) A ban on lingering in certain public places,

(g) A ban on visiting certain restaurants or public houses,

(h) A ban on taking alcohol home,

(i) A ban on associating with certain persons or providing certain persons with accommodation,

(j) A ban on employing persons under eighteen in the home or in a commercial enterprise,

(k) A ban on riding, driving or using vehicles of all kinds,

(l) A ban on using certain means of public transport,

(m) A ban on carrying or possessing weapons,

(n) A ban on advertising with a box-number or placing advertisements with a certain content,

(o) A ban on corresponding by poste restante,

(p) A ban on establishing groups for correspondence or marriage,

(q) A ban on producing and possessing obscene texts, illustrations and representations,

(r) A ban on producing, possessing and disseminating objects that are used for sadistic or masochistic purposes,

(s) A ban on keeping animals, especially dogs and cats,

(t) An obligation to make a serious effort at work.

(2) If further bans and obligations become necessary to implement the regular supervision, they require the approval of the Reich Criminal Police Bureau.

2 (1) Regular supervision lasts for as long as its purpose requires. Supervision measures should not go beyond what is necessary to achieve their purpose and must be framed in such a way that they do not bar the way to honest labour and do not have a detrimental effect upon current employment.

(2) After twelve months of supervision it must, and before that it may, be verified whether its continuation is still required. If further supervision is considered necessary, the twelve-month period begins again with that decision.

II. *Preventive police detention*

(a) Implementation

   (1) Preventive police detention shall be enforced in closed reform and labour camps, or in other ways by order of the Reich Criminal Police Bureau. It lasts for as long as its purpose requires, but in cases A II 1f for no longer than four weeks unless the Reich Criminal Police Bureau extends the period in exceptional cases.

   (2) To ensure that dependants of detainees do not get into economic difficulties through no fault of their own as a result of the enforcement of preventive police detention, it must be checked immediately after the arrest whether dependants are in a situation of need. If so, they should be made known to the appropriate NSV [National Socialist People's Welfare] office within forty-eight hours so that they can be given appropriate help.

   (3) After two years of detention at the latest, but not before twelve months have elapsed or three months in cases under A II 1e, it should be verified whether its continuation is still required. If the detention is maintained, a decision should be made after each further 12 or 3 months respectively about the continuation of detention. [...]

[49] Guidelines of 4 April 1938 relating to the decree 'Preventive Combating of Crime by the Police'
(Extracts)

B I 1(1) ff – Clause II 1 of the Guidelines involves a ban on lingering in such public places as: railway stations, post offices, banks, schools, swimming baths, public conveniences, children's play areas, fixed-price and cooperative stores, employment exchanges, pawnbroker's rooms, warehouses, certain streets, roads used by prostitutes, arcades, racetracks, betting offices, public gardens and parks, etc. The prohibited places should be clearly specified in the provisions of the order. [...]

B I 1(1) ii – The ban on associating with certain persons or providing certain persons with accommodation should mainly be applied to individuals who carry out their offences together with others (e.g., thieves, receivers), but even more so in the case of sex offenders and the like (e.g., homosexuals, pimps). The category of persons must be precisely identified. It should be explained to the individual in question that 'associate' refers to the establishment and maintenance of relations of any kind (including by letter or telephone, for example).

B I 1(1) jj – The ban on employing persons under eighteen in the home or in a commercial enterprise applies only to individuals who have exploited such minors for criminal offences or committed such offences on them (e.g., sex criminals) [...]

I 1(1) nn – The ban on advertising with a box-number or placing advertisements with a certain content should chiefly be applied to fraudsters, as well as individuals who use newspaper or magazine advertisements to initiate illicit sexual relations. This refers especially to the often well-disguised advertisements used to bring about perverse sexual intercourse or obscene correspondence.

I 1(1) oo – This ban is directed against the same category of persons as in (o) [not shown]. Poste restante correspondence refers not simply to the possibility of collecting postal items from a poste restante, but also to correspondence conducted through a poste restante card. The use of a PO box or box-number does not come under this heading. But cases where the offender has items meant for him sent on to a cover address should be treated as poste restante correspondence. [...]

A13 B I 1(2) The insertion of a general clause makes it possible to impose further bans and obligations with the approval of the Reich Criminal Police Bureau, or to place under supervision individuals whose previous record does not satisfy the formal requirements. This gives the necessary flexibility to regular police supervision. In this way, for example, an order specifying certain dress can be imposed on persons who offend public decency.

B I 2(1) Regular police supervision is not restricted in time. So that it is not extended for longer than necessary, however, the decree specifies a time limit for compulsory verification. It is also possible that orders will be gradually relaxed or temporarily made more severe. [...]

II. Implementation

1 Preventive police detention shall, unless the Reich Criminal Police Bureau decides otherwise, be enforced in reform and labour camps (concentration camps) on professional and habitual criminals as well as people constituting a danger to the public and anti-social elements.

In the case of men
from districts coming under the Criminal Police Headquarters of
Königsberg, Berlin, Stettin [Szczecin], Hamburg, Bremen, Breslau
[Wroclaw] and Hanover, currently
  at Sachsenhausen near Oranienburg
from districts coming under the Criminal Police Headquarters of
Dresden, Düsseldorf, Halle and Cologne, currently
  at Buchenwald near Weimar
from districts coming under the Criminal Police Headquarters of
Munich, Stuttgart and Frankfurt am Main, and Jews from all districts, currently
  at Dachau near Munich

In the case of women
from the whole territory of the Reich, currently
  at Lichtenburg near Prettin/Elbe.

2 The length of preventive police detention is not restricted in time;
but in the case of detention for the purpose of establishing identity
it may not exceed four weeks. In the latter case the Reich Criminal

---

Subject: Pederasty
Kr.R. III 2228/35

Leipzig Police Headquarters, Crime Bureau, Department F, 18.9.35

A confidential agent has reported here that homosexuals gather every
evening at Peter's Automat, make acquaintances and go off with
them to engage in sexual relations.

While we were on patrol at about 22.30 the agent pointed us to a
table with four allegedly homosexual men who were regularly to be
found in Peter's Automat. The four were taken to police headquarters. When we checked their details we ascertained that one of
them was already on the index of pederasts: namely, the hairdresser
F., first names: Willy Rudolf, b. 17.7.02 in Leipzig, resident here at
his mother's address, Tauchaer Str. 46/II. The others were not yet on
record and denied that they had homosexual tendencies. They were
released. [...]

F., who is on the index of pederasts, is not yet under a soliciting
ban. There are no unfinished proceedings or investigations. There
were no grounds for arrest, and after questioning he was released.

Patzner
Main Police Station

Staatsarchiv Leipzig PP-S 7923

Police Bureau may grant an extension of detention, if extensive and complicated enquiries are necessary at home and abroad. [...]

[50] Police officers as *agents provocateurs*
Observation of traps in Frankfurt am Main

[50a] *Letter from the Reich Minister of Justice to the Reichsführer-SS, dated 24 January 1938 (Extract)*

A series of legal proceedings for offences under §175ff. of the Penal Code, which have recently become known to me from the district prosecutor's office in Frankfurt a/M, prompt me to draw your attention to the highly questionable methods of investigation used by certain officers to secure the conviction of offenders.

1. Case against K. – 9 K LS 14/37 StA. Frankfurt a/Main. The judgement refers to the following facts:
'At about 21.00 on 7 April 1937 the defendant approached the 17-year-old journeyman G. He said that he liked G. and wanted to photograph him. The two then went to the Konstablerwache. On the way G. mentioned that he might have nowhere to stay for the night. The defendant then offered to meet him again at 0.30, when he would either give him money for the night's accommodation or take him home to sleep. The defendant gave G. money for a cup of coffee; then they parted.
This conversation had been watched by a police officer. The officer stopped G., pointed out that the defendant was probably a homosexual, and got G. to keep the appointment and go along with the defendant's wishes.
G. followed this advice and, having met the defendant as arranged, went home with him that night. There they both undressed and went to bed. According to the testimony of the aforenamed, G. put his hand on the upper part of the defendant's body, cuddled up to him and made restrained movements with his own body against him. The defendant then kissed G. on the cheek and stroked his head and body. Next he took his aroused sexual organ and held it for a while in his hand. G. then got up, put his clothes on and prepared to leave. The defendant apologized, offered him another mark for a night's accommodation and accompanied him to the door. At the main door he was then arrested by the waiting police officer.'

The officer was Police Prosecution Assistant Wildhirt.

Subject: Suspected pederasty
Kr.R. IX 1035/36   Custody!
                                        Arrested on 15.4.36, 13.45 hrs.

Leipzig Police Headquarters, Crime Bureau, Department 'F', 15 April
1936

During the period from 13.15 to 13.45 Candidate Detective *Riemer*
and myself kept under observation a man who was idly loitering at
the public convenience at the New Theatre. We suspected him of
being a pederast. The still unidentified man repeatedly went into the
aforementioned convenience. Eventually he came out behind a
soldier. The soldier went through Schwanenteich Park towards the
main station, immediately followed by the unidentified civilian. In
Schwanenteich Park the civilian drew closer to the soldier. But we
could not see them talking. The two then went almost together by a
roundabout route through the Wintergartenstraße entrance to the
main station. Inside the main part of the station they went together
to the convenience located on the east side. They stayed there for
approximately three minutes. When they came out they went across
the station to the convenience located on the west side. Here too they
remained for approximately three minutes. Afterwards they went still
talking down the steps to the station lobby (west side). They
separated at the entrance. The soldier came back and again went to a
convenience. The unidentified civilian went to the station concourse.
    Here he was stopped by Candidate Detective *Riemer* and taken to
the station police. When the soldier came out of the convenience,
I stopped him and asked him to come quietly to the station police.

Staatsarchiv Leipzig PP-S 6458.

2. Case against N. – 9 K Ms 36/37 StA. Frankfurt a/Main. The
judgement refers to the following:
'At about 20.00 on the evening of 25 June 1937 the defendant left
home and went to the adult education centre. At 21.00 he left the
centre and went via the Hauptwache and Zeil in the direction of his
home. Where the Zeil meets the Friedberger Anlage he entered the
public convenience to answer a call of nature. Apart from the
defendant there were two men in the convenience. The younger of
the two left the convenience first. The defendant followed him and
saw him standing on the Friedberger Anlage. As the defendant had
reason to believe from the man's behaviour that he was willing to
get sexually involved with him, he twice went over to the man,
looked at him in an ostentatious manner and indicated that they
should go and sit on a bench on the other side of the Zeil. After a

certain time the man sat down next to the defendant, who soon took hold of his right knee. When the man did nothing to resist this, the defendant felt for the man's sex organ, undid his trousers, took out his sex organ and put it in his mouth. At that point the man stood up, identified himself as a police officer and took the defendant to the police station, where he was placed under arrest.'
The officer was Sergeant Gorius. [...]

5. Charge against D. – 9 Js. 843/37 StA. Frankfurt a/Main – Police Sergeant Gorius gave the following outline of the case:
'At about 21.00 on 18 December 1937 D. was loitering in the manner of a rentboy inside and against the outside of the Opernplatz public convenience. When he left the urinal for the last time, he asked the undersigned for a light so as to get into conversation. He asked the undersigned whether he would like to drink a glass of beer together, whereupon the undersigned gave the answer: "Sure I would." D. followed the undersigned and we drank two glasses of beer on Große Bockenheimer Straße. Each paid for his own beer. The undersigned wanted to go home from there. D. asked if he might accompany the undersigned for part of the way. The undersigned said in reply: "I don't mind."
At the Gallustor he asked the undersigned to sit down with him on a bench – which is what he did. On the bench he pressed his legs against the undersigned, took hold of his bottom and tried to work his way under to his genitals. I asked him in a harmless enough way to come with me. D. then made the remark: "Let's go down to the Main." D. then staggered alongside the undersigned as far as the police station at 11 Neckarstraße. In front of the station the undersigned identified himself as a police officer and arrested him.'

Although I do not deny that a ruthless struggle against homosexuality is urgently required to maintain the strength of the German *Volk*, I consider it intolerable for the reputation of the police that officers should put up their own bodies to trap homosexuals. It may be left open whether it is permissible for police officers to encourage third parties to connive in illicit acts by homosexuals; but it can never be justifiable that young persons, who are easily influenced by others and face an especially grave danger of corruption, should be made use of to trap offenders in the manner outlined in case (1). [...]
I should be grateful for an early communication of your views.

Homosexual 'criminals', from *Kriminalität und Gefährdung der Jugend. Geheimbericht*, published by the Youth Führer of the German Reich, no date or place, [Berlin 1942].

[50b] *Himmler's answer of 7 June 1938*

I am also unable to approve of steps taken by some police officers in Frankfurt/Main to trap homosexuals.

I have arranged for the officers in question to be taught that their behaviour is unacceptable, so that in future such methods of trapping homosexuals will no longer be employed.

'[...] As the Frankfurt chief of police reported on 26 April 1937, the Reichsführer-SS, at a conference shortly before in Berlin, had among other things stated that in future he would judge the activity of the Criminal Police by its success in relation to homosexuality and abortion. This expression of will has apparently been misunderstood by some officers. [...]'

From the report of 2 September on the general situation in the area of the Supreme Land Court in Frankfurt am Main, BAK R22/1460, fol 18.

[51] 'Some say that some of the sentences are too high, others that they are too low'

Extracts from the situation report by the Thuringia Prosecutor's Office to the Prosecutor-General 1938/39

Prosecution Department at the Gotha District Court
Ilmenau Branch

Ilmenau, 17 January 1938

[...] In the preliminary proceedings mentioned in the last situation report against Hilpert and others for offences and crimes under §§175, 175a of the Penal Code, the proceedings have now been concluded.

Five of the culprits have already been duly convicted by the court in Ilmenau. They received sentences of between two and eighteen months' imprisonment. In two further cases proceedings were discontinued. In a further two cases, where proceedings were discontinued, the public prosecutor lodged an appeal. One further case is still pending with the court in Ilmenau. Two cases at the 29th Divisional Court had to be abandoned because the culprits are currently serving as soldiers. The trial of the main culprit, Hilpert, is being heard before the chief crime division in Gotha. [...]
(fol 7)

Chief Prosecutor at the Meiningen District Court
Sonneberg Branch

Sonneberg, 19 January 1938

[...] The 36-year-old man from Schalkau mentioned in section 4 of my last report was sentenced for offences under §175a Clause 3 and §175 of the Penal Code to two and a half years' imprisonment with five years' loss of civil rights and to preventive detention. [...]

Gera Chief Prosecutor   Gera, 16 March 1938

[...] this nationally damaging epidemic [has] also spread to the area of the Schleiz court. A whole series of homosexuals have been caught there. Roughly thirty have been prosecuted. They include a number of juveniles. Some of them have since become soldiers. In the case of one waiter the proceedings have been passed on to Gera. The most seriously incriminated have been taken into custody for questioning. Against one culprit twenty-one illicit sex acts with males have been proven. With two exceptions the partners had normal sexual tendencies. If some of the cases fall under the statute of limitations, this whole action shows that the public is in part much too indifferent about such matters. Otherwise the unbridled instincts of two of these criminals would certainly have long since been reported. [...]
(fol 28)

Weimar Chief Prosecutor   Weimar, 19 March 1938

In 1938 the Weimar Justice Department has so far had to deal with 380 new cases and has brought 151 prosecutions. This increase over the previous year is mainly to be explained by the fact that around the end of the year there was greater proof of homosexual associations, but also by the fact that the effects of the 1934 and 1936 impunity laws are gradually beginning to diminish. [...]
(fol 37)

Homosexuals in penal institutions and prison camps serving the administration of justice. Letter from the Reich Minister of Justice, 15 December 1939, to the Reichsführer-SS and Head of the German Police.

The principles of penal law in the Reich (see also now the announcement of 22 February 1939, p. 389 of the official decrees for the Sudeten German territories) contain the following provision in §45 para. 1 of the principles for the enforcement of custodial sentences: 'Prisoners of whom it is feared that they will exercise a harmful influence on other prisoners are to be kept, wherever possible, in solitary confinement or in cells.'

In accordance with long-standing penal practice, it is above all convicts serving time for homosexual activity or otherwise known to be homosexuals who should be separated from other prisoners, at least on any occasion when there is a danger of an approach being made. Usually, therefore, homosexuals will also be kept separate from their like so that, even where corruption does not have to occur first, the opportunity is blocked for the resumption of homosexual activity.

This was and is unconditionally applicable in institutional practice. Insofar as its framework allows for outside work – in the sense of the employment of prisoners outside the limits of the institution – a harmless relaxation has recently been permitted in the interests of a salutary drawing of homosexuals into hard labour in the open air. A short time ago, in reply to a query, I provided information about the rules to be observed in such a situation to the Head of the Security Police and the Security Services, and I would refer you to my letter of 4 December 1939 – IIIs[1] – 1589/39 – to IV (II H3) – B Nr.- 382/39.

When camp sentences first appeared and began to be served on a large scale, it proved unfeasible to refuse any involvement of homosexual prisoners. Thus, homosexual prisoners have been admitted to the camps in the Bavarian Ostmark, in Rodgau and Emsland. In the Ostmark camps, with the help of a hut containing single-sleeper cells developed at Tegel prison, it has been possible to keep homosexual prisoners separate during the night; the experiences are considered to be extremely favourable. In Rodgau too, some of the homosexual prisoners are put at night in a large hut containing single cells (or in the cells of a former workhouse). In the Ems camps, and in Rodgau where night-time isolation cannot be assured, practice favours the so-called 'dilution principle'. This principle consists in distributing homosexuals so that everywhere they are faced with a great majority of non-perverts who keep them, as well as each other, under control, out of a healthy abhorrence of homosexuality that is very widespread among prisoners as well. This system is completed by putting them in a part of the hut that is especially easy to watch and on the upper bed where there are bunks, and by carefully selecting the hut elders. In the allocation of work, it is important to ensure that homosexual prisoners do not have the opportunity to be with other individual prisoners without being under constant and direct supervision; for this reason they should not be used for kitchen or storeroom duties. May I further point out that youths, as well as other young prisoners who are part of the juvenile penal system, are not admitted to the camps. To put homosexuals together in isolation from other prisoners, apart from offering the opportunity of secret homosexual activity, would appear to contain the risk that a 'homosexual atmosphere' will take shape which drags the individual still deeper into homosexuality. If experiences on the ground contradict this assumption, I should be grateful to be informed of it.

BAK B 22/1261 fol 154–156.

Survey by the Reich Statistical Bureau of Sentences for
Unnatural Sex Acts (§§175, 175a, 175b) other than Offences with
Children under Fourteen (§176,3)

Year	Duly convicted persons	Of which, minors aged 14 to 18	Minors as % of total
1931	665	89	13.4%
1932	801	114	14.2%
1933	853	104	12.2%
1934	948	121	12.8%
1935	2106	257	12.2%
1936	5320	481	9.0%
1937	8271	973	11.8%
1938	8562	974	11.4%
1939	7614	689	9.1%
1940	3773	427	11.3%
1941	3739	687	15.7%
1942	2678	665	24.4%
1943[1]	2218	500	22.5%

[1] Figures for the first half-year doubled for the sake of comparison. All figures for the years 1940 to 1943 refer to the 'Old Reich', without the annexed eastern territories and without the 'Ostmark' [i.e. Austria].
Source: *Kriminalität und Gefährdung der Jugend*, op. cit., p. 89. Figures for the years 1940 to 1943 have been completed from details given by the Reich Statistical Bureau.

Gera Chief Prosecutor   Gera, 16 May 1938

[...] Sex crimes have still not subsided. As before their number is
frighteningly high. I should like to mention here a few especially
striking cases. [...] A Labour Service sergeant in Saalburg, basely
and contemptibly abusing his position on numerous occasions, sexually assaulted a number of healthy, irreproachable workmen.
[...]
(fol 55)

Chief Prosecutor at the Weimar District Court
Jena Branch
                                                         Jena, 20 July 1938

[...] On the other hand, crimes and offences involving unnatural
sex acts have somewhat declined. Two major cases are still under
way under §175a of the Penal Code. One involves an artist Dr T.
from Grimma/Sachsen who was restoring paintings in the Town

Museum on the instructions of Jena Town Council. Dr T. seduced a large number of boys under twenty-one to have unnatural sexual relations with him. [...]
(fol 102)

Chief Prosecutor at the
Weimar District Court   Weimar, 18 July 1938

[...] The fewer number of criminal cases against homosexuals shows that the scourge is being successfully combated, at least in this district. It is repeatedly heard from convicts, however, that they feel their sentences to be unjust, because prominent homosexuals are allegedly not being prosecuted. The main people named in this connection are State Councillor Dr Ziegler and Prussian State Councillor Gründgen. [...] (fol 111)

Chief Prosecutor at the
Altenburg District Court   Altenburg, 10 November 1938

[...] Sex crimes still constitute a major area of criminal cases. Only in a very small number of cases are trials still pending for unnatural sex acts. [...]
(fol 157)

Rudolstadt Chief Prosecutor   Rudolstadt, 9 November 1938

[...] On 1 October the businessman Otto K. was arrested here for offences under §§175a Clause 3, 175, 176 Clause S of the Penal Code. Gradually he admitted having masturbated with 14 school-boys under fourteen years of age and 15 youths aged between fourteen and seventeen, in the period from 1937 until October 1938. In earlier years (1924–1932) K. had done the same with a master dressmaker Sch., a motor vehicle driver Sch., a wire-weaver E. and a Dr V. In the course of further enquiries the following were arrested:
on 21.10.38 the businessman Erich H. and the dressmaker Sch.
on 22.10.38 the representative Hugo M., the greengrocer Bruno T. and the 81-year-old retired civil servant S., the last-named being subsequently declared unfit for detention
on 29.10.38 the chemist Erich B.
on 3.11.38 the senior primary school teacher Hugo H.
on 7.11.38 the representative Heinz R.
In addition, similar cases are pending against a few others. [...]
(fol 174f.)

Letter of 12 July 1942 from the NSDAP local group in Wesenberg, Stargard district (Mecklenburg) to the district leadership (Source: Mecklenburgisches Landeshauptarchiv Schwerin. STA/LG Neustrelitz 301).

Subject: Petition from Mrs . . ., Wilhelmshöhe

'I enclose herewith a petition from Mrs . . . in Wilhelmshöhe b/Wesenberg for the release of her father from preventive detention, with a request that it be dealt with further.

'The father of Mrs . . . from Wilhelmshöhe b/Wesenberg has served a long custodial sentence for an offence under §175 and apparently a preventive detention order has now been made. . . ., who is a mason by trade, used to be a respectable and highly capable person who rapidly advanced thanks to his mental alertness. Unfortunately, as a result of the painful aftermath of world war and the ensuing inflation, he completely went off the rails. In my opinion he was led into his sex offence by his completely degenerate life-style. At that time he showed absolutely no consideration for his highly capable wife and two children (both girls), and by his wild life he completely ruined relationships within the family. In his case it is not a question of an inherited tendency, for his parents were decent, respectable people and his children also show only the best inclinations. The elder daughter lives married in Neustrelitz. Her husband is currently on active service with the Waffen-SS. The second daughter has taken over the completely ruined Wilhelmshöfe farm and is making hard and honest efforts to get things under control. She is divorced from her husband, who I'm afraid was also a thoughtless character. One day the farm will go to the boy produced by the marriage.

'If, as a result of this petition, . . . were to return to his former property and thus to his family, it would only represent a further burden for that family. It can be excluded that . . . will reform. And he has caused his dependants so much sorrow that there can be no question of harmony being restored in the family. From personal experience I have known the situation at the Heidenreichs very well for more than thirty years. The origin of this petition is only a certain sense of duty in relation to the father. But I know that no one in the family wishes the husband and father to return: his presence could only lead to further afflictions.

'In view of the sketch I have given, I would therefore ask you to pass on the petition with a recommendation to reject.'

Heil Hitler!
Signed: illegible

Rudolstadt Chief Prosecutor   Rudolstadt, 16 January 1939

[...] On Wednesday and Friday of last week [...] the trials of 8 persons charged of offences under §§175f. took place at the Criminal Assizes. Sentences ranging from a fine of 300 Reichsmarks to four years' imprisonment were handed down [...]. Two of the defendants [...] are still waiting to be sentenced. Views are divided about the level of the sentences. Some say that some of the sentences are too high, others that they are too low. Otherwise the whole business was more an occasion for rather pointed humour, insofar as the week in which the trials took place was generally known as Rudolstadt's 'hot week'. [...] (fol 214)

Gera Chief Prosecutor   Gera, 16 March 1938

[...] As I have always stressed in my reports, sex crimes are not subsiding in this district. Proceedings were taken not only under §§175, 176 Sect. 1 No. 3 of the Penal Code but also §§172, 173, 177, 182 and 183. The shamelessness of men with unnatural tendencies is shown by a case in which two men relieved each other in a wine bar in the presence of other customers. In another case a homosexual in a public house followed a non-commissioned officer who was a complete stranger to him into the toilets. There he took the other's hand and guided it to his sex organ. Later it was possible to arrest under §175, 3d of the Penal Code a head waiter who had earlier been active in Zeulenroda. He must be declared a thoroughly dangerous 'friend' of young people. [...] (fol 235)

Chief Prosecutor at the Gotha District Court
Ilmenau Branch
                                         Ilmenau, 20 July 1938

[...] Second hearing against minors for offence under §175 of the Penal Code.
A centre of the epidemic was recently discovered in Arnstadt. Approximately forty youths were mixed up in the affair. Some of the cases formed part of a whole together with offences under §176 of the Penal Code. The investigations have been concluded. In most cases, given the young age of the accused, it was decided not to bring charges and the proceedings were abandoned with the agreement of the juvenile judge after the accused had been warned by the court. Charges were preferred only against those who had been identified as corrupters.

The offences of the accused go back to schooldays. Most of the accused belonged to a school class which had been confirmed at Easter 1937. The mutual masturbation carried out there was mostly kept up after they left school. [...]
(fol 293f.)

[52] '[...] the sad lot of these hapless people should be made a little more bearable'
Letter from one Erich Müller to the Reich Ministry of Justice, 4 December 1939

To the
Reich Ministry of Justice
Berlin   Berlin, 4 December 1939

In the last few years especially heavy sentences have been passed for offences under §175. This has prompted me to write these lines today.

There is hardly anyone who does not condemn it if an adult sexually assaults a young or even mentally subnormal person, just as it is reprehensible if one individual exploits another's plight. It is therefore welcome to all if the most severe measures are taken against such elements. But the situation is quite different where two adults act in full conjunction.

Unfortunately the law-makers show that they are quite incapable of putting themselves in the position of such people who suffer so much as a result of this unfortunate predisposition and who, with the best of wills, cannot find any lasting cure to the disease. A custodial sentence may not be a means of curing this disease. People with this inclination suffer from a lasting sense of inferiority and yet fully discharge their duties at work – indeed, one could say that by far the majority of them are exceptionally capable and hard-working and therefore enjoy the esteem of their superiors and workmates. Such people may at least be able to claim a modest place in the sun for themselves; they are not criminals, they cause nobody any harm, nor do they deceive or steal from anyone. It is a crime if they enter a marriage, however, for either they make their wife still more unhappy, or any children produced by the marriage later experience in themselves through inherited troubles the whole tragedy that their father has already lived through. If the present lines could help prevent further prosecutions of such people, if, as I said at the beginning, mutual understanding is possible so that they do not constantly have that terrible sense of being tormented and repressed which paralyses the creativity at work which matters so much nowadays, then I can be sure that it is not unworthy national comrades to whom such kindness and understanding is being given. It is really not an unreasonable demand to make.

Especially in hard times like those of today, when we Germans must stand together all the more to defeat our external foes, may I perhaps address to the competent authorities a modest request that the sad lot of these hapless people should be made a little more bearable. Always to have to live in fear of coming into conflict with the law – that is a terrible and ultimately intolerable feeling, of which someone with normal tendencies can hardly have any idea. It is not surprising that over time something like that wears people down, for in the end it is not just their own fate but that of their closest kin which is at stake.

Because I know that many thousand German national comrades would sign this letter with the greatest enthusiasm, I have been able to find the courage to write to you. I implore you to give this letter your serious consideration.

Heil Hitler!
Signed: Erich Müller

Part IV
Intensified Persecution after 1939

(a) 'Ruthless Severity' in the Wehrmacht

Universal military service was reintroduced in 1935, covering all males from the age of 18 to 45, or up to 60 in the case of officers and NCOs.[1] A year later the strength of the army already stood at 550,000 men, and by August 1939 a total of 2.6 million soldiers came under the Wehrmacht High Command (OKW).

Such a concentration and isolation of men must have seemed to the rulers particularly conducive to the phenomenon they termed 'epidemic spread'. And yet, in the newly drafted code of military penal law there were no specific provisions against homosexuality. In the Wehrmacht as in civilian life, pertinent behaviour was dealt with as an offence under §175 or §175a of the Penal Code. In formal legal terms nothing changed in this respect up to the end of the war. But there were efforts to push through special regulations for the Wehrmacht and to express these in the practice of military courts.

Fears that the concentrated isolation of men in the army, navy and air force would lead to homosexual behaviour on a massive scale were not confirmed by the number of trials of members of the Wehrmacht. A comparison of sentences in the civilian and military spheres shows that things developed in more or less the same way. 'In 1940, 3773 adult and 427 juvenile civilians were convicted of homosexuality in the Reich. This figure was lower than the 3841 adults and 263 juveniles in 1939. On the other hand, offences under §§175, 175a of the Penal Code increased in the Wehrmacht because of the enlistment of numerous homosexuals; 1134 sentences were handed down in 1940. In 1941 there was no significant change in the number of civilians convicted. A total of 3739 sentences were passed on adults and 645 on juveniles. In the Wehrmacht in the same year, the number of convicted soldiers rose by nearly fifty per cent to 1700. Roughly speaking, that is the level at which it remained until the end of the war.'[2]

According to Wehrmacht crime statistics there were a total of just under 7000 relevant convictions in the period from 1 September 1939 to 30 July 1944 (after which no figures are available) (see table on page 163). Given the strength of the army this figure is very low, even if (fortunately for the men concerned) a number of cases went undetected.

Until 1942 the judgement of members of the armed forces was governed by the same criteria as in civilian life. Thus, the decisive factor in convictions and sentence levels was the extent to which the military court (and, in some circumstances, army doctors involved in the

[1] For the text of the decree see *Reichsgesetzblatt* 1/1935, p. 375.

[2] F. Seidler, *Prostitution, Homosexualität, Selbstverstümmelung. Probleme der deutschen Sanitätsführung 1939–1945*, Neckargmünd 1977, pp. 205f.

	Convictions	Of which, officers	Of which, NCOs
1939 (from 1.9)	242	6	40
1940	1134	126	273
1941	1700	50	443
1942	1578	63	436
1943	1473	n/a	n/a
1944 (to 30.7)	830	n/a	n/a

Source: BA-MA H 20/479.

decision-making) thought they could establish whether the accused had acted 'out of an incorrigible disposition' or whether he had 'healthy' sexual feelings but had been 'seduced or had erred through sexual overexcitement'. In the first category the norm was a prison sentence or, if there had been an abuse of authority, penal servitude followed by detention in a camp. Defendants who had been 'seduced', however, could reckon on a return to active service after completing their sentence. This was supposed to give them the chance of 'proving themselves' in face of the enemy. But both categories of men convicted under §§175, 175a were considered unsuitable for duties involving leadership.

No secure criteria were available to make the required identification of men born with the 'defect' of homosexuality. Already before the outbreak of war, it was clear that intensive studies of the supposedly inherited causes of homosexuality – a pet theme of Himmler's supported by the Reich Office for the Combating of Homosexuality and Abortion – were not yielding the anticipated results. Medical knowledge, which at the time was expected to elucidate the problem, had not made any real headway since 1933, and the leading lights of biology, endocrinology and psychiatry were as ever at odds with one another over the explanation.

During the war there were stronger demands for criteria of differentiation that would be of pragmatic use. Both ideological and practical needs played a role in this.

In August 1941, at a consultation meeting in the Führer's headquarters, Hitler denounced the 'plague of homosexuality' and called for 'ruthless severity' in the Wehrmacht, the Party and the Hitler Youth. Three months later an order was issued for 'the SS and Police to be kept pure'; it prescribed the death penalty and stepped up the pressure on judges and expert witnesses.

In the summer of 1942 the Wehrmacht leadership found itself compelled to carry out thorough checks on the practice of military courts. An officer convicted under §175 had turned to Hitler with a plea for clemency and asked to be allowed to prove himself on parole at the front. The Führer, dismissing the plea, demanded that the sentence should be served in full and the officer then discharged from the army. At the Reich Chancellery this decision was treated as precedent, although it remained unclear whether in future any member of the armed forces convicted under §175 would be punished so rigorously and whether the distinctions envisaged in Göring's decree of 17.1.1942 were no longer valid.

To clarify matters the OKW initiated a confidential survey among representatives of the Reich Ministry of Justice, the Gestapo, the Reich Criminal Police Bureau and the Army Medical Inspectorate, with the aim of establishing the various opinions on the question. The Wehrmacht legal department insisted on a decision.

The Ministry of Justice, seeing a danger in every convicted soldier, essentially opposed any setting aside of sentences or a general amnesty and argued for expulsion from the army. The Gestapo and Criminal Police, by contrast, supported for the armed forces too the old distinction between those who were homosexually 'inclined' and those who had 'misbehaved' or been 'seduced' on one occasion. Reform and prevention, as well as a return to active service, were supposed to be possible in the latter case.

Towards the end of 1942 a working committee was set up to clarify the different positions. Much space was given over to discussions of the concept of 'criminal tendencies' [*Hangtäterschaft*], rekindling the pre-1933 controversies between medical and legal experts about the causes of homosexuality. Judges tended to interpret the 'tendency' towards homosexuality as an inclination to become a so-called 'habitual criminal'. The experts involved in the debate could not agree, however, what exactly should qualify as a homosexual tendency: something more or less innate, or a sexual inclination acquired through 'corruption'. The recommended solutions differed accordingly. Even a study commissioned by the Wehrmacht into the extent of 'infection' in the army – and written up by Otto Wuth in February as an aide-mémoire – threw no definitive light on the subject. Wehrmacht crime statistics recorded a total of nearly six thousand convictions by March 1943.

Two different sets of guidelines were eventually adopted as a result of these disputes.

- On 19 May 1943 the OKW Chief, General Keitel, issued 'Guidelines for the Handling of Criminal Cases of Unnatural Sex Acts'.
- On 7 June 1944 the head of the Luftwaffe Medical Corps, Schröder, passed a fourteen-page directive of his own, the 'Instructions for Medical Doctors on How to Evaluate Homosexual Acts'.

The OKW guidelines drew a sharper distinction between 'criminals by inclination' and those who had been 'seduced' or doubtful cases, with a corresponding difference in the sentences to be meted out. In 'serious cases' involving 'criminals by inclination', there was provision for penal servitude or exceptionally the death penalty under §5 of the Wartime Penal Ordinance. After completing his sentence, the prisoner would not be considered fit for service but would be sent for 'reform' in a concentration camp. Corrupted men ran the risk of imprisonment, followed by 'parole in face of the enemy'. In case of doubt the person in question might be deported to a field punishment camp or ordered to serve his sentence in a field prison camp.

The 'Instructions' issued by the Luftwaffe Medical Corps are of interest more in historical terms than for any practical effect on the soldiers' everyday life. They give us an insight into the different views of rival groupings within the decision-making bodies. For as the 'Instructions' used some officially disapproved psychoanalytic notions – the result of collaboration with the Reich Institute for Psychological Research and Psychotherapy, whose director was Matthias Heinrich Göring, a favourite nephew of Reichsmarschall Göring – the psychiatrist Max de Crinis, who succeeded Wuth on his retirement in November 1944, ordered that the 'Instructions' should no longer be distributed. In December he again called a committee together to tackle what had not yet been achieved: a uniform basic orientation for expert assessment of homosexual acts, which would preclude any special regulations for people whom the regime labelled as criminals. With military disaster looming over more clearly in late 1944, this was also a desperate attempt to make up for the massive casualties by mobilizing some final reserves.

[53] The Führer on the plague of homosexuality in the Wehrmacht and Party
Memorandum from the Führer's headquarters, 19 August 1941

Yesterday evening the Führer spoke for a long time about the plague of homosexuality. He said that we must prosecute it with ruthless severity, because there was a time in youth when boys' sexual feelings could easily be influenced in the wrong direction; it was precisely at that age that boys were corrupted by homosexuals. More often than not, a homosexual seduces a huge number of boys, so that homosexuality is actually as infectious and as dangerous as the plague. But our youth must not be lost to us – on the contrary, it must be brought up properly. So wherever symptoms of homosexuality appear among the youth, they should be attacked with barbaric severity.

Precisely our state and our order can and must be based only on the performance principle. Any kind of favouritism is to be rejected; we want no specially protected children and so on.

A homosexual, however, does *not* judge other men by their performance: he dismisses the most capable men even though, or even because, they are not homosexual; for he prefers homosexuals. In the Röhm case and others we saw that a homosexual will fill all positions of authority with other homosexuals.

Especially in the Party and its various organizations, as well as in the Wehrmacht, it is necessary to act with ruthless severity against any case of homosexuality that appears in its ranks. If this is done the state apparatus will remain clean, and it must remain clean.

In *one* organization, however, any case of homosexuality must be punished with death, and that is in the Hitler Youth. If it is to be the elite of the nation, then misconduct in its ranks must never be given any other sentence.

[54] Dealing with sex offences between men
Decree of the Luftwaffe commander-in-chief Reichsmarschall
Hermann Göring, 17 January 1942

The Reich Minister for Air Travel   Berlin W 8
and Commander-in-Chief of the Luftwaffe   17 January 1942
– Legal Department –
B 14f 11, ZA/R IV B 140/42

Subject: Cases involving sex offences between men (§§175, 175a Reich Penal Code)

The Reichsmarschall wishes the following principles to be applied in the handling of sex offences between men. A distinction should be drawn between:

(1) offenders who have contravened §175 out of a predisposition or a clearly incorrigible drive,

(2) offenders who basically have healthy sexual feelings but have been seduced or have erred through sexual overexcitement.

In cases under category (1) a prison sentence should be passed, with detention in perpetuity in a penal camp. The same applies to all sex offences with men committed through *gross* abuse of authority.

Culprits falling under category (2), including officers punished with loss of rank, are to be taken back into the service after they have completed their sentence. On principle they should be given the chance to prove themselves on parole in face of the enemy.

German soldiers in the Soviet Union, 1943

The decision whether (1) or (2) applies cannot be taken in general but only in each individual case, with reference to all the circumstances of the offence – one criterion being that offences committed by superiors with respect to subordinates should be dealt with more harshly. The temptation should be avoided of automatically taking in mitigation the fact that an offence was committed under the influence of alcohol.

Implementation of these principles presupposes that in future court sentences, it will be established in each individual case to which of the aforementioned categories the offender should be allocated in accordance with the conclusions of the trial. The investigation should already consider things from this point of view in the preliminary proceedings.

p.p.
Signed: Dr Baron von Hammerstein, assistant secretary

[55] No mercy. The Führer stands firm
The decision on a plea for clemency and its consequences

Notes: Dr Lehmann for the Field Marshal, Head of the Wehrmacht, 12 August 1942

According to a report from Captain von *Puttkammer*, when the Führer was presented with a plea for clemency from a former lieutenant convicted of unnatural sexual acts, he expressed his astonishment that the rest of the sentence should be suspended for the lieutenant to prove himself in face of the enemy (his offences being based on a *predetermined tendency*). The Führer argued that a person's disposition cannot be changed, and that it is therefore wrong to allow parole in the face of the enemy. As a matter of principle the sentences must be served in full and at the end the culprits must be definitively discharged from the Wehrmacht.

On another occasion Major *Engel*, the head of P 2, reported the Führer's views as follows. Anyone convicted of unnatural sex acts, even in a drunken stupor, must never be put on parole in face of the enemy and be granted rehabilitation. It is not known here whether this second expression of the Führer's will referred to *innately* determined offences or also to a single act of misbehaviour.

The report of the Führer's will first gave reason to obtain expressions of opinion through confidential personal enquiries with the Reich Ministry of Justice, the Secret State Police Bureau, the Reich Criminal Police Bureau and the Psychiatric Adviser of the Army Medical Inspectorate. The enquiries have produced a *variety* of views.

1 In the view of the Reich Ministry of Justice any homosexual act on the part of an *adult* indicates with near certainty a predisposition. The culprits will constantly represent a danger to those around them. A less extreme view can be entertained only in relation to misbehaviour in adolescence, when a healthy development of feelings can take place after a suitably long period of time.

2 The Secret State Police Bureau thinks it is possible to draw a distinction between people with homosexual tendencies and those who err or are seduced on one occasion. Elements with unnatural tendencies are a danger to the community, and in their case one has to reject the idea of reform or parole. As to those who err or are seduced once, experiments can be made with milder treatment and reintegration into the national community. The specialist at the Secret State Police Bureau has estimated the number of those with

homosexual inclinations (including borderline cases) at roughly four *million*.

3 The Reich Criminal Police Bureau distinguishes between environmentally determined and predisposed cases of unnatural sexual practices. In practice it works in accordance with the following guidelines. One-time misbehavers are at first placed under supervision. If there are repeated convictions or seduction of several partners, an order is made for preventive police detention. The inmates of concentration camps are to a considerable extent homosexuals. Major Dr *Göring* at the Reich Ministry for Air Travel is using psychotherapeutic research to attempt the reintegration of such people into the national community and he has had some good results.

In the personal view of the specialist at the Reich Criminal Police Bureau, the exclusion of homosexuals from the Wehrmacht is not to be recommended. The Criminal Police has already released homosexuals from preventive detention to perform military service. In police terms a danger arises in the Wehrmacht too only in the case of repeated convictions or of offences committed with different persons. If homosexuals are in future discharged from the Wehrmacht after serving their sentence, preventive police detention should be provided. But there is hardly enough room in police camps, and accommodation in Wehrmacht punishment camps would have to be considered.

4 The psychiatric adviser at the Army Medical Inspectorate was of the view that any conviction for unnatural sexual practices (even in a drunken stupor) indicated with a greater or lesser degree of certainty the presence of an unnatural inclination. Only homosexual misconduct in adolescence could be regarded as not being out of the ordinary. It would not occur to an adult male with normal feelings, even when blind drunk, to engage in unnatural activity.

From a psychiatric point of view, there should only be a firm warning of discharge following completion of the sentence. If it was already known, there would be a danger that soldiers whose position in civilian life carried no particular obligations would commit a homosexual act against their own nature so as to gain a discharge following completion of a short sentence. Other authorities also regard this as a serious danger.

The *Party* takes the position on principle that comrades who have unnatural *inclinations* or who *act* unnaturally should be expelled from the Party. The *SS* and police courts mete out punishments of death in cases involving unnatural sexual practices. Given these completely different views and evaluations, I consider it necessary to bring about an *official* position of all the authorities involved, before a regulation corresponding to the Führer's reported will is established for the armed forces. I would ask the Field Marshal to authorize the securing of an *official* position of all interested authorities. That will take some time, because the authorities to be consulted will most carefully weigh their official expressions of opinion.

Until then, things should be done in such a way that soldiers who have committed homosexual acts out of a *tendency* are not released on parole. The Field Marshal's guidelines of 10 June 1942 for the completion of custodial sentences stipulate that persons who have been given long terms of imprisonment for unnatural sexual practices between men, and who are expected to be a permanent threat to discipline, should be transferred to a field punishment camp. This principle is also upheld by a decree of the Reichsmarschall dated 17 January 1942, a copy of which is enclosed and which I intend to forward to the army and the navy.[3]

Furthermore, a directive to Wehrmacht courts might be considered to the effect that, in serious cases involving unnatural sexual practices where a long term of penal servitude is deemed necessary according to the provisions of general penal law, the death penalty should be inflicted on disciplinary grounds under the extended range of sentences provided for by §5a of the Special Wartime Penal Ordinance.

Signed: Lehmann

[3] See Document 54.

[56] Aide-Mémoire: Offences under §175 of the Penal Code
Military Psychiatrist Prof. Otto Wuth to the Wehrmacht Command, 24 February 1943

Psychiatric Adviser   24 February 1943
at the Army Medical Inspectorate
Academy of Military Medicine
25/42 geh.

To the
Wehrmacht Command
attn. Second Army Staff Officer
Major Risch
Berlin W 35
Bendlerstr. 35   Secret

As per telephonic consultation, you will find enclosed the material on sex offences between men that could be gathered at the present time from various authorities, together with a breakdown according to year of birth. It is in the nature of such material that one can never fully quantify all possible or actual perpetrators. To some extent it would have been possible to establish the number of homosexuals in the army, if my proposal at the time had been accepted.[4] It is incomprehensible why that advice was rejected on the grounds that the victims of corruption could be branded as a result, for it was precisely to avoid this that only rentboys and corrupters of youth were mentioned.

Some explanations are appended to the enclosed figures. The notes and references make some points that should be worthy of attention.

Signed: Wuth
Colonel in the Medical Corps

– 1 communication – (aide-mémoire)
– 2 loose enclosures – (1 drawing)
                    (1 copy)[5]

Aide-Mémoire
Subject: Offences under §175 of the Penal Code. Statistical and other remarks submitted by Prof. Dr. O. Wuth, Colonel in the Medical Corps.

The following table uses Reich Statistical Bureau surveys to

[4] See Documents 42a to 42c.
[5] Neither of the loose enclosures was found in the file.

provide figures for the number of persons *convicted* of any offence
and for those convicted under §175, in both cases for adults and for
young persons under eighteen years of age.

	Total convicted adults	§175 adults	Total convicted juveniles	§175 juveniles
1932	564 479	801	21 529	114
1933	489 090	853	15 938	104
1934	383 885	948	12 294	121
1935	431 426	2106	17 038	257
1936	385 400	5320	16 872	481
1937	438 493	8271	24 562	973
1938	385 665	8562	19 302	974
1939	335 162	8274*	17 444	689
1940	264 625	3773**	21 274	427
1941	318 293	3753	37 853	687

* Includes the annexed Eastern Territories and the 'Ostmark'.
** Excludes the annexed Eastern Territories.

The sharp decline in the number of adults convicted under §175
from 1939 to 1940 is mostly to be explained by enlistment into the
armed forces. Thus the §175 cases handled in those years by *all the
police organizations in the Reich* included the following figures for
those against whom accusations were made in the civilian sector:

1937 – 32 360, of whom 308 belonged to the armed forces;
1938 – 28 882, of whom 102 belonged to the armed forces;
First half of 1939 – *16 748*, of whom 327 belonged to the
armed forces.

Then the surveys were suspended until:
First half of 1942 – 4697, of whom 332 belonged to the
armed forces.

The number of persons accused thus fell to almost a quarter.
Some of the difference can be put down to the fact that from 1940
any homosexual who seduced more than one partner was handed
over to a concentration camp. The lowest figure for this category
from 1940 on was 2284, but it must now be somewhat higher.
Of the total figure, accusations were made against:

Corrupters of youth		1937 – 7452	Rentboys – 800
Corrupters of youth		1938 – 7472	Rentboys – 587
Corrupters of youth	First half	1939 – 4162	Rentboys – 300
Corrupters of youth	Second half	1942 – 1257	Rentboys – 114

Here again we see a reduction to approximately a quarter.

It should be stressed that the figures are for persons *accused* not for those actually *convicted*. There must also be a considerable number of unreported cases. The *Reich Youth Leadership* reported the figures for criminals, i.e. for juveniles, on the basis of material from the Reich Statistical Bureau. Per 100,000 convicted juveniles these came to:

1936	11.5
1937	20.5
1938	20.9
1939	15.0

Using material from the Reich Criminal Police Bureau, the Reich Youth Leadership reported per 100,000 investigated juveniles:

1936	33.8
1937	61.1
1938	40.3
1939	54.5

With the large number of unreported cases, it is impossible to identify figures for persons in the armed forces who *might* commit offences under §175. Again what is most instructive is to note that by 1942 the numbers accused at the Reich Criminal Police Bureau had fallen to a quarter of the figure for 1939. Some of these will, it is true, have been recorded in the armed forces under the appropriate offence.

The Wehrmacht crime figures show the following breakdown:

from 26.8.39 to 31.12.39 –	185	condemned under §175, 175a
from 1.1.40 to 31.3.40 –	229	condemned under §175, 175a
from 1.4.40 to 30.6.40 –	241	condemned under §175, 175a
from 1.7.40 to 30.9.40 –	291	condemned under §175, 175a
from 1.10.40 to 31.12.40 –	373	condemned under §175, 175a
from 1.1.41 to 31.3.41 –	405	condemned under §175, 175a
from 1.4.41 to 30.6.41 –	474	condemned under §175, 175a
from 1.7.41 to 30.9.41 –	451	condemned under §175, 175a
from 1.10.41 to 31.12.41 –	370	condemned under §175, 175a
from 1.1.42 to 31.3.42 –	401	condemned under §175, 175a
from 1.4.42 to 30.6.42 –	403	condemned under §175, 175a
	3823	condemned under §175, 175a

The number of §175 convictions in the armed forces cannot be explained either by a fall in Reich Statistical Bureau figures for convicted adults or by an increase in juvenile convictions. Even for those who show up in police figures as having been accused, there is no absolutely clear explanation. Examination of all these statistics creates the impression – even if it cannot be expressed in figures – that offences under §175 are actually rolled back under the conditions of military service. This is not so surprising if one thinks of the strain and effort to which combat troops are subject. A study of the files also leaves the impression that such offences are more likely to be committed at the rear and under the influence of alcohol than among combat troops.

If one were to draw a conclusion from these rather speculative considerations, it would be that §175, 175a offenders should, if possible, be posted among combat troops.

As for detention in a punishment camp or prison, experience suggests no reason for misgivings if such offenders are visibly identified by a certain colour affixed to their uniform. It has been shown in concentration camps that such criminals as burglars or thieves reject §175 prisoners in the sharpest manner. Such a means of identification, which can be seen by all inmates, also makes it impossible for them to form groups and cliques.

Precise figures for potential offenders can obviously never be established. A few years ago *Das Schwarze Korps* estimated the number of homosexuals in Germany at 2 million, while the Gestapo expert Fehling puts it at between 1 and 2 million. This is probably too high, as the Reich Criminal Police Bureau, which now has specialists working in the field, also accepts.

As I have already explained, recidivism and other indices of criminality are high, especially among corrupters of youth.

Medically speaking, it must be stressed that 'homosexuality', like other sexual perversions, does not have an effect on the military fitness rating, except in the case of acts committed in the state defined in §51.1 or 51.2, when the fitness rating should take into account the underlying disorder (e.g. manic-depressive psychosis).

There has often been talk of sexual exigency, by analogy with homosexual offences between sailors, long-term convicts, etc.; but such exigency is probably present only in exceptional cases, and anyway combat troops should not experience it, nor, for different reasons, should those on duty at the rear. It is better to speak here of surrogate behaviour.

If an offender approaches someone normal among the troops, that person will give him a piece of his mind and report him. If he approaches a like-minded person, they will both be liable to punishment.

Detention in a punishment camp from the beginning of the sentence, and only after the war is over, would be an unjust exacerbation not provided for by the law.

It should be considered that someone placed on parole among the troops may no longer have the incentive to prove himself if he sees that, whatever he does, he cannot achieve anything – for in general homosexuals are not suited to become superiors (leaders and examples to the men), except in unusual cases of, for example, first offences committed when blind drunk by someone who otherwise is an excellent leader and has a blameless sex life.

So only few homosexuals are suited to serve parole among the troops, unless some kind of incentive, some goal worth the effort, is given to them there.

Among young people, perhaps those still in late adolescence, one should be careful not to break them more than is necessary for correction.

Sex education seems important here, but it should never be done by means of texts or at mass assemblies. It should be carried out by doctors in the context of education about venereal diseases, but the subject should not be blown up out of all proportion.

Many young people were seduced into homosexual offences by Magnus Hirschfeld, Blüher and the Wandervogel movement and the Bund Youth. In the nature of things this still has its effect today, when the one-time seduced have now become seducers. It is out of the question, however, to accept that the German *Volk* is heading for homosexual practices. For this reason – and especially because of the enemy propaganda (to which England has the least right, given its high number of homosexuals which Havelock Ellis puts at 3 to 4 million) – it seems advisable to stop the publication of scientific and pseudo-scientific material in this field in specialist journals. Scientific experience can be exchanged between the Wehrmacht and the Party and its component divisions.

From the experience so far, emasculation appears to offer lasting success in a high percentage of cases of chronic recidivism. This should not, in my view, make a person unfit for the army, since otherwise the shirking of military service would be encouraged.

[57] New guidelines for the Wehrmacht
Chief of the Wehrmacht High Command (OKW), General Keitel,
19 May 1943

Chief of the Wehrmacht   Führer's Headquarters
High Command   19 May 1943
14 n 19 WR (II)
58/43g

Guidelines
for the Handling of Criminal Cases of Unnatural Sex Acts
(§§175, 175a and 330a of the Reich Penal Code)

(A)

A distinction should be made between:

I. offenders who have acted out of a predisposition or an acquired and clearly incorrigible drive;

II. offenders who have strayed on only one occasion, especially if they were seduced;

III. offenders in whom a tendency remains a matter of doubt.

On I:

The tendency must be established in the judgement. The most careful enquiries are necessary, already in the preliminary stages and not only at the main hearing. Questioning of comrades, including from the Wehrmacht reserve. Perhaps evidence going back to the period before military service. If there are doubts, the offender may be placed in the reserve. The court in the person's home area has more opportunity, in cooperation with the Reich Office for the Combating of Homosexuality and Abortion at the Reich Criminal Police Bureau, to arrive at the necessary conclusions.

In the case of serious crimes, long sentences of penal servitude are appropriate. In especially serious cases the death penalty may be imposed, in accordance with the more severe range of sentences allowed under §5a of the Special Wartime Penal Ordinance. Convicts should be discharged from military service, if they are not already ineligible as a result of a verdict having the force of law. If the execution of sentence is not directly transferred to the public authorities, the judge shall request that they take over the execution of sentence.

On II:

Once again the most careful enquiries. That the offence [was] committed under the influence of alcohol is not by itself proof that no tendency is present. Special vigilance in offences by superiors against subordinates. To conclude that no tendency is present is just as fraught with consequences as a positive conclusion.

German soldiers in the Soviet Union, 1943

Such convicts should be treated in accordance with the general provisions, and so are eligible for parole in the face of the enemy after completion of all or part of the sentence.

On III:
In these cases detention in a field punishment camp or completion of sentence in field penal units. Strictest supervision necessary both there and after release among the troops. If unusable for military

---

Re: Guidelines for the Handling of Cases of Unnatural Sex Acts
(§§175, 175a and 330a of the Reich Penal Code)

Enclosed are the guidelines of the Chief of the Wehrmacht High Command for the Handling of Cases of Unnatural Sex Acts (§§175, 175a and 330a of the Reich Penal Code). The guidelines have been submitted to the Führer and approved by him.
Chief of the Wehrmacht High Command
p.p.
Signed: Dr *Lehmann*

Communication from the OKW dated 22 May 1943, BA – MA H 20/479.

---

purposes, discharge and transfer to Reich administration of justice for further serving of sentence. Treat repetition according to I.

(B)

Cases judged before these guidelines were decreed should in general also be handled in accordance with them. This applies especially to the question of whether the man may or may not remain in military service. If, contrary to I. of the guidelines, the man has been kept on duty, he should be discharged even if he has proved himself as a soldier. An exception may be made only if such a soldier has behaved irreproachably over a long period of time, so that as far as anyone can judge a repetition is not to be looked after [sic].

(C)

It is recommended that confirmation is still reserved for a person in higher authority.

Signed: Keitel.

[58] Cannon fodder. Male convicts in penal battalions
A proposal of the SS-Legal Headquarters, 14 September 1943

The Reichsführer-SS   Munich, 14 September 1943
SS-Legal Headquarters
IIIb 366 (Bd. III)

To the:
SS-Judge attached to the Reichsführer-SS
and Head of the German Police
SS-Obersturmbannführer Bender
Berlin

Subject: Assignment of persons convicted of unnatural sex acts to
          the Dirlewanger special SS unit

In minor cases of unnatural sex acts, involving convicts who were seduced at a young age, the Reichsführer-SS has already decided that they may be assigned to a special unit of the Waffen-SS (labour section, parole section or special unit of the SS Police Division), if their personality and conduct during the offence offer an assurance that their misbehaviour was a single aberration and that there is no reason to fear a repetition.

In serious cases, on the other hand, where a predisposition or acquired tendency to unnatural sex acts can be demonstrated in the culprit, the sentence should be served in a concentration camp – with no account taken of time served at war in the case of penal servitude, and with a preventive camp order in the case of imprisonment, so that they are kept in detention until the end of the war and beyond.

Between these two groups, however, there are intermediate cases where, from the verdict, the offence and the culprit's personality, as well as from observation during the period of detention, it cannot be said whether the case is minor or serious in the above sense. In such intermediate cases, where a repetition can be excluded with great probability but not with certainty, it would often be advisable to place the culprit on parole for further opportunities to present themselves, but it then seems advisable to assign them to a special unit of the Waffen-SS.

In such intermediate cases, therefore, consideration has been given to the assignment of relevant culprits to the Dirlewanger special SS unit. It is requested that the approval of the Reichsführer-SS be obtained for this regulation.

Chief of the SS-Legal Headquarters
p.p. [illegible]
SS-Obersturmbannführer and Head of Department.

[Handwritten note:]
For attention RF-SS [Reichsführer-SS]:
No need for such a regulation.
Serious cases to be eradicated.
Minor ones to special unit of Waffen-SS.
Intermediates to concentration camp or Dirlewanger.
15/10. Be [= Bender][6]

[59] Concentration camp for 'incorrigibles'
Secret decree of the Head of the Security Police, 12 May 1944

The Head of the Security Police   Berlin, 12 May 1944
and Security Service

V – B3 – Nr.189/44g   Strictly confidential!

To:
Criminal police (regional) headquarters
Copies to:
(a) officials I [...], III [...], IV [...], V [...]

---

[6] SS-Oberführer Bender, chief liaison officer from SS-Legal Headquarters to the SS Judge, Himmler.

(b) top leaders of the SS and Police
(c) inspectors in the Security Police and Security Service
(d) commanders of the Security Police and the SD in Prague, Krakow, Strassburg [Strasbourg], Metz [...]

Subject: Preventive measures against homosexuals discharged
from the Wehrmacht

In accordance with a decree of the Chief of the OKW, members of the armed forces who have committed homosexual acts out of a predisposition or an acquired and clearly incorrigible drive (those with a criminal tendency) are to be discharged from the forces. Wehrmacht courts are required to establish in their judgement whether or not the offender has clearly incorrigible criminal tendencies. A positive decision, which will usually be reached in conjunction with the Reich Office for the Combating of Homosexuality at the Reich Criminal Police Bureau, must include an assessment that the culprit is a dangerous habitual criminal who, even after completing his sentence, will be a continual danger to the community.

After being discharged from the armed forces, or immediately after the sentence which in many cases will remain to be served in public penitentiaries, such offenders should be taken into preventive police detention as dangers to the community, in accordance with Clause A II 1d of the decree of the Reich Ministry of Justice dated 14.12.1937 (Pol S Kr 3 Nr. 1682/37 – 2098) regarding the combating of crime by the police (document series 15). The custody papers should be submitted in the usual way to the Reich Criminal Police Bureau.

The Reich Office for the Combating of Homosexuality forwards to the competent regional headquarters of the Criminal Police, for further action in the sense of this decree, the reports which regularly come into it from Wehrmacht authorities concerning homosexuals with criminal tendencies who are approaching their time of release. The decree is not suitable for publication or for transmission to local police authorities. If necessary, they should be confidentially briefed at official meetings or on suchlike occasions.

Signed: Dr Kaltenbrunner

[60] Separate guidelines for the Luftwaffe
Instructions for medical officers on the assessment of homosexual acts (Extract)

The Head of the Luftwaffe   Saalow (Zossen-Land)
Medical Corps   6 June 1944
AZ 49a Nr. 28 500/44 (2G)
                                                           Only for official use
[...]
(C) Duties of the medical officer

Basic principles
I. The interests of the war effort, military discipline and protection of the youth, as well as considerations to do with population policy, imperiously require the ending of all homosexual acts, the identification of homosexuals and their punishment and removal from the armed forces.
II. Born homosexuals are essentially 'incorrigible' in respect of their instinct, but not in respect of their behaviour. An attempt must be made to teach them self-control and responsibility. This is the goal of punishment. Emasculation is in order for behavioural defectives, recidivists and individuals without a sense of responsibility.
III. Those who have become homosexuals should essentially be regarded as curable. Specialist psychotherapeutic treatment is necessary. In their case a court sentence has the educative purpose of making them aware of the necessity of treatment and strengthening their will to recover. Emasculation is biologically pointless and eugenically questionable for those who are capable of being cured.
IV. Illusory homosexuals require special education, guidance and care. Insofar as they are inferior characters, or above all 'homosexuals of convenience', it is essential to remove them from the armed forces.

These basic principles give rise to the following duties for medical officers:

1 Prevention of any kind of homosexual activity.

2 Accurate assessment of homosexual behaviour and correct advice to the commanding officer about the measures to be taken.

3 Prevention of relapses.

On 1:
The danger of homosexual activity is especially great wherever healthy, sexually needy young men live together in close physical

and psychological companionship and have no opportunity to engage in sexual intercourse or forge relations of friendship with women. This is as true of young people's homes, youth camps and monasteries as it is of barracks and other shared military accommodation. Life at the front, away from the main combat area, has a beneficial effect. The danger is especially great when soldiers have not been adequately or correctly educated in sexual matters, when the physical companionship is excessively close and an overheated sexual atmosphere develops.

The preventive action of the medical officer should therefore concentrate on:

(a) Proper instruction
The form of education depends on the particular external circumstances and the men's age and average level of education. Informal talks and individual instruction are both possible. They should essentially be given by the medical officer himself, within the framework of other sex education. It is forbidden for instruction to be given by other ranks in the medical corps. Nor is instruction by superiors an advisable practice, as it is really a matter for doctors.

The instruction must retain a strictly medical character and accord with the seriousness and dignity that sexual life should have for soldiers. It calls for objectivity and discretion, psychological understanding, tact and comradeliness. It should be neither dry nor slovenly in form. Things must be called clearly and simply by their right name, without prudishness and without sensational flourishes. Trivialization is just as dangerous as exaggeration. Facetious and brash ways of speaking are to be avoided. Noncommissioned officers should be instructed separately and told of the need for strict but unobtrusive supervision. It must be made clear to them that expressions such as 'pansy' [*warmer Bruder*], 'homo' or 'arse-fucker' are not allowed when speaking of sexual matters. That kind of slang is poisonous precisely for young soldiers. The aim should be that anything suspicious is reported to the medical officer, so that he can then intervene.

The medical officer must also inform officers – in a suitable way and in consultation with the unit commander – about the whole complex of issues relating to homosexuality, and emphasize the medical nature of the problem.

(b) Proper organization of the soldiers' communal life
Here the medical officer should work closely with the commander, the officers and the NCOs. Each soldier must on principle have his

own place to sleep. If sleeping together in one bed cannot be avoided because of conditions at the front, provision must be made for sufficient clothing. Mutual warming under the covers without closed items of clothing is especially dangerous for young soldiers. But a watch should also be kept on older soldiers who want to sleep with younger ones. The men should be prevented from suspiciously lying together in a half-awake state or during the day. Joint use of a sleeping-bag should be forbidden and made subject to punishment. If special circumstances make this unavoidable, the wearing of closed items of clothing (swimming trunks, gym shorts) is an indispensable condition. The men must leave the sleeping-bag immediately after they wake up. It should never be forgotten that to sleep in close physical companionship with a man is just as difficult for a man with homosexual tendencies as the corresponding arrangement with a woman is for a man with normal feelings. In both cases it would be asking too much to demand complete self-control. Illusory homosexuals, and homosexuals who basically do not want to give in to their instincts, would inevitably go astray in such a situation, while malicious homosexuals would be offered a welcome opportunity and an equally welcome excuse.

It is also necessary to keep an eye on communal life outside night quarters. It is thoughtless and foolish to allow young soldiers to go around in their quarters completely or partly undressed without reason or to lie about in the sun in that state. A healthy sense of shame is just as necessary as a healthy lack of inhibition. Soldierly comradeship and naturalness should not degenerate into a cult of nudity. Provocative nudity is not a necessary condition for sport and physical exercise, any more than flirting with 'sporty' trousers and shirts. Care should be taken that styles of dress and undress are plain and practical. Trunks are appropriate for swimming and sunbathing. A sauna must not become a hotbed of conscious or unconscious eroticism. Games which are on the fine line between the harmless joy of youth and sexual tickling are to be avoided: 'ham tapping', above all, must be looked out for, especially where it takes place in a 'narrow circle' perhaps of just two people, so that the basic idea – to guess the person giving the slap – does not apply. Even wrestling can be used as camouflage or lead to unintended effects. Naturally the medical officer must steer clear of prudishness and over-timidity, and must avoid making a laughing stock of himself. But nor should he fall into the opposite error of treating as harmless things which are not harmless at all.

Experts for homosexual offences
Establishment of expert advisers to the
HR [= *Heeresrechtsabteilung* (Military Justice Department) ?] for
homosexual offences, for the purpose of differentiating between
isolated acts and a determining tendency

Military District No.		
I	Med. Lieutenant Prof. Dr Mauz	Königsberg, University Psychiatric Clinic
II	Med. Colonel Dr Franckenberg	Stettin Hospital I, Dept. f., Psychiatric & Mental Diseases
III	Prof. Müller-Hess	Berlin N W 40, Hannoversche Str. 6, Inst. for Forensic & Social Medicine, Berlin University
IV	Med. Captain Dr Carrière	Westewitz
V	Med. Lt-Colonel Prof. Dr Bostroem	Strassburg, University Psychiatric Clinic, Civil Hospital
VI	Captain Dr Panse	Ensen near Cologne
VII	Ministerial War Physician Prof. Dr Bumke	Munich, Nußbaumstraße 7
VIII	Med. Colonel Prof. Dr Villinger	Breslau [Wroclaw], Auenstraße 44
IX	Med. Colonel Prof. Dr Kleist	Frankfurt a.M., University Psychiatric Clinic
X	Med. Captain Prof. Bürger-Prinz	Hamburg, University Psychiatric Clinic
XI	Med. Captain Prof. Dr Ewald	Göttingen, University Psychiatric Clinic
XII	Med. Colonel Prof. Carl Schneider	Heidelberg, University Psychiatric-neurological Clinic
XIII	Navy Med. Colonel Prof. Dr Meggendorfer	Erlangen, University Psychiatric Clinic
XVII–XVIII	Med. Lt-Colonel Dr Fuchs	Vienna 13, Riedelgasse 5
XX–XXI	Med. Colonel Dr Otten	Riesenburg

Gen. Gouv. [German occupation authority of Poland] for VIII –
Colonel Prof. Dr Villinger

BA – MA H 20/479.
The document is undated. It was compiled by Otto Wuth.

(c) Avoidance of an overheated sexual atmosphere

Conversation about sexual matters, jokes, stories and ribald songs cannot be avoided in the communal life of soldiers. In themselves they are harmless. What is not harmless, however, is excess and the not uncommon tendency to 'teach' young inexperienced comrades, to impose on them, to tease and harass them. Care should therefore be taken that, especially before bedtime in the men's quarters or even in bed, there is not too much of a good thing and tendencies become apparent which could lead to fateful consequences. Ribald conversations about homosexual matters are precisely what should not take place, for their generally erotic or sexual character may be sufficient to pave the way for homosexual aberrations. Especially dangerous are pulp literature, pictures and handwritten concoctions, which pass from hand to hand and excite young soldiers. Erotic gramophone records then do their bit to create a dangerous atmosphere. A single irresponsible lad can infect the whole quarters. Such elements must be uncovered and rendered harmless.

In the highest degree dangerous are certain performances that take place in the framework of forces entertainment. Here things may be presented to young soldiers which go far beyond the limits of what is responsible. Not only is healthy love life cynically stripped of illusions; but double-entendres with a homosexual content, spread under the cover of art, enter the soldiers' stock of anecdotes and persist even outside the performance hall. There can be no doubt that many a young soldier has more easily fallen victim to homosexual enticement because it came after a queer 'cabaret performance'. Much that would at home merely have been among a host of similar surface impressions to be rapidly forgotten, leaves a firmer mark on the uniform life of the troops. What is there a passing stimulus here turns into poison. The big mistake of many entertainments at the front is that their organizers select them from the viewpoint of the soldiers' home, without considering their often young age, their hunger for stimuli, their sexual tension and their readiness to accept everything coming from civilian life. The medical officer must pay careful attention to theatre programmes and those who organize them, and immediately intervene where he sees a danger to the sexual health of the troops. In this way he will be doing an essential service not only to them but also to forces entertainment. It goes without saying that a special eye must be kept on alcohol and its effects.

On 2:

The medical officer must be clear in his own mind that the same behaviour should be assessed in very different ways according to the culprit's personality. He must make an effort to determine in each case whether it involves a homosexual or an illusory homosexual (especially someone who has been seduced), whether aberrations are just the result of sexual need or whether the greed of a rentboy and the sordid calculation of an unscrupulous place-hunter are concealed beneath the acts. He should report accordingly to the unit commander, who will then make the right decision about the measures to be taken, especially about the type of punishment (disciplinary sanctions, report to a military tribunal), and will be able in his own report to a tribunal to give valuable indications about the specificities of the case. The correct diagnosis is often difficult to make. How to proceed and from what point of view are therefore discussed at length in Section B. To know all the possibilities is to take a great step closer to the truth. Everything else is learnt from experience and further personal training. Sexual psychology and pathology is still today a poor cousin of the art of healing. Unjustly so. It is not so rare for it to provide the key to real knowledge and thus to therapy and human conduct. In every case where the medical officer does not feel sufficiently certain, he must

---

Letter dated 9 December 1944 from the Psychiatric Adviser of the Army Medical Inspector/Military Academy Office to the Army Medical Inspector/WIGIb

Subject: Instructions for medical officers in assessing homosexual acts

Wider distribution of the instructions cannot be recommended, since the views set down within them are very controversial. Among other things, they make use of the insights of depth analysis and psychotherapy. Besides, attempts are currently under way – starting from psychiatrists in military district III in collaboration with the Central Army Court – to develop a uniform forensic position on homosexuals. After the discussions have been concluded a proposal will be issued to this end. The idea is then to work out new army guidelines for the assessment and handling of homosexuals.

Signed: Prof. Dr de Crinis
Med. Colonel
H/Gi

BA – MA H 20/479.

turn to a psychiatrist for advice. This applies especially if differences of opinion develop between himself and the commanding officer. Then the views of a specialist usually help to settle the differences. The request for a psychiatrist may be made from the Luftwaffe district doctor or the air fleet doctor.

On 3:

The prevention of recidivism essentially calls for the same measures as in the curbing of homosexual activity per se. Additions are: the breaking up of an infected or corroded group of men, removal of troublesome soldiers or unsuitable other ranks, and prevention of the appearance and spreading of rumours, gossip and wrongful suspicions. The events must be briefly, clearly and truthfully made known to the troops, in a plain and unsensational manner. Veiled hints and half-measures are usually the germ cell of rumours. If an occurrence has to be kept secret for military reasons (discipline, strike power of the troops), care should be taken to ensure that absolutely nothing leaks out. The principle must be that the incident should disappear again as rapidly as possible from the men's conversation – otherwise there will always be the danger of further aberrations. If culprits are allowed to remain in the armed forces, they must on no account return to their old unit.

There can be no general instructions on how to handle men who, having been seduced or having strayed on only one occasion, did not receive a sentence or have been transferred after the sentence from other units. Here everything must be left up to the medical officer's sense of tact and knowledge of men. What has happened and been punished, or what has not been considered worthy of punishment, should not be raked over any more. In particular, there must be no teasing or innuendoes on the part of comrades and other ranks. The necessary supervision must be operated in a skilful and not wounding manner. Otherwise young people can easily be driven into a defensive reaction and acts of defiance which pave the way for further aberrations.

It is wrong to think that illusory homosexuals can be 'cured' in brothels and with prostitutes. In particular, in the case of a young man who has not yet had relations with the other sex, it would be outrageous to seek to arrange his first 'amorous experience' with hired women. That would have precisely the opposite result. Apart from any other psychological effects, he would certainly develop a hard-to-overcome aversion to the female sex and hence a renewed danger of turning his still unfixed drive towards other men. This is also true of young soldiers who have not yet strayed or been seduced homosexually. Brothels are a necessary evil. But they are only for older, sexually experienced men with a fixed drive. It is just as questionable to advise masturbation. For there is a grave danger that a preoccupation with one's own genitals will again throw a bridge to other men and encourage a relapse. Young soldiers who are mentally and instinctually labile must rather be taught self-control and a sublimated enjoyment of natural heterosexual eroticism. Respect for women, and joyful anticipation of a clean and natural sex life suffused with spiritual warmth that will one day be realizable, is the surest defence against homosexual aberrations.

Signed: Schröder[7]

Distribution
All health offices
medical officers and NCOs of the Luftwaffe

[61] New recommendations for the assessment of criminal cases involving unnatural sex acts
Communication from Prof. Dr de Crinis to the Army Medical Inspectorate, 23 December 1944

Psychiatric Adviser   Berlin NW 40, 23.12.1944
to the Army Medical Inspector   Scharnhorststraße 35
Academy of Military Medicine
Nr. 3194/44

Subject: Experience with the implementation of the 'Guidelines for
             the Handling of Criminal Cases of Unnatural Sex Acts'

To
the Army Medical Inspector
Berlin
by Educational Group C
Internal

A working committee has met at my suggestion to exchange experiences regarding application of the Guidelines for the Handling of Criminal Cases of Unnatural Sex Acts. Following a number of discussions, the enclosed proposals were presented to me. I am fully in agreement with them and would ask you kindly to secure their implementation. In accordance with Clause 3 of the proposals it is

---

[7] General Oskar Schröder, head of the Luftwaffe Medical Corps.

suggested that Res. Captain Prof. Dr Zutt, Hospital 122, should be employed at the Central Army Court.

Signed: Prof. Dr de Crinis
Chief Physician

– Enclosure –
Enclosure 1
New Recommendations for the Assessment of Criminal Cases involving Unnatural Sex Acts

To the
Psychiatric Adviser   Berlin, 15 December 1944
to the Army Medical Inspector
Berlin NW 45
Please forward

In order to review in a medical, juridical and criminological light the experiences that have grown up out of more than a year of applying the Guidelines for the Handling of Criminal Cases of Unnatural Sex Acts (Chief of the Wehrmacht High Command 14n 19 WR (II) 58/43g), a working committee has met comprising a delegate of the Psychiatric Adviser to the Army Med. Inspector and Waffen-SS, a delegate of the Legal-Medical Adviser to the Army Med. Inspector, a delegate of the director of the Reich Institute of Psychotherapy, the Psychiatric Adviser to the Dep. Gen. Cmd. of Dist. III, a delegate of the Chief Judge of the Central Army Court and a delegate of the Reich Criminal Police Bureau.

You are requested to secure measures that will give effect to the following proposals coming out of the work of the committee.

Under the Guidelines for the Handling of Criminal Cases of Unnatural Sex Acts (§§175, 175a and 330a of the Reich Penal Code), the court must decide in relation to every homosexual offence whether a homosexual tendency is present in the offender. In establishing possible criminal tendencies, the judge looks to the individual's mode of life and general personality and to the facts of the case; but the doctor who is not familiar with the concept rather inclines to regard as a tendency, in the special case at issue here, a constitutionally innate or acquired sexual peculiarity. If the judge nevertheless turns to an expert, as he often does, with the question whether the defendant is a man with criminal tendencies, he is evidently seeking to ascertain whether the offender has a personality of the type of a habitual criminal. But the medical expert replies in accordance with his different (biological) perception of the concept of tendency. As many examples show, these dissimilar notions of a criminal tendency also make it difficult for medical experts to arrive at a uniform position. This gives rise to the following basic proposals:

1. For the court the question of criminal tendencies should no longer be addressed to the medical experts, for their positive answer (in the sense of the Guidelines) should be seen as a criminological conclusion.

As the Reich Criminal Police Bureau (Reich Office for the Combating of Homosexuality) conducts wide-ranging enquiries in this connection beyond the actual facts of the offence, the Bureau is by virtue of its special experience in the best position to assist the judge with a report on the matter of tendencies.

In previous experience, the judge generally considers that a tendency is present if the offence displays the associated personality traits and if the assumption of incorrigibility appears to be justified. The requirements of Clause I of the Guidelines are thus satisfied for the judge if the offence is to be regarded as a realization of stirrings which are characteristic of the overall personality and which, owing to their strong inner impetus, constantly assert themselves over any restraining factors. Thus a criminal by tendency is a category that can apply both to a predisposed homosexual – which is at least very rare – and to someone who was sexually normal at first but who, as a result of seduction in early youth and subsequent habitual homosexual activity or because of suchlike external developments, is so deeply involved in homosexual experiences and the corresponding gratification of urges that he can no longer give up this perverse form of sexual activity.

2. The basic medical viewpoints in the forensic assessment of homosexual offences should be brought into line with each other. The starting-point here should be that, medically speaking, there is no reason to support special treatment for homosexuals as opposed to other criminals (for example, in the framework of §51 of the Penal Code).

The question of consulting a medical expert therefore comes up if pathological disturbances of the intellectual faculties, the will or the character can be regarded as the cause of the crime. He should always be involved if there is a suspicion of mental illness (e.g. schizophrenia, manic-depressive psychosis, mental disorders resulting from infectious diseases etc.) or of an organic illness of the brain (e.g. softening of the brain, a brain tumour, conditions resulting from brain disorders of various origins etc.) or of illnesses of glands with internal secretion (e.g. the testicles, the pituitary gland, the thyroid gland etc.). It is also recommended that an expert be consulted if the offences have always taken place under the influence of alcohol, if they have occurred in a state of drowsiness, or if the offender is a person under twenty-one years of age.

3. A suitable medical corps officer (specialized in psychiatry) should be posted to work at the Central Army Court Dept. IX. His job should be both to propose timely consultation of a medical expert and to prepare the registration and medical evaluation of accruing material, with reference to the drawing up of future practical reports.

Signed: Prof. Schulte, Lt-Col.; Dr Becker, Lt-Col.; Dr Rodenberg, SS-Col.; Dr Frenzel-Beyme, Col.; Dr Felix-Boehm, Res. Capt.

Copies to:
Chief Judge of the Central Army Court
Head of the Reich Criminal Police Bureau

(b) The Death Penalty for Homosexuals in the SS and Police

On 18 August 1941, as we have seen, Hitler made his fateful declaration: 'Especially in the Party and its various organizations, as well as in the Wehrmacht, it is necessary to act with ruthless severity against any case of homosexuality that appears in its ranks. If this is done the state apparatus will remain clean, and it must remain clean.' Three months later this prompted a secret order for the cleansing of the SS and Police. With barbaric brevity this document stated over the Führer's own signature: 'A member of the SS and Police who commits unnatural acts with another man or lets himself be abused for unnatural acts shall be punished with death.'

The despotism expressed in this nakedly dictatorial measure involved the bypassing of legal provisions currently in force and a radical shift of legal perspective in the case of members of the SS and Police. The competence of the regular courts was immediately revoked. Public prosecutors had to declare their lack of competence through appropriate procedures and to hand cases over to the special courts – a flagrant breach of the law.

The decree did not subsequently appear among the published directives and announcements of the Reich Ministry of Justice. Indeed it was subject to strictly confidential treatment by the public prosecutor's office. The constituents of the SS and Police were notified that only oral instruction should be given, and that the passing of information to anyone outside the SS and Police was strictly forbidden.

The reasons for this order should probably not be sought mainly in the wish of the Nazi leadership to avoid legal discussions about the permissibility of its practices. With this blatant perversion of the course of justice Hitler again asserted what he later had the Greater German Reichstag confirm on 26 April 1942: namely, that his judgement stood qualitatively higher than that of any court. The Nazi jurist Carl Schmitt justified this in advance with the words: 'The Führer safeguards the law from the worst abuse when, at the moment of danger, he uses his leadership as supreme judge to make law directly. The true Führer is always also a judge. Being judge flows from being Führer.'[8] Rather, the strict secrecy was supposed to prevent the public – above all abroad – from especially associating the elites of the SS and Police with homosexuality. The Nazi leadership had itself unintentionally fostered such prejudices with its moral defamation of the SA leaders in 1934, who were said to have started building a sect around certain inclinations. Each case involving homosexuality in the SS threatened to

[8] C. Schmitt, *Positionen und Begriffe im Kampf Weimar-Genf-Versailles 1923–1939*, Hamburg 1940, p. 200.

confirm these prejudices if it became public, and that had to be avoided at any event. For the SS, originally founded as a bodyguard for the Nazi leader, had been upgraded in propaganda as the 'elite of the nation'. Together with Heydrich's Security Service (SD), into which it was itself integrated, and the Secret State Police, the SS was the main support of the system of terror. As the rulers saw it, members of the SS should be 'the vanguard of the struggle to eradicate homosexuality in the German *Volk*'.

The transfer of these matters to the competence of special courts threw open the door to arbitrary practices. Judicial personnel were replaced by SS Justizführers directly under the discipline 'of the Reichsführer-SS,[9] who could thus mark up a further major increase in his powers. The degree of arbitrariness can no longer be reconstructed. There are no known statistics on the verdicts of SS or police courts in cases involving homosexuality.

[62] Death penalty for members of the SS and Police
Decree of the Führer for the cleansing of the SS and Police,
15 November 1941

The Führer   Headquarters of the Führer
                                                     15 November 1941

In order to keep the SS and Police clean of vermin with homosexual inclinations, I hereby resolve:
I. For members of the SS and Police the following sentences shall apply instead of §§175 and 175a of the Reich Penal Code:
A member of the SS and Police who commits unnatural acts with another man or lets himself be abused for unnatural acts shall be punished with death.
In less serious cases penal servitude or imprisonment of not less than 6 months may be imposed.
Where a member of the SS or Police was not yet twenty-one years of age at the time of the offence and was seduced into it, the court may in especially minor cases refrain from punishment.
II. Imposition of the sentences threatened under I. is independent of the offender's age.
III. The crimes designated under I. come under the jurisdiction of special SS and Police courts in accordance with the provisions applying to them. The competence of Wehrmacht courts is not affected.

[9] See the 'General Directive on the Competence of Special Courts in Criminal Cases involving Members of the SS' [...], *Reichsgesetzblatt* 1/1939, p. 2107.

IV. The provisions necessary to enforce and supplement this decree shall be ordered by the Reichsführer-SS and Head of the German Police at the Reich Ministry of the Interior.

The Führer
Signed: Adolf Hitler

[63] From the correspondence of the Reichsführer-SS

[63a] *Letter from the Reichsführer-SS to the Head of the Reich Chancellery, Dr Lammers, 16 December 1941*

Berlin SW 11, 16.12.1941
Prinz-Albrecht-Str. 8
Headquarters of the Führer

Dear Reichsminister,
    I am most grateful for your letter of 10 December 1941 and the authenticated photocopy of the Führer's decree of 15 November 1941 on keeping clean the SS and Police, as well as for the two circulars of your letters to the Reich Minister of Justice and the Chief of the Wehrmacht High Command.
    I specially thank you, however, for the efforts you made in bringing about this decree. Naturally I shall forward in advance for your comments any provisions for enforcement and supplementation under Clause IV of the Führer's Decree.

Heil Hitler
Respectfully yours
Signed: H. Himmler

[63b] *Letter from the Reichsführer-SS to the Head of the Reich Chancellery, Dr Lammers, 7 March 1942*

Temp. Headquarters of the Führer, 7 March 1942
Confidential!

Subject: Führer's Decree on keeping clean the SS and Police

Dear Reichsminister,
    It was so kind of you to send for my comments the directive being considered by the Reich Ministry of Justice in relation to the above decree. I thank you most cordially.
    After examining the draft I have come up with the following amendments that I should like to see made, and I should be most grateful if you would plead for them with the Reich Minister of Justice.

1 I do not consider it necessary to obtain an official notification from the Reich Ministry of the Interior vouching for the competence of the SS and Police courts. In my opinion, a written declaration by the competent public prosecutor should be sufficient. If this is not enough, however, I suggest that the notification be obtained from your ministry.

2 The instruction under Clause 3, para 2 is not useful. Appropriate here would be a regulation such as one finds for the special courts in 15, para. 2 of the competence order of 21.2.40 (*Reichsgesetzblatt* I p. 405). I hold to the view that the Reich Minister of Justice is competent to originate this regulation within his own sphere by means of a circular directive, without the need for further legal provision. The directive should read: 'If another punishable offence is factually connected with a crime or offence of this kind, the proceedings for that offence may in conjunction be placed under the authority of the SS and Police court.'

There also needs to be some reference to the fact that under §11 of the law of 16.9.1939 (*Reichsgesetzblatt* 1 p. 184), where more than one person is involved in a punishable offence the proceedings may be referred to the SS and Police court.

3 The circular directive of the Reich Ministry of Justice contains mention of an appendix which was not enclosed. If this refers to the actual announcement of the decree of 15.11.1941, I do not think that it corresponds to the Führer's intention or that it is necessary. Apart from the announcement of judicial competence, all that needs to be said is that the decree is not retroactive and that therefore only offences committed after 15 November 1941 come under the jurisdiction of the SS and Police courts.

Since you have asked me, Reichsminister, to give you the opportunity to comment on any decree of provisions for enforcement and supplementation, may I report the following to you:

(1) If the directive of the Reich Ministry of Justice takes my wishes into account, I intend to make it known to the courts and to inform them that it is being issued with my agreement. Technical provisions for supplementation and enforcement would then hardly be necessary for the present.

(2) I have arranged for the Führer's Decree to be made known within the SS and Police by means of the enclosed order, which complies with the Führer's wishes as you have reported them to me.

Once again, dear Reichsminister, I thank you most cordially for your kind endeavours in this regard, and may I ask you to inform me of what the Reich Minister of Justice thinks of my requests. SS-Obersturmbannführer Bender is at any time at the disposition of yourself or your specialist staff.

Heil Hitler
Respectfully yours
Signed: H. Himmler

'[...] We are still getting one case of homosexuality a month in the SS. Over the year there were roughly eight to ten cases in the SS as a whole. I have now reached the following decision. In each case, of course, these people will be publicly stripped of their rank, discharged and handed over to the courts. After serving the sentence handed down by the court, they shall be taken on my orders to a concentration camp and there shot while attempting to escape. Each time this will be announced on my orders to the unit to which the individual belonged. In this way I hope to tear every last man of this kind out of the SS, so that at least we can keep clear the good image we have in the Schutzstaffel, and the new kind of recovery through blood that we are cultivating for Germany [...]' (pp. 97f.).

Heinrich Himmler, speaking on 18 February 1937 to SS-Gruppenführers at Bad Tölz, quoted from B. F. Smith and A. F. Peterson, eds., *Heinrich Himmler: Geheimreden 1933–1945 und andere Ansprachen*, Frankfurt/Main 1974, pp. 93–104.

'In sixteen cases railway police sergeant E. seduced or tried to seduce members of his battalion into unnatural sex acts. He thus shamelessly exploited his position as superior in relation to young recruits. In every case he cunningly set about arousing his victim through allusions to normal sexual intercourse, so that he could then have an easy time of it. Only after a long time did a man appear who acted properly and immediately reported the matter. In an extension of the normal range of sentences, E. was condemned to death under §5a of the Wartime Penal Ordinance because his behaviour undermined discipline. A leader who engages in homosexual activity cannot count on any mercy. The sentence was carried out.'

Hauptamt SS-Gericht. Mitteilungen über die SS- und Polizeigerichtsbarkeit, vol. 1, July 1940, p. 116. BAK NSD 41/3 – 1940/41.

Mitteilungen

über die ⚡⚡-und Polizeigerichtsbarkeit

Herausgegeben vom Reichsführer-⚡⚡ und Chef der Deutschen Polizei, Hauptamt ⚡⚡-Gericht

Heft 1	Vertraulich!	Juli 1940

Zur Einführung.

Das Hauptamt ⚡⚡-Gericht gibt in Zukunft fortlaufend Mitteilungen über die ⚡⚡- und Polizeigerichtsbarkeit heraus.

Zweck der Mitteilungen soll sein:

1. Die ⚡⚡- und Polizeigerichtsbarkeit als solche durch praktische Hinweise auf ihre Notwendigkeit und Bedeutsamkeit den mit ihr befaßten ⚡⚡- und Polizeidienststellen näher zu bringen,

2. durch Erläuterungen besonders bemerkenswerter Fälle aus der strafrechtlichen Praxis zu einer weltanschaulichen einheitlichen Rechtsprechung in nationalsozialistischem Sinne beizutragen.

Die Mitteilungen wenden sich daher nicht nur an die Gerichtsherren und Richter der ⚡⚡- und Polizeigerichtsbarkeit, sondern auch an alle Einheiten-Führer und Dienststellenleiter, denen die Erziehung ihrer Mannschaft zu anständigen und sauberen ⚡⚡-Männern und Nationalsozialisten obliegt und denen schon dadurch mindestens mittelbar im Rahmen der Sondergerichtsbarkeit eine wichtige Verantwortung zufällt. Denn so notwendig es im Interesse von Disziplin, Anstand und guter Sitte ist, strafbare Verfehlungen zu sühnen, so ist es noch wesentlich wichtiger, strafbaren Verfehlungen, soweit irgend angängig, vorzubeugen. Das kann nur durch erzieherische Einwirkung der Vorgesetzten auf ihre Untergebenen geschehen. Sie erfolgt durch Belehrung und Beispiel.

Eine Unterstützung der Belehrungen sollen die Mitteilungen des Hauptamtes ⚡⚡-Gericht über die ⚡⚡- und Polizeigerichtsbarkeit bieten.

Ihr Inhalt kann sich, wenn dieser Zweck erreicht werden soll, nicht nur auf Hinweise beschränken, wie man es machen soll, sondern auch, wie man es nicht machen darf.

The introductory page to a periodical series of reports on the activity of the SS and Police courts – marked 'Confidential!' The intended readership was not only judges but 'all unit commanders and section leaders whose duty it is to educate their men to become pure and upright SS men and National Socialists, and who thus at least indirectly have an important responsibility within the framework provided by the special courts'.

[64] The SS and Police as 'the vanguard of the struggle to eradicate homosexuality in the German Volk'

Order of the Reichsführer-SS and Head of the German Police, 7 March 1942

The Reichsführer-SS and   Berlin, 7 March 1942
Head of the German Police
at the Reich Ministry of the Interior

H. A. SS-Gericht Ia 121 Tgb. Nr. 287/41

Confidential!

Subject: Decree of the Führer on keeping clean the SS and Police

1 In order to keep the SS and Police clean of vermin with homosexual inclinations, the Führer has resolved by a decree of 15 November 1941 that a member of the SS or Police who commits sex offences with another man or lets himself be abused for sex offences shall be punished *with death*, regardless of his age. In less serious cases penal servitude or imprisonment of not less than six months may be imposed.

2 The Führer's Decree is not being published, because that might give rise to misunderstandings.
Homosexual misconduct has been *extremely rare* in the ranks of the SS and Police. But it must be punished with ruthless severity, because the Führer wants the SS and Police to remain absolutely pure. Every means must therefore be used to keep them clean of this dangerous and infectious plague. Any member of the SS and Police must immediately report any indecent approach of this kind, even if it is made by a superior.

3 SS and Police courts are competent *for the whole of the SS and Police* with regard to offences of this kind committed after 15 November 1941. Offices of the SS and Police must therefore refer reports of this kind exclusively to the competent offices of the special SS and Police courts.

4 This order shall be verbally communicated to *all* members of the SS and Police, with notice that it is forbidden to give any information about it to anyone outside the SS or Police.
The order should be read out and discussed in a special class to be given by the immediate superior.
It should be pointed out that all members of the SS and Police must be in the vanguard of the struggle to eradicate homosexuality in the German *Volk*. Superiors have a responsibility to ensure that the

order is promptly made known to everyone joining the SS or Police. This order should also be repeatedly raised at future official classes or official discussions.

The Reichsführer-SS and
Head of the German Police
Signed: H. Himmler

'The thirty existing courts of the SS and Police had more work in 1941 than in the previous year. The first reason for this is that the category of people coming under the special courts became greater than in the preceding year. Above all, however, most of the leaders responsible for the reporting of punishable offences have attained the necessary understanding of the requirements of a powerful system of wartime courts. They have accordingly forwarded more reports of offences to the courts than in 1940. [...]

Punishable acts of an indecent nature make up less than three per cent. A good half of these involve sex offences between men – which at 1.6 per cent are now rare enough to be disappearing. Even with other offences of indecency we are talking only of rare, though usually serious, exceptional cases. Regrettably there were also some cases of sex offences with children and under-age dependants. [...]'

From 'Die Straffälligkeiten im Jahre 1941', in *Mitteilungen des Hauptamtes SS-Gericht*, vol. 3/1, 1942, pp. 35, 37. BAK NSD 41/3 – 1942/43.

(c) Action in the Occupied Territories

Little is known of the fate of homosexual men in the lands conquered by the Nazis. Territories annexed to the Reich, such as the large parts of Poland renamed West Prussia and Posen [Poznan], or the Belgian frontier districts of Eupen, Malmédy and Moresnet, were subjected to the penal definitions of the 'Old Reich'. Even if the long-term aim may have been to impose them on all the occupied lands, all we have proof of at present is the special provisions for the prosecution of homosexual men in the 'Protectorate of Bohemia and Moravia', the 'General-gouvernement Poland', the Netherlands and the occupied zone of France.

What is clear, however, is that the actions against homosexual men were in no way comparable to the persecution of Jews in the occupied territories. The reasons why this was so can still only be conjectured. On the one hand, there was the fact that legislative activity was unable to keep pace with the occupations: in the period from 1 September 1939 to 6 April 1941 the fascists invaded Poland, Denmark and Norway, Belgium, Holland and Luxembourg, Yugoslavia and Greece as well as France. On the other hand, there were eugenic considerations – especially the insane distinction between superior and inferior races – which spurred the Nazis on to take various forms of action. On the question of the punishability of homosexuality, even before 1933 not a few countries had a different tradition from that of German jurisprudence. Romance countries such as France, Belgium or Italy, which had undergone the influence of nineteenth-century French liberal legislation, did not have prosecutions for so-called simple cases of homosexuality (sex acts between consenting males), whereas these were punishable in the countries of the Anglo-Saxon legal sphere (e.g. Germany, England, Sweden, Czechoslovakia and Austria).

This inevitably complicated matters, but the Nazis relied on the help of prosecution authorities – both the local police and the judiciary. We learn something about discussions in this field from a controversy unleashed shortly after the outbreak of war by an article in the official paper of the SS, *Das Schwarze Korps*. The occasion was a ruling by the Sixth Criminal Division of the Reich [Supreme] Court on 17 October 1939, whereby a male defendant was released in the annexed 'Ostmark' (= Austria) because there was no evidence against him of intercourse-like acts. The basis of the verdict was 129 1b of the Austrian Penal Code. *Das Schwarze Korps* demanded strict application of the tighter clauses entered in the penal code of the 'Old Reich' on 28 June 1935. A year or so later, on 27 November 1940, Chief Public Prosecutor Brettle had the 'honour of informing' Dr Freisler, State Secretary at the Reich Ministry of Justice, that 'the Sixth Criminal Division of the Reich Court now followed the interpretation of the law of the other divisions with regard to the concept of a sex offence between persons of the same sex'.

The practice was different in the 'Generalgouvernement' administering the rump of Poland. In a confidential directive of 22 January 1941 to provincial prosecutors, Freisler called for the adoption of a eugenic perspective in deciding whether a prosecution should go ahead. German nationhood [*Volkstum*] would not be in danger 'if a Polish woman aborted her unborn child [. . .] or if Polish men committed homosexual acts with one another'. He argued for decisions to be made case by case – a recommendation which must evidently have led to contradictory verdicts. In March 1942 Himmler felt compelled to issue a directive whose explicit purpose was to standardize police practice regarding abortion and sex offences between Polish men. It laid down that no charges should be preferred if all the parties involved in offences under §§175 and 218 were Poles. Cases were supposed to bypass the public prosecutor and be reported directly to the regional headquarters of the Criminal Police for a decision on how to proceed. After a dispute with the Reich Ministry of Justice and the NSDAP Central Office, who saw their competences being ignored, a rider was added in September 1942 to Himmler's directive. On grounds relating to the 'politics of nationhood', abortion and sex offences between men were not to be prosecuted if those involved were Poles. But they would have to reckon with being deported from Poland, because the Nazis saw them as a danger to 'Germanhood'. It is not known how far the German prosecution authorities kept to the letter of the directive. But under the 'Criminal Justice Provisions against Poles and Jews in the Incorporated Eastern Territories', issued on 4 December 1941 (*Reichsgesetzblatt* 1, 1941, p. 759), the SS and Police had the general powers for arbitrary action, including imposition of the death penalty. Within this framework, if a Polish male homosexual was apprehended or denounced, it was very probable that he would come in for special SS measures and be shipped off to a concentration camp.

The practice was different again in the Netherlands and the occupied territories of France. In both countries male homosexuals had not been prosecuted since the beginning of the nineteenth century. In the Netherlands a special article, 248b, introduced into the penal code in 1911, had made it an imprisonable offence for an adult male to have sexual relations with a male under the age of twenty-one. But there was no provision in the law against homosexual prostitution. On 31 July 1940, ten weeks after the occupation began, the Reichskommissar issued Order No. 81 on the Combating of Unnatural Sex Offences, which transferred the severe legislation valid in Germany. At the same time, Art. 248b of the Netherlands Penal Code remained in force. Prosecution was the responsibility of the Dutch police authorities – except where a defendant was involved together with a member of the

German SS or Wehrmacht. According to research done by Pieter Koenders, the occupation forces were not very happy with the results and blamed the Dutch authorities for poor investigative work and a lack of professional zeal in the prosecution of homosexuality. During the period from 1940 to 1943 proceedings were initiated against 138 men, and 90 were found guilty by Dutch courts.[10]

In annexed Alsace-Lorraine, in an operation prepared as early as June 1940 against 'anti-social or work-shy elements, vagrants, beggars, pimps and gypsies', the German authorities also began to deport identifiable homosexual men (probably with previous convictions) to the unoccupied but German-controlled South of France. Between June 1940 and April 1942 a total of 95 homosexuals (plus 19 dependants) were expelled from Alsace, 9 were temporarily interned in the Vorbruck detention camp, and one man had a preventive detention order (= concentration camp) imposed on him. It is not known how many Frenchmen were prosecuted in the Vichy zone, where on 6 August 1942 – a hundred and fifty years after penal sanctions had been abolished – Marshal Pétain signed Law No. 744 (§334 of the Code Pénal) prescribing imprisonment of between six months and three years for male homosexuals. (It was preserved by de Gaulle after 1945 and only repealed under Mitterrand in 1982.[11])

Austria

[65] Demands for more radical action in the 'Ostmark'
Article from the official SS paper Das Schwarze Korps, *15 February 1940*

A few days ago a criminal sentenced to death as an anti-social pest was executed. He had indecently assaulted two boys and in the case of one of them – whose father is at the front – paired him off with a woman in the absent father's home.

The wiping out of this creature has been a source of unmingled satisfaction in the German *Volk*. The executed man lost his life because he committed one of his crimes on a child whose father and protector, serving his homeland at the front, was not in a position to watch over the child. A soldier at the front must be able to live in the certainty that the homeland is prepared to protect his wife, children and possessions under any circumstances and by any means.

[10] P. Koenders, *Homoseksualiteit in bezet Nederland*, Amsterdam 1984, pp. 86–117; and *Het koninkrijk der Nederlanden in de tweede wereldoorlog. Deel 14*, The Hague 1991, pp. 556–558.
[11] J. Boissons, *Le triangle rose. La déportation des homosexuels 1933–1945*, Paris 1988, pp. 114–116.

If this criminal had not indecently assaulted the child of a front-line soldier, and if the judge had not thus been given the chance to treat him with the merciless severity of the law against anti-social pests, he would no doubt have escaped with his life. But we would have hardly found it understandable if he had then only received a light sentence. For his crime as such does not change with the circumstances. It is and remains a crime against the German youth.

We saw recently where crimes of this kind can lead, when a large number of so-called '*youth leaders*' had to be tried and expelled from the national community because their criminal inclination and activity ended up in a separatist political association.[12]

In all such cases one should concern oneself less and less with the external circumstances and more and more with the offender's cast of mind. Only that is consistent with National Socialist conceptions of the meaning of criminal justice. Antiquated notions of law coming from the age of liberalism must therefore be cleared away. A judge from Styria has brought such a mistake to our attention.

In its Vienna edition the magazine *Deutsches Recht* regularly publishes judges' verdicts and documentation from the Old Reich, from which an Ostmark [= Austrian] judge can see how he should apply the provisions of Austrian criminal law according to the legal conceptions current in the Old Reich. On page 12 of the edition of 20 January, there is a discussion precisely of §129 of the Austrian Penal Code and the concepts of 'sex offence', 'sexual abuse', 'immoral conduct'. The judge is thus told what is to be understood by these terms. For obvious reasons we cannot reproduce it word for word but only give the approximate sense as follows.

Not every indecent contact with the body of a person of the same sex is an illicit act in the sense of §129 Ib of the Penal Code – not even if the relevant bodily parts of the other person are felt and if the act of feeling is due to arousal of the sexual instinct or is intended to arouse or gratify it. Only if there is an intention (!) to carry out an act that goes beyond temporary contact [...] can there be an attempted offence under §129 Ib of the Penal Code.

Next comes the application of this legal knowledge to a case in practice. It emerges from the account that a defendant pressed to himself and kissed the 'body of his object of attack' and touched the relevant bodily parts. But this was not enough to establish 'a sex offence in the sense of §129 Ib of the Penal Code'!

And that is a ruling by the Reich Court dated 17 October 1939, 6 D 559. Austrian criminal law, however, tersely stated: '§129. – The

---

[12] The reference is to the trials of Bund Youth members in the Sudetenland. See Document 81.

following kinds of illicit acts shall also be punished as criminal offences: 1. Illicit acts contrary to nature, that is, (a) with animals, (b) with persons of the same sex.'

With that the judge could have got something going. He was not tied to quibbling with words. He could himself decide what was an 'illicit act' and punish any character who abused others for the arousal or gratification of his unnatural urges, whatever the other circumstances.

This is not to say that he would always have done that. But if a judge, thinking and acting in a National Socialist spirit, is able to apply this all-embracing section, no individual with unnatural inclinations will ever slip through his fingers.

Only in the criminal justice system characteristic of liberalism could the viewpoint of Jewish lawyers spread itself around – a viewpoint for which a sex offence is only a sex offence if certain conditions are fulfilled. That is why, in the liberalist state, unnatural sex acts were also something like a gentleman's crime. 'One' found nothing wrong with them, and criminal justice was quite happily bound down.

In the National Socialist state, however, a different wind is blowing. The hugely successful struggle against the cliques and clubs and quiet corners of homosexuals and their 'intellectual' champions, against depraved monks, priests and 'youth educators', would have got stuck at square one if those who conducted it had put on the learned spectacles of theoreticians divorced from the real world.

The judge who put an end to the criminal mentioned at the beginning presumably also wanted to wipe out a criminal cast of mind that was hostile to the people, and that is why he did not care whether the violator of youth corresponded to all the restrictive provisions of venerable legal minds.

Our principles of legality must be protected from complicated constructions, especially in areas where force has to be a means of struggle against enemies of the people – and nothing else! One does not approach an enemy with the long-tressed wig of secluded objectivity. In war live ammunition is used.

[66] Hectic reaction at the Reich Ministry of Justice

[66a] *Letter from the Reich Ministry of Justice, State Secretary Dr Freisler, to Chief Prosecutor Brettle, Leipzig*

Berlin, 20 February 1940
Personal!

Dear Chief Prosecutor,

The chairman of the Reich Court visited me today and spoke with me about the practice of the Austrian courts, and thence also of the Sixth Criminal Division, in cases involving homosexual offences. The reason was the short article, well known to yourself, which appeared in the last issue of *Das Schwarze Korps*. The chairman of the Reich Court regarded the *Schwarze Korps* criticism as substantively correct: i.e., he regretted that the Sixth Division could not decide to return to the Ostmark administration of justice that prevailed until 1905. Considering that, in a political matter which is also so important especially with regard to the protection of the youth, it is not unacceptable for the Ostmark administration of justice to be counterposed in this way to that of Germany as a whole, I should be grateful if you would take the opportunity to bring the next appropriate case before the Grand Court. I discussed this too with the chairman of the Reich Court.

Heil Hitler!
Respectfully yours
Signed: Dr Freisler

[66b] *Memorandum of a telephone conversation of the chairman of the Reich Court, Dr Bumke, with the Reich Ministry of Justice, assistant head of department Dr Grau*

1. Reich Court chmn. Dr Bumke rang me this morning and reported the following:
In a case from the Ostmark currently pending in his court, a Cath. priest is being prosecuted for an offence under §129 Ib of Aust. Pen. Code. The verdict under appeal narrowly interpreted §129 Ib (just as in the case described in No. 7 of *Das Schwarze Korps*, 15.2.1940, 'That's just what is lacking!'). The Court is unsure whether it is better to endorse the narrow interpretation and thus perhaps provoke fresh attacks from *Das Schwarze Korps*, or to choose another interpretation in conformity with the law in the Old Reich and thus risk that in future too many cases are started under this provision.

In his view, it would be best if an act of legislation were to introduce the new version of §175 as rapidly as possible in the Ostmark. When I remarked that hopefully we could bring the whole of German criminal law into force in the Ostmark by the end of the year, he said that the interval was really too long and that during it there could be still be too much damage with the current Ostmark law.

I promised in-house report and also promised that Reich Court chmn. Bumke will receive telephonic advice of the decision.

2. To Head of Dept. Suchomel for reasons of competence.

Berlin, 15 March 1940
Signed: Grau

[66c] *Memorandum from the Reich Ministry of Justice on the disputed ruling of the Sixth Criminal Division at the Reich Court*

1. Observation:
From the proceedings of Dept. III, which were communicated to be by senior adviser Klemenz on 14.3.1940, the following conclusions emerge:
In the case against theology professor Dr Franz Linninger, the Sixth Criminal Division of the Reich Court by a decision of 17.10.1939 – 6 D 559/39 – quashed the guilty verdict of the Linz Court for the offence of illicit act contrary to nature under §129 Ib of the Aust. Pen. Code, acquitted the defendant of the charge under this offence, but rejected the appeal of invalidity against the guilty verdict for the offence of seduction into illicit acts under §132 III of the Aust. Pen. Code.

The verdict concluded that the defendant, who as governor of a Catholic boys' association was responsible for the religious and moral education of its members, and who as cellarer of the St. Florian seminary was in charge of the cellar boys, did firmly press several 14 to 17-year-old members of the association against himself, whereupon one of the boys felt a hard object against his thigh which he took to be the defendant's member; that he did further kiss the boys, feel their clothing above the thigh in the genital region, and manually assault them above the clothing over the genitals but without taking hold of the genitals or remaining there for a long time. Only in the case of one boy did he feel his naked body at the pubic hair and touch his naked member for a moment.

The verdict concludes that the defendant committed these acts out of sexual excitement and in order to gratify his sensuality.

The Reich Court gave the following essential reason for its acquittal on the charge of illicit homosexual acts:

'According to the provisions of §129 Ib of the Penal Code, which is substantially in accord with §175 of the Penal Code (old version), the expression used here "illicit act contrary to nature" covers only intercourse-like and onanistic acts – that is, acts which are such as normally to bring about sexual gratification corresponding to that associated with natural sexual intercourse.

'Not every indecent contact with the body of a person of the same sex is an illicit act in the sense of §129 Ib of the Penal Code – not even if the relevant bodily parts of the other person are felt and if the act of feeling is due to arousal of the sexual instinct or is intended to arouse or gratify it.

'Of course, if there is an intention to carry out a masturbatory act that goes beyond temporary contact, there may be an attempted offence under §129 Ib.

'According to the facts of the case established in the verdict, the court did not accept that the acts with which the defendant was charged were intended by him to be the prelude to the carrying out of an onanistic act and that the realization of such an intention was thwarted only by one of the circumstances indicated in §8 of the Penal Code. It was therefore also not possible to accept that there had been an attempt in the sense of §129.'

In its issue dated 15.2.1940 *Das Schwarze Korps* criticized the decision of the Reich Court. The chairman of the Reich Court, in a discussion with State Secretary Dr Freisler, stated that the opinion of *Das Schwarze Korps* was substantively correct and regretted that the Sixth Division 'did not return to the Ostmark administration of justice that prevailed until 1905'. The State Secretary instructed Dept. III to issue a directive to the Ostmark prosecution authorities that they should support the standpoint which the Ostmark administration of justice took up until the year 1905. [...]

[67] The standardization of judicial practice

Letter from Chief Prosecutor Brettle to the Reich Ministry of Justice, State Secretary Dr Freisler, 27 November 1940

The Chief Prosecutor   Leipzig C 1, 27 November 1940
at the Reich Court   Reichsgerichtsplatz 1

To:
State Secretary Dr Freisler
at the Reich Ministry of Justice
Berlin W 8

Dear State Secretary,

With reference to your helpful personal letter of 20 February 1940 and the verbal discussion of this matter, I have the honour of informing you that the Sixth Division of the Reich Court now follows the interpretation of the law of the other divisions with regard to the concept of a sex offence between persons of the same sex. I venture to refer to the Reich Court judgements of 4.6.1940 – 6 D 121/40 –, 9.7.1940 – 6 D 261/40 – and 24.9.1940 – 6 D 361/ 40 –, copies of which I enclose herewith.

It was not necessary to call on the Grand Court.

Heil Hitler!
Respectfully yours
Signed: Brettle

The 'Protectorate' of Bohemia and Moravia

[68] Order of 2 October 1942 regarding the sentencing of dangerous habitual criminals and sex offenders in the Protectorate of Bohemia and Moravia

By virtue of the decree of the Führer and Reich Chancellor on the Protectorate of Bohemia and Moravia dated 16 March 1939 (*Reichsgesetzblatt* I p. 485), it is hereby ordered in agreement with the Reich Protector in Bohemia and Moravia:

§1

§1 of the law of 4 September 1941 altering the Reich Penal Code (*Reichsgeseztblatt* I p. 549) and the provisions of the Reich Penal Code against dangerous habitual criminals are valid in the Protectorate of Bohemia and Moravia, also for persons who are not German citizens.

§2

In the sense of §20a of the Reich Penal Code deliberate, legally punishable violations of Protectorate law are on a par with deliberate offences, with the exception of violations of §§1 to 4 and 6 of the Vagrancy Act of 24 May 1885 (*Österr. RGBl. No. 89*) and the like, which carry the threat only of detention up to six weeks or a fine or both.

§3

In the Protectorate of Bohemia and Moravia a sex offender is defined in accordance with §§125 to 128 of Austrian penal law, except insofar as the provisions of Reich law are to be applied.

Berlin, 2 October 1942
The Reich Minister of Justice
Dr Thierack

The Reich Minister of the Interior
p.p.
Dr Stuckart

Persons duly convicted of offences under §§175, 175a + b: Protectorate citizens, Poles and Jews 1941 to 1943

	Total	Protectorate citizens	Poles and Jews	Pure-bred Jews
1941	210	–	–	–*
1942	112	24	86	2
1943**	48	17	28	–

* No further details could be obtained for 1941.
** Only the first half of 1943

Statistisches Reichsamt: *Die Kriminalität im Großdeutschen Reich*
Landeshauptarchiv Sachsen-Anhalt, Magdeburg Rep C 127 Nr. 799, fol 195f., 215ff.

Poland

[69] Handling of abortion and sex offences among Poles
Confidential circular from the Reich Minister of Justice to provincial prosecutors, 22 January 1941

The Reich Minister of Justice   Berlin, W 8, 22 January 1941
9170 Ost/2–III a⁴ 144.41

To: Provincial prosecutors   Confidential!

Copies to:
The chairmen of the Reich Court and
the People's Court,
The chief prosecutors at the Reich Court
and the People's Court,
The chairmen of provincial high courts

Subject: Criminal proceedings against Poles

The sentencing of Poles must take account of whether the German penal norm mainly serves to protect the *German* people, whereas the offence is directed not against German but against Polish nationhood. There is no danger to German nationhood if, for example, a Polish woman aborts her unborn child or is guilty of infanticide or if Polish men commit homosexual acts with one another. Insofar as such misconduct, both directly and in its effects, is exclusively directed against a different nation, it should normally be punished more leniently than in similar attacks against German nationhood. In cases where such acts committed by Poles nevertheless affect by contagion the interests of the German *Volk* – for example, this viewpoint does not apply to *commercial abortions* – a heavy sentence will be more appropriate.

I would ask chief prosecutors to ensure that this viewpoint is taken into consideration and in all such cases to inform me before themselves bringing an official action on such matters.

p.p. Signed: Dr Freisler

[70] Investigative bureaucracy
Circular directive issued by the Reichsführer-SS, 11 March 1942

In order to assure uniform police handling of abortion and sex offences among Poles, the following measures have been decided.

1 All reports or investigations concerning offences under §§173, 174 clause 1, 175b, 217 and 218 para. 1 of the Penal Code should first be

forwarded without discussion to the competent (regional) headquarters of the Criminal Police where the offenders (persons involved) are Poles.

2 For offences under §§175, 175a and (in cases of wage-abortion)
218 of the Penal Code, if the offenders and their 'partners' or
'victims' are Poles, cases should first be forwarded to the competent
(regional) headquarters of the Criminal Police after the most essential investigations have been carried out to establish the facts. The
competent (regional) headquarters of the Criminal Police should be
rapidly informed of the arrest and its instructions should then be
awaited.

3 Offences under §§174 clauses 2 and 3, 176, 177 of the Penal Code
do not come under the provisions of this directive, even if all those
accused are Poles.

4 In case of doubt a decision should be obtained from the competent (regional) headquarters of the Criminal Police.

5 The (regional) headquarters of the Criminal Police and the State
Crime Department shall proceed in accordance with the instructions separately communicated to them.

6 All protected and stateless persons of the Polish nation shall count
as Poles.

[71] Objections on 'nationhood policy' grounds
*Letter from the manager of the Party Central Office, Martin
Bormann, to the Reich Minister of Justice (Extract)*

National Socialist German Führer's Headquarters
Workers' Party 3 June 1942
Head of the Party Central Office
III C – Ku. 2655/1/49

To the:
Reich Minister of Justice
Berlin W 8
Wilhelmstraße 65

Subject: Prosecution of abortion and sex offences in the
incorporated eastern territories

In accordance with para. 2 clause IV of the criminal justice order
against Poles and Jews in the incorporated eastern territories, dated

4.12.1941 (*Reichsgesetzblatt* I p. 759), the public prosecutor prosecutes offences committed by Poles and Jews when he considers their punishment to be in the public interest.

This requirement makes it possible to gear criminal justice to the needs of nationhood policy in the incorporated eastern territories. [...]

This applies especially to the prosecution of crimes against the seeds of a new life and related offences. Here German courts, like other official bodies, must take care that their decisions do not promote the biological strength of the alien (particularly Polish) nationhood – especially as it puts its vitality more strongly to proof in the eastern territories than does German nationhood. [...]

It will not be possible, however, to disregard altogether offences which only affect Polish nationhood. The life of the Polish national group in the incorporated eastern territories is not so detached from German national life that signs of decay among Poles are without any danger for Germans coming into contact with them. This applies above all to the question of homosexuality. [...] The head of the Security Police and the SD therefore intends to ensure, by means of appropriate guidelines, that such elements are taken after their arrest to areas where there are no doubts about tolerating homosexuality and wage-abortion in view of the nationhood policy conditions obtaining there. For implementation of clause IV of the Polish criminal justice order, the prosecuting authorities should be instructed by guidelines on how to deal with such cases.

These guidelines should be approximately as follows:

1 The maximum penalty must be passed on Polish men or women who carry out abortions on German women, and offenders must be eradicated as elements hostile to the *Volk*.
Even the death penalty should be considered against Polish abortionists, for in each case they carry out an assault on German life.

2 If offences under §§173, 174 clause 1, 175b, 217 and 218 of the Penal Code involve self-abortion, they should not be prosecuted when the offender or other persons involved belong to the Polish national group and German citizenship has not been and will not be granted to them.

3 Offences under §§174 clauses 2 and 3, and 176 of the Penal Code should be prosecuted in the usual way if the offender belongs to the Polish national group.

4 In cases where offences under §§175, 175a and 218 involve wage-abortion, charges should not be preferred if the offender and other

parties all belong to the Polish national group. Instead, the competent headquarters of the Security Police should be informed and the offender should be taken there as soon as possible by individual transport.

I should be grateful if you would send me your views on the requests expressed above.

Heil Hitler
Signed: M. Bormann

[72] Reply from the Minister of Justice
Letter to the manager of the Party Central Office, 30 June 1942 (Extract)

Reich Minister of Justice   Berlin, 30 June 1942
9170 Ost/2–III a²/1267/42

Ref. St. Sec. Dr Freisler

To the:
Manager of the Party Central Office
Munich
Führerbau

Subject: Prosecution of abortion and sex offences in the
             incorporated territories

Ref. your letter of 3.6.1942 III c/Ku 2655/1/49
[...] Your proposed guidelines thus correspond to the basic position I have already adopted. In particular, I agree with you that especially heavy sentences must be passed on Poles who carry out abortions on a German woman – which is possible in every case under the general range of sentences in the Polish Criminal Justice Order which goes right up to the death penalty. I also concur with your view that self-abortion or infanticide by a Polish woman, or sex offences under §§173, 174 cl. 1, 175b committed by a Polish offender, should not normally be prosecuted – unless the way in which the offence was committed and its becoming public knowledge carry the risk of contagion to the German population as well. I could therefore declare my agreement with non-prosecution of such offences only if the offender really is deported as rapidly as possible to a region where there is no danger at all that the German population will be contaminated. [...]

The decision whether a particular offence should be prosecuted and punished is the responsibility of the public prosecutor. [...]

[73] The regulation
Memorandum of the Reich Ministry of Justice, 18 September 1942 (Extract)

Submitted to the Minister
– via the State Secretary –

[...]
(2) Decree of the Reichsführer-SS, 11.3.1942, on the prosecution of abortion and sex offences among Poles.
   For reasons of nationhood policy:
   (a) Incest, sex offences with dependants (§174 No. 1), sodomy, infanticide and self-abortion should not be prosecuted where the offenders are Poles;
   (b) Sex offences between men and wage-abortion should also not be prosecuted where offenders and other parties involved are all Poles. (The offenders should, however, be deported to areas outside the Reich where they will not be a danger to German nationhood.)
   Reported to the *Minister*. [...]

Netherlands

[74] Order No. 81 of the Reich Commissar for the Occupied Netherlands Territories on the Combating of Unnatural Sex Acts
31 July 1940

By virtue of §5 of the Führer's Decree of 18 May 1940 on the exercise of governmental authority in the Netherlands, I hereby order:

§1

(1) A man who commits a sex offence with another male or allows himself to be abused for a sex offence shall be punished with up to four years' imprisonment.
(2) Where a party was still a minor at the time of the offence, he may in especially trivial cases be exempted from punishment.

§2

A man who, by abusing dependence based upon a relationship of service, work or subordination, induces another male to commit a sex offence with him or to allow himself to be abused for a sex offence shall be punished with up to six years' imprisonment.

§3

(1) A sentence of up to ten years' imprisonment shall be passed upon:
1. a man who seduces an under-age male to commit a sex offence with him or to allow himself to be abused for a sex offence;
2. a man who, in pursuit of gain, commits sex offences with males or allows himself to be abused by males for sex offences or solicits for such purposes.

(2) In cases coming under Section 1 Clause 2, persons capable of work may also be sentenced to a term of up to three years in a state workhouse.

§4

Acts falling under §§1–3 count as crimes.

§5

German citizens continue to come under the provisions of the Old Reich existing at any given time.

§6

This order came into force on the day of its proclamation.

The Hague, 31 July 1940
The Reich Commissar
for the Occupied Netherlands Territories
Signed: Seyss-Inquart

[75] 'Results practically zero'
From the General Commissar for Administration and Justice in the Occupied Netherlands to the Chief Medical Officer of Health, Dr Reuter, January 1941

The successful combating of homosexuality is possible only if the Netherlands police takes the appropriate initiatives and does not wait for chance reports. Measures absolutely necessary for the successful combating of homosexuality – such as the investigation of pubs favoured by homosexuals, the surveillance of people who frequent them, the questioning of rentboys, etc. – require experience, investigative skill and professional zeal. These three conditions are not present in the Netherlands police, however, when it comes to the question of homosexuality.

[76] Trials and sentencing of male homosexuals during the Nazi occupation of the Netherlands, 1940–1943

Trials and sentences in the Netherlands under Order No. 81 of the Reich Commissar (Sex Offences between Men), 31 July 1940. Years 1940 to 1943

Year	Number of trials	Of which, guilty	Of which, prison
1940	11	10	7
1941	36	26	16
1942	46	26	10
1943*	45	28	21
Total	138	90	54

* No details are available after 1943

Trials and sentences under Art. 248b of the Netherlands Penal Code (Sex Offences with Minors of the Same Sex). Years 1940 to 1943

Year	Number of trials	Of which, guilty	Of which, prison
1940	47	28	26
1941	49	23	22
1942	36	21	15
1943*	32	16	14
Total	164	88	77

* No details are available after 1943.

Deportations from Alsace to France

[77] Registering for deportation
Order of the commander of the Strassburg Security Police,
18 November 1940

Commander of the Strassburg Security	Strassburg
Police and SD	18 November 1940
IV – Schm/Hl. 8000	Erckmann-Chatrian-Str. 2

To the:
Regional Commissioners
in Erstein, Hagenau [Haguenau], Molsheim,
Schlettstadt [Sélestat], Strassburg Region,
Weissenburg [Wissembourg], Zabern [Saverne]

Subject: Professional criminals, anti-socials, homosexuals etc.

The high level of crime in Alsace requires the toughest action against professional and habitual criminals, among whom should be included anti-social or work-shy elements, vagrants, drunkards, beggars, pimps, homosexuals, gypsies and people who wander around like gypsies. As it is still possible at the moment to remove these undesirable elements from Alsace, I am attempting to identify professional criminals, anti-socials etc. and to register them on local council lists. The lists must contain the following columns:

(a) Surname
(b) First names
(c) Occupation
(d) Date of birth
(e) Place of birth
(f) Married, divorced, widowed, separated
(g) Number of dependent children
(h) Home address
(i) Whether professional criminal, anti-social etc.

Would you please forward the lists by 5.12.1940, to Task Force 1, Strassburg Security Police and SD, Sängerhausstraße 10, together with brief notes on each person in which previous sentences are also mentioned. Security police checks will in each case be carried out by Task Force 1. As the decision on future treatment of the professional criminal, anti-social etc. must be taken soon, the deadline of 5.12.1940 must be strictly adhered to.

Signed: Dr Scheel
SS-Oberführer

[78] Announcement of group transport

Security Police   Strassburg, 14 December 1940
Task Force 1/III
Criminal Police

To:
Security Police and SD commanders in Alsace

Subject: Deportation of professional criminals, homosexuals, gypsies and anti-socials
Ref.:   Order of 18.11.40 IV Schm./Hl. 800

I enclose a copy of a list of persons who will be deported in the next few days by group transport to central France. They are people who, on the basis of the published decree, were recorded in lists and reported to us here by urban and rural commissioners in Lower Alsace. By including wives and children who will at any event also be deported, we reach a total of approximately six hundred. The lists received from urban and rural commissioners also contain a large number of anti-socials etc. whom it did not seem necessary to deport but whom it would be in order to send to a detention camp. I shall report at the appropriate time about the results of the measures taken against them.

With two lists for the manager of the executive office, with a request for further dispositions. The lists have been drawn up from the point of view of the practical registration of place of residence.

The Commanding Officer
Signed: Landgraf
SS-Sturmbannführer and
government adviser

Persons evacuated by the Criminal Police

Professional criminals	out of town	7
Professional criminals	Strassburg	42
Anti-social elements	out of town	146
Homosexuals	out of town	9
Homosexuals	Strassburg	27
Francophiles	out of town	1
Poachers	out of town	28
Poachers	Strassburg	1
Dependent women and children		403
		664

This figure is included in the totals reported by the task force.

[79] Internal statistics on deportations
From 27 June 1940 to 27 April 1942

Security Police
Criminal Police Mülhausen i./Elsaß [Mulhouse]   Mülhausen
Tgb. Nr. K 435/42   27 April 1942

Statistics
on preventive police action in Upper Alsace
from 27.6.1940 (date of entry) to the present.

1 Evacuated to unoccupied France:
a) Professional criminals, anti-socials, pimps   230 persons
   Not returned from French evacuation   120 persons

Number of evacuated family dependants, incl.

non-returnees (not fully registered by name)   *c.* 260 persons
b) Homosexuals   95 persons
Number of evacuated family dependants   19 persons
c) Gypsies   42 persons
Number of evacuated family dependants   *c.* 240 persons
(not fully registered by name)

2 In detention:
a) Still at Vorbruck detention camp are:
Professional criminals and anti-socials   33 persons
Homosexuals   5 persons
b) Formerly at Vorbruck camp and released
after a varying length of time
Professional criminals and anti-socials   60 persons
Homosexuals   9 persons
(1 anti-social died at Vorbruck)

3 Preventive police detention ordered against:
a) Professional criminals and anti-socials   11 persons
(of which, 6 persons died in a concentration
camp)
b) Homosexuals   1 person
4 Protective custody ordered against:
Professional criminals and anti-socials   3 persons
5 Police custody for educational reasons up to 3
weeks:
a) Work-shy, drunkards and other anti-socials   154 persons
b) Prostitutes   91 persons
6 Regular police supervision ordered against:
a) Poachers in   227 cases
b) Since rescinded in   79 cases
c) Still in force in   148 cases

Note: Persons evacuated to unoccupied France were arrested before their evacuation and mostly held at Vorbruck detention camp for evacuation. The gypsies were directly evacuated from here.

7 *Prisoners*:
In the case of prisoners held at Mülhausen and Kolmar [Colmar] prisons, checks are made both on admission and before their release as to which preventive measures are to be taken.

[80] Preventive struggle against crime

Express letter from the commander of the Strassburg Security Police and SD to the Reich Security Headquarters, Bureau V, Berlin, dated 29 April 1942

As early as July 1940, in one of the first and most urgent measures of the German Criminal Police in Alsace, an order was given for the registration of professional and habitual criminals, anti-socials, homosexuals, poachers, gypsies, etc.

It was executed in such a way that all gendarmerie and police stations in Alsace were instructed to report all persons of the above kind to the task forces in Strassburg and Mülhausen.

The criminal records kept at the prosecutor's office of the Alsace regional court had been partly carried off to France, so that the registration then had to be undertaken with the personal police files still available and was inevitably incomplete.

As a result of these measures a total of 2115 persons were deported in several stages to France. During this time 151 persons were sent to Vorbrück detention camp, most of them for six months. At present 66 Criminal Police detainees are still there.

Furthermore, in late 1940 a total of 348 poachers were placed under preventive police detention. It has since been possible to lift this measure in the case of 140 persons.

Since the provisions valid in the Reich for the preventive combating of crime have been introduced into Alsace by the head of the civilian administration in Strassburg, a further 2 Reich German professional criminals have been placed under regular police supervision and 13 persons committed to Dachau or Flossenbürg concentration camp.

As is well known, in comparison with judicial practice in Germany the sentences passed by French courts were too light, and so it was necessary to apply an especially strict standard in assessing those with previous sentences. For this reason persons were also registered who did not always meet the requirements of the directive of 14.12.37 in respect of sentence levels.[13] A further far-reaching registration is currently under way on the basis of the criminal records which have since been returned to Alsace.

[13] See Documents 48 and 49.

(d) Combating 'Homosexual Transgressions' in the Hitler Youth

From the beginning the Hitler Youth leadership made no secret of the fact that its proposed struggle against all symptoms of degeneracy included radical action in its own ranks against 'homosexual corrosion', with the aim of finally 'eradicating' it.

After the outbreak of war it appeared as if, despite all the rigorous measures, the goal was still a long way off. Two phenomena caused the rate of prosecution to be stepped up.

1. *Rising crime figures among young people.* Homosexual offences were especially important here according to the official version. If the proportion of juveniles (14 to 18 years) in the total convicted under §175 stood at roughly 12 per cent in the years from 1933 to 1939, it rose in 1941 to just under 16 per cent and in 1942 to 24 per cent. Even discounting the decline in the number of persons convicted in the civilian sphere – and there was no increase here either in the absolute figures for 1941 and 1942 – the Reich Youth Leadership saw the rising number of juvenile convictions as sufficient proof that homosexuality had had a considerable effect on juvenile delinquency since the beginning of the war.

2. *The formation of illegal groups, mainly by ex-members of long prohibited youth associations.* From 1936 the Hitler Youth leadership waged a fierce struggle against the Bund Youth, and only a few months before the outbreak of war Himmler confirmed its prohibition. At the same time, he forbade on pain of severe penalties the continuation of old traditions by the German Volunteer Corps, the Young National Volunteers, the Greater German Bund, the German Boys' Brigade, the Austrian Boys' Corps, and so on. And yet, in 1941 a secret report by the Reich Youth Leadership stated: 'The Bund Youth problem appears to be of only historical significance. But the results of surveillance show that this question is still of the utmost importance today.'[14]

It can be inferred from a report of 1940 in the SS paper *Das Schwarze Korps* that tried and tested tactics were used against youth groups which involved themselves in political opposition. A Sudeten German Youth League founded by prominent figures from German high schools in Prague, which, among other things, preached the separatist idea of a Sudeten German stock, was regarded as a danger for the Sudeten German branch of the NSDAP. As there were no legal grounds on which the founders could be dealt with, they were eliminated in the manner already successfully used against the Nerother Wandervogel in 1938 – that is, by means of criminal proceedings under §175.

[14] *Kriminalität und Gefährdung der Jugend. Lagebericht bis zum Stande vom 1. Januar 1941,* published by the Youth Führer of the German Reich, edited by Bannführer W. Knopp, marked 'Strictly confidential. Only for official use!', no date or place (Berlin 1942), p. 99.

Today we can only very seldom distinguish between real and arbitrarily concocted events in cases involving youth leaders, who were always charged as youth leaders and therefore had to reckon with the most severe sentences. Tough action was easier whenever they invoked the kind of political romanticization of homosexuality that had been introduced into the Wandervogel movement by Hans Blüher and was still alive. In this, Nazi judges found absurd but fateful confirmation of the view that homosexuality fostered political conspiracies. Or as the previously mentioned secret report put it: 'Owing to the interaction between criminal/anti-social activity and politically oppositional views, homosexuality leads at the end of the day to political subversion. Homosexuals, like all anti-social elements, have a tendency to form cliques which always also lead to political opposition.'[15]

Measures discussed and proposed in the early forties had the aim of perfecting the system set up within the Hitler Youth to hinder or uncover sexual activity among young males. As a rule there was intensive surveillance, and a duty to report was introduced as early as 1936. As soon as suspicions were aroused, the young person would be removed from leadership positions. And if they were confirmed, the public prosecutor had to be informed. Court convictions resulted in a police order for registration by the Reich Office for the Combating of Homosexuality and Abortion. But the Hitler Youth also had a special data-transmission system which warned its members, as well as the Nazi Party, that a particular individual had a record. From 1938 each annual intake at Hitler Youth district leadership schools, from the rank of company or troop leader upwards, were given instruction in matters regarding §§174 to 176. They had to sign a declaration which was put in their personal file and which, in the event of pertinent disciplinary proceedings, made it impossible for them to plead that they had not known such acts were punishable.

In October 1942 Arthur Axmann – Baldur von Schirach's successor in the office of Youth Führer of the German Reich – submitted a proposal to the Minister of Justice that a special 'study-group for the combating of homosexual transgressions in the youth' should be established within the framework of the nation-wide 'Working Group for the Care of Young People'. *All* youth education institutions, including those which did not come under the appropriate Hitler Youth leadership, were supposed to send a representative to this 'working group'. It thus embraced the 32 national-political approved schools (which in 1941 had some 6000 pupils aged between 10 and 18), the arts Gymnasiums, orchestra schools and various establishments coming under the Wehrmacht, as well as boarding schools and special-needs schools and apprenticeship hostels. The Reich Youth Leadership saw the task of the study group as the discussion and issuing of special guidelines for the combating of

15 Ibid., p. 99.

homosexual transgressions. A draft was prepared in collaboration with scientists (Otto Wuth, director of the Institute for General Psychiatry and Military Psychology at the Academy of Military Medicine in Berlin, and Matthias Heinrich Göring, director of the German Institute for Psychological research and Psychotherapy, Berlin), police officers and SS members of the Reich Security Headquarters, and was issued by the study group at the beginning of 1943.

The aim of the guidelines was both to standardize and to tighten up methods of surveillance. It was laid down that accusations against juveniles should in principle be handled by Hitler Youth's surveillance personnel and justice department. Investigations were to be carried out exclusively by the Security Police. Local police forces were not to be involved, so as not to put confidentiality at risk. The juvenile himself was not at first informed of the suspicions, and his parents were supposed to be gently notified as soon as possible by a Hitler Youth superior involved in the enquiries. With regard to the surveillance, every leader had the duty to know 'each boy inside out, with all his weaknesses and strengths'.

In general, one can say that the number of juveniles convicted between 1933 and 1943 of offences under §175 was not very high. (There are no corresponding figures for 1944 and 1945.) The total for those years came to just under 6000, out of roughly 21.4 million young persons in 1943. The Reich Office for the Combating of Homosexuality and Abortion reported that an average of 47 per hundred thousand juveniles were convicted under §175 – a figure which offers no support for the view of homosexuality as a special danger to the youth which served to justify the 'eradication policy' of the Hitler Youth leadership.

[81] 'Annihilation of national pests.' Prominent members of the Bund Youth convicted in the Sudetenland

The official SS paper Das Schwarze Korps *on the trials of 1938/39*

A complex of homosexuals [Homosexualkomplex] in the Sudeten-land

The effects of Bund ideas and the need to combat them is stressed in the following article from *Das Schwarze Korps*, which deals with Bund Youth members in the Sudetenland.

'The regional courts in Dresden and Böhmisch-Leipa [Česka Lipa] have sentenced a number of not exactly nameless men to penal servitude or prison for homosexual offences. They include such people as Rudolf Gärtner, Dr Walter Brand, Rupert Glaas, Dr Josef Suchy, Wilhelm Zimmermann, Dr Ernst Leibl, Ernst Plischke, Justin Siegert, Anton Pleyer, Friedrich Wagner-Poltrock, Professor Anton Purkl, Professor Waldemar Fritsch and Professor Karl May.'

The culprits, who were expelled from the national community, committed far more than what the court describes and punishes as 'homosexual offences'.

They disguised their crimes against nature with the cloak of 'politics' and thus did terrible harm to the German national community. In our eyes they are not only criminals but much more: *political criminals*.

Already in the autumn of 1937 the architect Heinrich Rutha was arrested for homosexual offences. Rutha found death by his own hand on 5 November 1937 in the court cells at Böhmisch-Leipa.

He would have been the main defendant in the trials. The crime reached ever wider circles, spreading out from him as the central point of crystallization.

Rutha came from the muddled circles of the so-called 'Bund Youth', which did its mischief throughout the area of Greater Germany in the grim post-war years. One of its prophets was the Wandervogel apostle, Hans Blüher, who may well be described as the classic corrupter of youth.

The title of Blüher's book – *The Wandervogel Movement as an Erotic Phenomenon* – is indicative of his criminal ideas. In dark times he openly (with hardly any disguise) declared homosexuality to be a precondition of loyalty to the league, making use of distorted, erroneous or anyway completely irrelevant examples from the history of Greek and Roman morals.

Heinrich Rutha was one of Blüher's leading parrots. In his depraved imagination Blüher's recommended pimping already took on 'political' forms.

His 'idea' was to build a 'homoerotic men's league as a state-like organization'. Such a notion crops up again and again among criminals. It can be dressed up in the phrase: All power to the criminal! Just as a gangster wishes for a state run by gangsters, so a homosexual wishes for one in which his vice is the constitution.

Rutha's 'ideas' had many points of contact with those of Professor *Othmar Spann* and his 'Spann Circle', which fought with a hazy male conceit against the National Socialist mass movement.

Othmar Spann's loyal helper, a certain Dr Walter Heinrich, built the bridges to Rutha and his circle and looked after the philosophical underpinning of Rutha's 'political' perversities. The ball travelled backwards and forwards between them. When Rutha proclaimed: 'The state is a sphere separate from the family, a kind of counterpole', Heinrich dug out Spann's saying: 'The state is a spirit', which Rutha then completed: 'Friendship (between men) is the basis, the fundament of the spiritual.'

We can see then how this 'philosophy' is at pains to alienate from family, mother or wife young males who vigorously strive for re-organization of the state, for power in the state, and to represent natural feeling as something unspiritual, as a matter for the dull masses not for leaders. [...]

Never have criminal desires been dragged with subtler methods into the seemingly inviolable sphere of 'the spiritual'. Even the swinish Jews around Magnus Hirschfeld, with all their brutal honesty, could not hold a candle to these highly talented, organized corrupters of the nation's youth!

Thus spake Rutha: 'In woman I honour the mother [...], and I also grant her the grown-ups [...], only youths and boys will I not allow her, and never the one eternal youth who turns boys away from her.'

The Rutha-supporter Dr Wilhelm Haberzeth expressed this rather more clearly in prison on 5 June 1939: 'The awakening of natural feelings had to be prevented; whoever said the wrong thing was considered an idiot.' Another corrupter of youth argued 'on political grounds' for the 'consecration of semen'. To consider it necessary to form a band through the 'consecration of semen' was supposed to be an educational rather than a homosexual method!

And the 'writer' Leibl backed him up, suggesting that it was a means of 'getting to know the most intimate emotional responses' – an act of inspection and testing, as it were.

And these individuals were none of them theoreticians, who might have been content to get drunk on perverse fancies in the quiet of philosophers' little rooms. *The number of their real-life victims was growing bigger all the time.*

They knew how to give the meaning of '*sacrifice*' to the devotion they demanded of their 'followers'. A fellow-culprit stated in custody that he had found quite repulsive the unnatural acts which Rutha demanded of him, but that Rutha had thereby gained 'new strength for his activity' – that is, for the false show of his advanced 'political' activity. And one Suchy presumed to claim that *intercourse with Rutha had been an honour for him.*
[...]

It is not only as a criminal phenomenon that the National Social-ist state combats homosexuality. It annihilates national pests who seek to divert our greatest possession, our young people, from their natural destiny. And it eradicates enemies of the state who are driven by human impurity onto the path of political eccentricity.

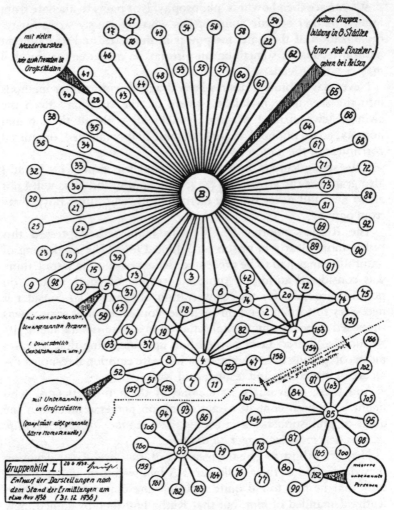

Diagram purporting to show the 'originating centre of a homosexual epidemic' and its supposed spread to other groups and towns by November 1936. From K. W. Gauhl, 'Statistische Untersuchungen über Gruppenbildung bei Jugendlichen mit gleichgeschlechtlicher Neigung unter besonderer Berücksichtigung der Struktur dieser Gruppen und der Ursache ihrer Entstehung' [Statistical Investigation of the Formation of Groups among Young People with Homosexual Tendencies, with Special Reference to the Structure of Such Groups and the Cause of their Emergence], Phil. Dissertation, University of Marburg 1940.

[82] Special committee for the combating of youth homosexuality

Letter from the Reich Minister of Justice to the Youth Führer of the German Reich, 7 February 1939

The Reich Minister of Justice   Berlin W 8, 7 February 1939
1051/S – IIIa⁴ – 107

To the:
Youth Führer of the German Reich
Berlin N W 40
Kronprinzen-Ufer 10

Subject: Combating of youth homosexuality
Ref: Your letter of 17 January 1939/IV J 3420/118/39

The experiences presented in your letter of 17 January 1939 have been confirmed in my special department for unnatural sex offences. It strikes me as useful to exchange experiences within a suitably composed committee.

I have therefore assigned my specialist on unnatural sex offences, Chief Prosecutor von Haacke, to serve on the planned committee. Insofar as the work of the committee refers to circles of the former Bund Youth, my specialist on that case, Chief Prosecutor Dr Joël, will take part in the committee's work.

Heil Hitler
p.p.
Signed: Dr Meggenburg

Re: SS-Untersturmführer Dr Günter Joël
      Reich Ministry of Justice

With effect from 30 January 1939 the Gruppenführer has taken charge of Cde. Günter Joël as Untersturmführer and assigned him to the SD Captain for collaborative work.

Chief Prosecutor Dr Joël is by agreement the direct liaison officer between C and the Reich Ministry of Justice on all matters concerning the Security Service and the Secret State Police.

12
Signed: Glatzel
SS-Oberführer

Memorandum Gestapo Headquarters 12, dated 7 May 1938, on the appointment of Dr Joël as Gestapo V-man [i.e. trusted agent]. BA-AH-ZB I 197, fol 10.

[83] Decrease in the number of proceedings under §175
*Memorandum on the 1st session of the Working Group for the
Care of Young People at the Reich Youth Leadership,
27 October 1941 (Extract)*

On Monday, 27 October 1941 the *Working Group for the Care of
Young People* appointed by the Reich Youth Leadership held its
first session in the meeting hall of the Reich Youth Leadership. The
chair was taken by the authorized representative of the Reich
Youth Führer, Stabsführer Möckel. Representatives from all Party
and state offices involved in youth care took part in the session. In
addition to the Reich Youth Leadership the following were represented: the Party Central Office, the NSV [National Socialist
People's Welfare], the DAF [German Labour Front], the Reich
Ministry of the Interior including the offices of the Reichsführer-SS
and Head of the German Police, the Reich Ministries of Labour,
Propaganda, Education and Justice, and finally the Reich Labour
Service and the Wehrmacht.

In his opening speech Stabsführer Möckel said, among other
things, that the working group should facilitate better cooperation
among all offices involved in youth care. It was intended to convene
the working group at certain intervals and to set up smaller working groups for discussion of urgent individual questions. Efforts
will be made to form similar working groups in districts where
cooperation among the various offices is also in urgent need of
improvement.

There followed reports from: Oberbannführer Schröder, head of
the Social Department of the Reich Youth Leadership and director
of the Youth Department of the DAF, who spoke on the 'nature
and significance of the Working Group for the Care of Young
People'; Bannführer Knopp, director of surveillance at the Personnel Department of the Reich Youth Leadership, on 'delinquency
and waywardness among young people'; Oberbannführer Tetzlaff,
director of penal provisions at the Hitler Youth Justice Department,
on 'Hitler Youth Justice and its Work'; and Bannführer Berge-
mann, director of juvenile law at the Social Department of the
Reich Youth Leadership, on 'youth waywardness and youth care'.

The following information and ideas should be emphasized from
the reports:

On the state of juvenile delinquency it was reported that as things
stood there was likely to be an increase in 1941 of roughly 20 per
cent over 1938. There had been a remarkable increase in delinquency among younger age groups, which was related to the gener-

ally earlier onset of puberty. Reference was also made to the rise in serious offences. Monitoring by the Reich Youth Leadership indicated a fall in the number of offences under §175 of the Penal Code. Unmistakable loose-living among young people should be seen as a reflection of the more general loose-living in sexual matters, just as the youth usually mirrors the nation's moral behaviour. Particularly lamentable was the moral waywardness of a section of female youth, which showed itself especially in dealings with members of the Reich Labour Service and the armed forces. In this connection it was requested that the Wehrmacht should put officers on patrol more often. [...]

Number of minors in care in special schools, 1938 to 1940

Reason for taking into care in Prussia	Year of referral					
	1938		1939		1940	
	m	f	m	f	m	f
Bodily injury/violence	106	9	68	3	98	8
Cruelty to animals	19	1	5	–	15	1
Arson	11	2	15	6	21	3
Offences ag property	2573	319	2523	357	3159	512
Begging	52	40	35	18	29	13
Vagrancy	45	5	43	5	41	3
Sexual waywardness involving:						
Prostitution	–	32	–	24	–	29
Homosexuality	171	–	110	–	85	–
	(3.4%)		(2.3%)		(1.6%)[1]	
Alcoholism	3	–	8	–	9	–
Work-shy/loitering/truancy	337	49	447	65	595	85
Bad conditions for bringing up	1327	1207	1221	1162	1170	1124
Total	4981	4160	4741	3960	5469	4614

[1] Percentage of all minors in residential care in the relevant year.
Source: Compiled from *Vierteljahreshefte zur Statistik des Deutschen Reiches. Die Fürsorgeerziehung im Rechnungsjahr ...*, Landeshauptarchiv Sachsen-Anhalt, Magdeburg Rep. C 127 Nr. 1145, fol 100/7, fol 157/7, fol 163/7.

'Homosexuality and Youth', an essay by Hitler Youth Oberbannführer Tetzlaff, from the title-page of *Der HJ-Richter* No. 5/1942.

[84]   Oberbannführer Tetzlaff: Homosexuality and Youth

An essay published in Der HJ-Richter, *an educational newspaper of Hitler Youth Justice, February 1942 (Extract)*

[...] Since 1936 Hitler Youth Justice has also been governed by the distinction between homosexual seducers and adolescent misbehaviour. Until 1936 we were under the spell of the Führer's decision of 30 June 1934. Up to then suspensions and expulsions for adolescent misbehaviour were the order of the day. The Supreme Party Judge, Reichsleiter Buch, is to be thanked for the fact that, by considering the frequency of such misbehaviour in cadet and other boarding schools, we came to realize that the great majority of boys inwardly get over such misbehaviour in a fairly short period of time and go on to become healthy, respectable men. Insofar as boys have not already developed a tendency to homosexual offences that represents a danger to the health of the community – in which case at least disqualification for a certain time will be necessary – the hoped-for educational results will probably best be achieved through the shock effect of official youth detention. Homosexual seducers present no problem for Hitler Youth Justice.

They are called to account with merciless severity, disqualified as potential youth leaders, and expelled from the Hitler Youth. All Hitler Youth regions and other divisions of the Party, as well as the Party itself, are sent lists warning them in case these persons should turn up again. It goes without saying that they are handed over to the public prosecutor for legal action to be taken. The Supreme Party Court has the same pitiless attitude toward adult homosexuals. In its directive of 19.12.1941 to lower Party courts it identified 'any kind of homosexual tendency or activity' as ground for immediate 'removal from the NSDAP, that is, at least expulsion without any question of parole at the front'.

Hitler Youth keeps a close watch out for the occurrence of homosexual offences. Already in 1936 it became obligatory to report homosexual offences on pain of disciplinary sanctions (Reich Order of 31.1.36, p. 55). In March 1938 the Reich Youth leadership ordered that at every district leadership school, each annual intake from the rank of company or troop leader upwards should be given instruction in matters regarding §§174 to 176 of the Penal Code. They have to sign a declaration which is kept under their name, so that in the event of disciplinary proceedings this becomes part of their disciplinary file and they can no longer plead that they had not known such acts were punishable.

On the other hand, the Reich Youth Leadership should refrain from mass instruction of young people themselves in this area as in the area of sex in general. Individual members of a yearly age-group are so different in their development and mental grasp that any mass instruction would lead to undesirable consequences. Such instruction must be given by the parents on an individual basis. No other educational institution can relieve parents of this naturally given task. Only they are fully suited to perform this task in their children's education.

With regard to homosexuality another demand should be made of the legislator – mainly the requirement of female honour that illicit sex acts between women should also be punishable under §175, as is already the case in the Ostmark [Austria].

The question of whether illicit sex acts are common between women can be left open, for that is no criterion of whether an offence should be punishable. In the Old Reich no figures are available because the criminal law does not apply. Since 1936 Hitler Youth Justice has sentenced four BDM [German Girls' League] members to expulsion and one BDM member to suspension because of homosexual acts (ages: 16 to 27 years). In the Ostmark there are no official statistics relating to this. But I am grateful to

Professor Grassberger from Vienna for the following figures.

In the years from 1922 to 1937 a total of 152 women were convicted of homosexual offences in the Ostmark – i.e. 9.5 per year. This low figure does not mean a lot, however. I agree with Prof. Grassberger's further remarks: 'The number of unreported homosexual offences between women is especially high. It is significantly less conspicuous for two women than for two men to live closely together without servants in one residence. Women generally live more secluded lives than men, even in their occupation, and so they are less subjected to critical observation.'

A sociological analysis of 110 cases showed the following characteristic picture:

Sixty-six per cent are repeat offenders and prostitutes, therefore criminals and anti-socials, as such offences largely originate in prisons or are to be found in convents. So the struggle against them is a struggle against abnormality and against anti-socials and criminals.

I shall end by considering together the reason why female homosexuality should be punished and the reason why a merciless struggle should be waged against homosexuality in general. Homosexuality does not weaken a nation only through the loss of births; it also involves a degeneration or inversion of normal feelings, a feminization of man and a masculinization of woman. It thus puts at risk a nation's healthy behaviour and therefore its very future. Young people, as bearers of this future, have a right to demand ruthless struggle against all symptoms of degeneracy.

Decisions of the Hitler Youth Supreme Court

1.

[...]

Stammführer A., who was 29 years of age at the time of his alleged acts, belonged since 1923 to the Bund Youth: first to the 'German National Youth League', and later to the 'Greater German Youth League' and the 'Young National Volunteers'. In 1931 he was a regional leader. In 1930 he had joined the Bund's 'Widukind' Students' Guild.

Already in 1936/37 A. was involved in criminal proceedings for unnatural sex acts with his Guild brother B., in which A was released for lack of proof.

In about April 1938 A. invited his Hitler Youth subordinate, platoon leader C., to stay overnight at his place. He slept with him in the joining beds, having moved his wife out. During the night A. felt

C. on the upper part of his body and talked with him about homosexual matters.

At Whitsun 1939 A. met C. and other Hitler Youth leaders to go together to the culture camp at W. On the way there they spent the night at D. and E.

On both occasions A. arranged things so that he would spend the night in the same room with C. At E., A. again felt C. on the upper part of his body, having first talked with him about the male–female relationship. At the culture camp itself A. arranged things so that C. came to lie beside him in the tent. At night there, after several preparatory acts, A. went on to hold C. by the genitals.

A. denies the acts of which he is accused, but C.'s testimony appears completely trustworthy.

What told against A. was above all the fact that he had already been involved in a trial for unnatural sex acts. It is not necessary to establish whether, because of C.'s testimony, the facts summarized in the regional court verdict of 2.4.1937 have been cast in a different light. At any event A. was already homosexually handicapped, and he had shown then that he lacked a healthy instinctive feeling of aversion to such acts. If A. had to admit that he had repeatedly slept in a double room with a comrade ten years younger than himself, this alone would have been reason to debar A. as a potential youth leader. For as a man who had been released for lack of proof in a case involving homosexual offences, he should afterwards have been especially careful and avoided the least appearance of wishing to act in a homosexual manner.

Furthermore, the Hitler Youth Supreme Court is of the view that A.'s disputed acts with C. did take place. The Hitler Youth Supreme Court cannot believe it was purely by chance that A., who had been involved in a trial for unnatural sex acts, slept together with C. on four successive occasions over a relatively short period of time. C.'s testimony shows, rather, that after A. got to know him he wanted them to be together – which made possible the carrying out of illicit homosexual acts. Only C.'s clear refusal then prevented A. from attaining his goal even before the events in the culture camp at W.

It is therefore established that A., in his capacity as a higher-ranking leader, tried to seduce a subordinate comrade into illicit sex acts. This crime, for which the sentence of the law is penal servitude, cannot be punished here with anything other than a dishonourable discharge from the Hitler Youth. In this decision no allowances at all can be made for A.'s undoubted service to the Hitler Youth.

A. was therefore stripped of his rank and expelled from the Hitler Youth.

Der HJ-Richter. Schulungsblatt der HJ-Gerichtsbarkeit, February 1942. BArch P, Film 14653.

The placing of minors in police-run youth detention camps

It will shortly be possible to begin placing minors in police-run youth detention camps. This will firstly involve under-age males for whom, despite their criminal or anti-social behaviour, care in a special school cannot be ordered or maintained because they show no prospects or have exceeded the age limit.

With reference to the reports made in accordance with my directive of 1.4.1940, I would ask you to propose minors for placement, initially from your police district. [...] The selection should mainly focus on 16-to-19 year-olds; anyone younger should be considered only if there are special reasons for doing so. [...]

With regard to a minor's arrest and the initiation of placement order and medical examination proceedings, instructions should be awaited from the Reich Criminal Police Bureau, these being a necessary condition for the ordering and enforcement of police placement. Until then the juvenile should not have any knowledge of the measures intended against him.

Otherwise – on matters of jurisdiction etc. – the provisions of Min. of Int. Directive of 14.12.1937 (Pol-S-Kr. 3 Nr. 1682/37 – 2098) and the supplementary guidelines of 4.4.1938 issued by the Reich Criminal Police Bureau shall apply accordingly to the proceedings.

The proposals should be presented from today, and no later than 20 July 1940.

Directive of the RSHA, 26 June 1940 (Extract). Collection of directives. Preventive combating of crime. IfZ Doc 17.02.

[85] 'The danger to German youth from homosexual offences requires special attention.'
The Youth Führer of the German Reich to the Reich Minister of Justice, 3 October 1942

The Youth Führer of   Berlin W 35, 3 October 1942
the German Reich   Kurfürstenstr. 53
Reich Working Group for the
Care of Young People   Strictly confidential!

To the:
Reich Minister of Justice
Berlin W 8
Wilhelmstr. 65

Subject: Reich Working Group for the Care of Young People
          Combating of homosexual offences

The danger to German youth from homosexual offences requires special attention and energetic measures, within the framework of close collaboration and uniform planning by all bodies involved in youth education.

In collaboration with leading scientists and the Reich Security Headquarters, the Reich Youth Führer has developed guidelines for the combating of homosexual offences in the Hitler Youth.[16] On the basis of the experiences of the past year, the guidelines contain all essential points concerning the preventive and investigative struggle. I enclose a provisional plan.

I consider it urgently necessary to apply the principles elaborated here to work on youth education for which the Hitler Youth does not have leadership responsibility. Particularly in:

Teacher training colleges
National-political training colleges
Arts Gymnasiums
Orchestra schools
Annual farm camps
Reich finance colleges
Preparatory schools for non-commissioned officers
Preparatory aviation schools
Music colleges of the Wehrmacht, Waffen-SS, Reich Labour Service
Boarding-schools, pupils' boarding-houses, vocational school hostels
NSV [National Socialist People's Welfare] youth homes
Special education schools
Apprentices' hostels etc.

In the framework of the Reich Working Group for the Care of Young People, a special group for the combating of homosexual offences has been created under the direction of Oberbannführer *Knopp*. I would ask interested bodies to participate in this special group. Implementation will be discussed at the next plenary session of the Reich Working Group.

Heil Hitler!
p.p.
Signed: Schroeder

[16] See Document 87.

[86] 'No dissection of the soul'

Report on the first session of the Study Group for the Combating of Homosexual Offences, 12 November 1942

Agenda: Distribution of guidelines
Present, among others:
Representative of the Wehrmacht High Command,
Lieutenant-Colonel Kretzschmer
Representative of the Navy High Command
Representative of the Air Force High Command
Representative of the Propaganda Ministry
Representative of the Reich Ministry of Justice
Representative of the Criminal Police
Representative of the Security Service etc.

The guidelines do not discuss the causes of homosexuality in any major detail. The main discussion concerned distribution of the guidelines. Some organizations wanted up to 12,000 copies. When I warned about discussing homosexuality too much all the time, and about the use which enemy propaganda would make of publication of the guidelines on such a scale, this view was endorsed by Lieutenant-Colonel Kretzschmer, Wehrmacht Propaganda, the Hitler Youth leadership, the Security Police, SD and Criminal Police. The guidelines should be issued as 'Strictly confidential, only for official use' and distributed only to leading bodies. Further instruction should be given by verbal means. Lieutenant-Colonel Kretzschmer and myself were both of the view that this is the concern of commanding generals or army corps doctors, and that the corps or military district doctors should pursue instruction by organizing lectures, and that only an appropriate quantity of the guidelines would be needed for the Wehrmacht, which should be issued by the head of Army Medical Service. Prof. Dr. M. H. Göring pointed out that if the directors of psychiatric clinics had to decide which case was suitable for expert assessment, they would also have to reserve for themselves a report about whether the case was suitable for assessment. (This refers to the fact that, at my prompting, directors of university psychiatric clinics are to be centrally involved in helping to draft the guidelines on page 38.) Crime Adviser Jakob, specialist on homosexuality at the Crime Department, thereupon asked Prof. Göring how he conceived of psychotherapeutic treatment of young adolescents. Prof. G. replied that in such cases psychotherapy could only be quite superficial. Crime Adviser Jakob and Obersturmbannführer Knopp then argued that it could also be undertaken by suitable youth doctors, leaders, educationalists and relatives. At any event they did not want any dissection of souls.

The guidelines are to be printed, and each authority should add an insert for its own purposes.

One copy of the draft guidelines is in my possession as a classified item. If desired, it can be produced at any time, with the request that it be returned.

Wuth
Colonel in the Medical Corps

[87] 'To keep German youth pure requires the sharpest repudiation of homosexual offences'

Special guidelines. The Combating of Homosexual Offences in the Framework of Youth Education. Published by the Reich Youth Leadership, Berlin, 1 June 1943 (Extracts)

I. General
I(a) Purpose of the Guidelines

To keep German youth pure requires the sharpest repudiation of homosexual offences, which are capable of destroying what edu cational work constructs. [...]

The following guidelines are designed to inform leaders and educators of the youth about the nature and consequences of homosexual offences, and to put them in a position where they can carry out their resulting duties. [...]

I(b) Announcement and Distribution of the Guidelines

1. Categories of individuals. The guidelines are to be announced to:
   (a) all full-time leaders and staff; all honorary leaders at headquarters;
   (b) leading personnel from company (troop) leader upward at leadership schools of the Reich Youth Leadership and districts;
   (c) all leaders, educators and administrators [...] at homes, schools and camps under the direction of the Hitler Youth where many young people are gathered together for a long period of time; especially at:
      halls of residence, youth hostels, Farm Service camps and schools, camps coming under the KLV, holiday camps, schools, leadership schools, Adolf Hitler schools, military training camps, harvest action camps, etc. [...]

IV Preventive Measures against Homosexual Offences

Preventive measures are of special importance. They should prevent homosexual offences from ever occurring or from involving a large number of people.

IV(a) Selection of Leaders

1 Careful selection of suitable faultless leaders and assistants is of the utmost importance in preventing homosexual offences. Leaders should not independently appoint the leader immediately below them (no favourites as junior leaders!!). Otherwise cliques might form, the dangers of which have been shown above. Leaders and junior leaders shall be selected and appointed by the regiment or district leadership. Before an appointment, leaders and assistants of the Hitler Youth should be verified in accordance with the 'Personnel Monitoring Guidelines'.

2 In the case of leaders, educators and assistants who are active in homes, further supervision is called for.
  (a) Home leaders should be married. Their wives should comply with the requirements of life in the home.
  (b) In homes no educational responsibility or leadership duties may be transferred to leaders under 18 years of age unless they are under constant invigilation.
  (c) Full-time educators at the home shall be appointed by district leaderships only with the approval of competent officials of the Reich Youth Leadership. Junior leaders may be appointed only with the written approval of the Hitler Youth body to which the home leader is responsible.
     For KLV and Farm Service camps the above orders are to be applied in accordance with their special requirements.

3 Persons about whom there are moral doubts, especially with regard to homosexuality, may not be utilized unless a different decision in accordance with the rules was made in personnel-monitoring or disciplinary proceedings in the case of earlier minor offences.
Leaders who deliberately or negligently fail to carry out their supervisory duties, or who permit the appointment or continued employment of leaders (assistants) whose incrimination is known to them, must expect the harshest of measures. [...]

IV(e) Preventive Supervision

1 Signs of homosexuality must be detected as early as possible, before actual offences if that is at all possible, but in any case before there is a further spread. The necessary attentiveness must not degenerate into compulsive suspicion and snooping. That would have a harmful effect on the community. In preventive supervision the competent youth or institution doctor can make an essential contribution.

2 Each individual boy should be under constant care and observation. That has nothing to do with snooping. But each leader must know each boy so well that it is possible to detect endangered or corrupted youths at an early stage, to give them help or to prevent a corrupting influence. However, anything like contact with or examination of sexual parts is strictly forbidden to leaders.

3 Especially at risk, and to be watched accordingly, are socially maladjusted juveniles, those who have lost one or both parents, illegitimate and single children, and so on. Further possible signs of general sexual, often homosexual, danger are: a feminine, affected character, conspicuous arrogance, separation from the community (particularly through clique formation), slackness in work and discipline, conspicuously shy behaviour, a dull and weary ('dissipated') aspect. Homosexual inclinations may also express themselves, especially among adults, in physical chastisement and cruelty (sadism).
From these and similar signs, however, it is never possible to draw definite conclusions; other causes may just as easily be present.

4 Boys' reading matter should be supervised. Unsuitable literature and pictures – e.g. pulp series, low-quality crime fiction, magazines and nude photos – should be confiscated. Among juveniles, sexual excitement often leads to homosexual acts as a substitute for unattainable natural activity.

5 In homes a watch needs to be kept for other things as well.
   (a) The youths should not be put two in a room. They must never, even in an emergency, sleep two in a bed. The beds should not be too close to each other. Youths must not be put together in a room with leaders and educators (except with junior leaders appointed from among the men, such as a dormitory prefect or a senior soldier in a barracks room).
   (b) After lights-out no boy may remain in the room of the leader or of other boys. The same applies to leaders, except in an

emergency. Checks after lights-out should be made every evening, usually by two leaders together. Bed checks (inspection of individual beds for signs of masturbatory activity, etc.) should not be carried out. They damage the trust between leaders and their entourage.[17]

(c) Contact with persons outside the home also requires supervision, where circumstances permit. Often adult corrupters of youth seek their victims among the inmates of homes. If such a suspicion arises, the police should be notified at once.

(d) Inspectors, outside leaders and so on are to be admitted only on the basis of an identity card, which should be presented without a need to request it and which should be carefully checked as to its validity. Outside persons should not be lodged in the home unless such lodging has been explicitly authorized by the superior body.

(e) Leaders must always unobtrusively keep an eye on junior leaders and their behaviour. The behaviour of technical and scientific auxiliaries (including women) should also be watched.

6 It is strictly forbidden for authorized personnel to entice suspects into attempted homosexual acts in order to secure a conviction (provocations). Such methods will be most severely punished both by the law and in disciplinary proceedings.

7 The monitoring of homosexual offences within the Hitler Youth shall be carried out by the Personnel Supervision Department of the Reich Youth Leadership and its offices in the localities and regiments, in collaboration with the Security Police and SD. The supervisory services of the Hitler Youth should here work very closely with all other bodies involved in youth education. They serve as central Hitler Youth agencies for the recording of all reports, whichever the body from which these come.

V. The Clearing Up of Homosexual Offences
V(a) Duties of Leaders

1 The duty to reveal. No homosexual offence may be hushed up, nor may it be passed over in silence by expelling those involved. Otherwise further offences would be encouraged and there would be reason to fear the consequences mentioned in Section II.

---

[17] The term *entourage* or '*Gefolgschaft*', with its intentionally pre-modern associations, was commonly used in Nazi parlance to denote the workforce or other group placed under a leader. *Translator's note.*

Rather, swift and ruthless action should be taken in each case. Comradely or other considerations (e.g. because of earlier merits or the prestige of the organization) have to be set aside. Negligent disregard of leadership obligations is also irresponsible and will be punished.

2 The duty to report. Leaders and educators are obliged to report immediately, if necessary by telephone, to their superior or to higher bodies any grounds for suspicion and any actual homosexual incidents. They should be reported to the Area Personnel Supervision Department if they occur in the home, or otherwise to the regiment. These bodies will make all further arrangements, inform the police, parents and so on. In the case of unclear suspicions the youth doctor may, if applicable, be brought in to express an opinion.

Failure to report will be treated as aiding and abetting and prosecuted both at law and in disciplinary proceedings. A report should be made even if other bodies have already opened an investigation.

If, in addition to the above report, immediate police assistance is exceptionally required (arrest, flight of the offender, etc.), the nearest police station (the Criminal Police in towns, the Gendarmerie in rural communes) should be directly alerted.

3 Ban on carrying out investigations.
Once leaders have drawn the *prima facie* conclusions necessary for the above report, they should immediately break off enquiries and stand apart from any further investigations.

4 Confidentiality.
Suspicions are to be handled in strict confidence, so that suspects are not prematurely alerted. Even when investigations are under way or have already been concluded, confidential handling of the case is necessary.

If, nevertheless, members of the unit (the home) or other persons learn of the situation, an unconditional obligation to silence should be imposed on them. The parents will be notified by the body carrying out the investigation. [...]

Arbeitsrichtlinien der Hitler-Jugend

Streng vertraulich!

4/43

Nur für den Dienstgebrauch!

Sonderrichtlinien

Die Bekämpfung
gleichgeschlechtlicher Verfehlungen
im Rahmen der Jugenderziehung

Herausgegeben von der Reichsjugendführung

Berlin, am 1. Juni 1943

Issue No. 4 in 1943 of the regular Working Guidelines of the Hitler Youth, marked
'Strictly confidential!' and 'For official use only!'. The title reads: 'Special Guidelines:
The Combating of Homosexual Offences in the Framework of Youth Education'.

Inhalt

2

The contents page of the 'Special Guidelines', with the chapter headings: 'I. General', 'II. What Is Homosexuality and Why Is It Combated?', 'III. The Criminal Nature of Homosexual Offences', 'IV. Preventive Measures against Homosexual Offences', 'V. The Clearing Up of Homosexual Offences', 'VI. Disciplinary and Educational Measures against Offenders', 'VII. Collaboration of Youth Doctors'.

Part V
Castration as an Instrument of Repression

Among the strategic instruments to fulfil demands for the 'eradication' of homosexuality or the 'reeducation' of homosexual men, castration was particularly inhumane.

Before 1933 there had been no agreement, among either forensic psychiatrists or criminologists, about its supposed benefits as a therapeutic, protective or prophylactic operation in the context of offences under §§174–176 of the Penal Code. Its 'effectiveness in the prevention of crime' was widely disputed. Not a few opponents of castration saw it as a largely inadequate method which did not extinguish the subject's sexual desires but 'only' dampened their force. In most cases, moreover, it was thought that depression and neurotic conditions would have to be reckoned with as effects of the irreversible and severely mutilating operation. Such arguments were not accepted by advocates of castration.

As part of the drive to use penal law to enforce the basic principles of Nazi population policy, the indications for compulsory castration in sex offences were considerably widened between 1933 and 1945. For the first time in German legal history judges were given the power to order compulsory castration in addition to custodial sentences. The 'Law against Dangerous Habitual Criminals and Measures for Protection and Recovery' (*Reichsgesetzblatt* I 1933, p. 997) laid down the appropriate regulations. But the operation was still tied to certain requirements. According to §42 k, para. I, cl. 1–2, it could be carried out only in cases of rape, defilement, illicit sex acts with children (§176), coercion to commit sex offences (§177), the committing of indecent acts in public (§183), and murder or manslaughter of the victim (§223–226), if they were committed to arouse or gratify the sex drive.

With regard to the different forms of homosexuality, the new regulations stipulated that an official castration order could be made in cases of sex acts with boys under fourteen (§176 1, 3) or homosexual exhibitionism (§183). The majority of men who became liable to punishment under §175, 175a did not fall under this regulation.

Even 'voluntary submission' to castration was not allowed at first. This possibility was only created with the 'Amendment to the Law for the Prevention of Offspring with Hereditary Diseases', dated 26 June 1935 (*Reichsgesetzblatt* I 1935, p. 773). The new Clause 2 of §14 permitted and regulated 'castration indicated by reason of crime' in the case of homosexual men. However, the consent of the person concerned was still a necessary requirement. The operation was permissible only if relevant convictions had already been pronounced or fresh ones were to be feared. It was also necessary for a medical officer or court doctor to give an assessment.

Under a directive of 23 January 1936 (RMBliV p. 258), it was explicitly laid down that the voluntary decision for castration must not be impaired by any coercion, even indirect. In particular, it was held to be impermissible to make the suspension of any part of a sentence conditional upon such consent.

Three years later, on 20 May 1939, Reichsführer-SS Himmler declared this last provision null and void. The necessity of consent was not challenged, he argued, if a person in preventive detention was told that his release would be possible after successful castration. It is very likely that in previous years homosexual men – especially those sentenced to penal servitude followed by preventive detention – had already consented to the severely mutilating operation. One could say that they hardly had any other choice.

It is not known how many men were forced to undergo the operation in this way between 1935 and 1945. A study published in 1944 by the psychiatrist Nikolaus Jensch – 'Untersuchungen an entmannten Sittlichkeitsverbrechern' [Investigations concerning Emasculated Sex Criminals] – stated that of the 693 mutilated men included in the study 285 had been sentenced as homosexuals and castrated in detention. This does not allow us to draw any conclusions as to the total number of homosexual men who had been made victims of this inhuman practice by that date.

Information about how the provisions of §14, Clause 2 of the above 'Amended Law' were applied in offences under §175, 175a might exist in Reich Health Bureau files, especially those relating to the forensic-biological research carried out after 28 November 1939. It has not been possible to trace one closed batch of such papers in the archives visited so far. In the late eighties 1137 personal files were discovered in Hamburg relating to the forensic-biological data-gathering centre at Hamburg prison, including some 600 castration cases (roughly 120 of them 'voluntary') from the years 1934 to 1945. According to the Hamburg doctor Friedemann Pfäfflin, a first perusal indicates three broad groups of cases.

'1. There is one group of cases where the cynicism of the Nazi dictatorship achieves undisguised expression, and it becomes clear that sterilization and castration could and did pass imperceptibly into extermination. Reports from this group best correspond to the image one commonly has of the Nazi state. An example may be the case of a seventy-year-old man who had been convicted twelve times of begging and six times of violating the provisions of §176.3 of the Penal Code. His last sentence was completed on 1.6.1934. Castration was ordered retroactively and carried out on 14.8.1934 in the framework of extra detention. The medical expert had reached the conclusion that castration was urgently necessary to protect the community, but he also pointed out that in view of the advanced hardening of the guinea-pig's arteries, the strong mental agitation associated with the operation might result in a heart attack. The ruling of the sole judge, Dr B., at the Hamburg district court read as follows: "Whilst the rigours of the operation are fully recognized, which for the defendant involve emasculation and possible consequences beyond its intended purpose, the risk that he represents to adolescent youth must, on the other hand, be taken so seriously that the somewhat additional harm to the defendant resulting from the operation counts for little in comparison. [...] The health and continuing purity of the German youth is a higher principle than consideration for individuals with unfortunate or depraved sexual tendencies."

'The man did not die of a heart attack during the operation, but hanged himself immediately afterwards.

'2. In a second, different-sized group of cases, it becomes clear that when medical experts had to choose between the legal alternatives of preventive detention and castration, they recommended the latter as the relatively lesser evil. The wordy emphasis on the beneficial therapeutic effects of castration is, in many reports at least, so exaggerated as to give the impression that the expert wanted to protect the subject from something worse.

'3. Finally there is a third group of cases, partly overlapping with the second, in which the reports seriously weigh up – sometimes with an extraordinary sophistication – whether castration is indicated and holds out some promise, and whether there are not other therapeutic possibilities. Some reports tersely stated that there were no objections to castration, while others put forward a detailed motivation which – as papers in the personal case-files seem to suggest – was also accepted by the object of the experiment. In many of the reports, arguments are put forward against the operation in general or in the particular case in question, with references to foreign specialist literature. There are also applications for castration, quite probably submitted voluntarily by guinea-pigs, which did not receive expert approval either because they did not meet the legal requirements or because they offered no prospect of success. Finally there are court rulings against castrations recommended by experts.'[1] The author goes on to quote in detail to show that a wide spectrum of justificatory arguments and actual interventions were employed.

Furthermore, in or around 1934, work was begun on a control system that was supposed to guarantee total registration and surveillance of castrated homosexual men. Operations were recorded on national standard forms, with follow-ups envisaged after four weeks, one year, three years and five years. After the end of 1937 registration was carried

---

[1] F. Pfäfflin, 'Chirurgische Kastration vor und nach 1945', in G. Kaiser/H. Kury/H. J. Albrecht, eds., *Kriminologische Forschung in den 60er Jahren. Projektberichte aus der Bundesrepublik Deutschland*, Freiburg 1988, pp. 597f.

out at 73 Forensic-Biological Research Establishments attached to penal institutions and concentration camps. Data were passed on to nine centrally organized regional forensic-biological centres, where they were examined, condensed and forwarded to the Reich Health Bureau. Plans were afoot to set up a Central Agency for Castration Research at the Reich Office for the Combating of Homosexuality and Abortion, but this failed to materialize because of the escalation in the war.

Under a decree of the Reich Security Headquarters dated 2.1.1942, convicted and castrated men were placed under regular police supervision. They had to report any change of residence to comply with all instructions of the competent health authority. In some cases – above all those which, on the evidence of the person's behaviour or the recommendation of a medical officer, 'presented, despite castration, a considerable danger to the community and especially the youth' – the Criminal Police could now order internment in a concentration camp without going through court proceedings.

As 'voluntary' castration was being carried out, there were also calls for its general application. The basis for these was research involving both legal and medical experts. In numerous particular investigations they attempted to justify official castration orders as being in the interests of the national community.

Such discussions, especially between the Reich Ministries of Justice and the Interior, intensified during the years from 1942 to 1944. An influential role was played here by the previously mentioned SS-Obersturmbannführer and doctor, Karl-Heinz Rodenberg. In 1943 the efforts converged in a draft law on 'the handling of social aliens [*Gemeinschaftsfremden*]'. The group of people denounced here as 'burdens' on the national community included so-called work-shy elements, grousers, vagrants, beggars, good-for-nothings, mental defectives and homosexual men. Even if the lurch into total war prevented it from coming into effect, the legal provisions were now ready and waiting for compulsory castration for offences under §175.[2]

The ministerial bureaucracy, then, continued to discuss with legal and medical experts whether the compulsory castration of homosexual men should be made available through a change in the criminal law, or whether it would be better to wait for the dreadful law on the handling of 'social aliens' to come into effect. But at the same time, by a secret order of 14.11.1942, the Economic and Administrative Headquarters of the SS – the central authority in charge of the concentration camps – gave the go-ahead for camp commandants to order castration in special cases not covered by the law. In this way the forced castration of homosexual men in concentration camps was 'legalized'. For years already they had been subjected to it without mercy.

---

[2] Cf. G. J. Giles, 'The Unkindest Cut of All: Castration, Homosexuality and Nazi Justice', *Journal of Contemporary History*, vol. 27, 1992, pp. 41–61.

[88] Blackmailing into voluntary castration
Decree of the Reichsführer-SS, 20 May 1939

The Reichsführer-SS and   Berlin S W 11, 20 May 1939
Head of the German Police
at the Reich Ministry of the Interior
S-Kr 3 Nr. 623/37 VI

To the Reich Criminal Police Bureau
Subject: Voluntary emasculation of persons in preventive
       detention

In the directive of the Reich and Prussian Minister of the Interior
and the Reich Minister of Justice, dated 23.1.1936 (RMBliV. p.
258), it is stated that the voluntary decision for castration must not
be impaired by any coercion, even indirect. 'In particular,' it says,
'it is therefore impermissible to make the suspension of any part of
a sentence conditional upon such consent.'

   In order to avoid a false interpretation of these provisions, I
would stress in agreement with the Reich Minister of Justice that
consent required under §14, cl. 2 of the Law for the Prevention of
Offspring with Hereditary Diseases is *not* challenged if a sex
offender in *preventive detention* is told that after castration has
been carried out it will *probably* be possible for him to be released
from preventive detention. I request you to proceed accordingly in
suitable cases.

RKPA. 60^{01}/426.39
§14 Clause 2 of the Law for the Prevention of Offspring with Hereditary
Diseases, 14.7.33, as amended by the Law of 26.6.35 (*Reichsgesetzblatt* I
p. 773), reads as follows: 'Removal of the gonads in a man may be
performed only with his consent, and even then only if, according to
reports by a medical officer or court doctor, it is necessary to free him of
a degenerate sex drive which gives reason to fear further offences under
§§175 to 178, 183, and 223 to 226 of the Penal Code. Emasculation
orders in criminal proceedings or safety proceedings are not affected.'

[89] Concentration camp for 'multiple seducers'
Reich Security Headquarters Directive, 12 July 1940

Reich Security Headquarters   12 July 1940
V B 1 Nr. 1143/40

To the State Criminal Police
Copy to: Secret State Police

I request that in future, after their release from prison, you should take all homosexuals who have seduced more than one partner into preventive police detention.

'Reports in the literature about the results of castration of homosexuals are so encouraging (Hackfield *et al*.) that we should recommend this operation to recidivist homosexuals more often than in the past, for it seems possible to protect them in this way from permanent institutionalization. Under the legal provisions currently in force, the castration of homosexuals cannot be ordered by a court; it is left entirely up to homosexuals to apply for castration during internment.'

R. Lemke, *Über Ursache und strafrechtliche Beurteilung der Homosexualität*, Jena 1940, p. 43.

[90] Ending of 'preventive detention' for castrated homosexual men
Decree of the Reich Criminal Police Bureau, 23 September 1940

Reich Criminal Police Bureau   Berlin, 23 September 1940
Tgb. Nr. Allg. 2057 B

To the Criminal Police departments
in [. . .]

Subject: Preventive combating of crime
Ref.:   Communication of 7.9.1940 – K Tgb. Nr. 6041

Preventive police detention should not be ordered against homosexuals who – as specified in the decree of 12.7.1940, V B1 Nr. 1143/40 – have seduced more than one partner but have been castrated, if in medical opinion the sex drive is completely extinguished and a relapse into homosexual misconduct is not be feared.

K.L. [Concentration Camp] Buchenwald   K.L. Buchenwald
'Garrison Doctor'   ·   12 Oct. 1937 – Off.
                                                           Weimar Post
S. Az.: 14/10.37

Subject: Sterilization or emasculation of prisoners
Ref.   None
Enclosures: None

To the:
Commandant's office of
Buchenwald K.L. [concentration camp]

In the case of the following prisoners, who have still to be given a
detailed medical examination so that an application for sterilization
or emasculation can be submitted, it is requested that they should not
be released from the camp for the time being: [...]

1.	F., Karl	No. 1254		16.	S., Friedrich	No. 2415
2.	R., Ewald	No. 595		17.	S., Emil	No. 1970
3.	A., Max	No. 232		18.	D., Nikolaus	No. 491
4.	S., Emil	No. 1957		19.	D., Josef	No. 669
5.	W., Oswin	No. 2243		20.	F., Nikolaus	No. 364
6.	R., August	No. 1956		21.	H., Albert	No. 752
7.	K., Friedrich	No. 2057		22.	F., Erich	No. 426
8.	M., Werner	No. 1672		23.	G., Otto	No. 427
9.	K., Karl	No. 2392		24.	G., Hans	No. 777
10.	K., Theodor	No. 1931		25.	K., Otto	No. 681
11.	R., Otto	No. 2086		26.	J., Ernst	No. 457
12.	G., Walter	No. 2410		27.	K., Albert	No. 759
13.	F., Peter	No. 2414		28.	S., Max	No. 201
14.	H., Karl	No. 2419		29.	L., Philipp	No. 2433
15.	M., Herbert	No. 2413				

(Admission stamp   Garrison Doctor
K.L. Buchenwald)   K.L. 'Buchenwald'
                                                         Signed (signature)
BAK NS 4/45, fiche 1   SS-Obersturmführer

[91] Total registration and supervision of 'emasculated men'
Decree of the Reich Minister of the Interior, 13 November 1941

The Reich Minister of the Interior   Berlin, 13 November 1941
IV b 2248/41 -/- 10796   N W 7, Unter den Linden 72

To:
Reich governors in the Gaus (regional governments)
Chairmen of regional councils
The chief of police in Berlin
The mayor of the capital of the Reich, Berlin
Public health departments

Subject: Examination of emasculated men

(1) By the directive of 30 November 1936 – IV a 15183/36/1079b – (not published) I ordered that examination of emasculated men should be carried out after one month, one, three and five years, both in the case of compulsory castration under safety proceedings and in that of persons who voluntarily allowed themselves to be emasculated on the basis of §14, cl. 2 of the Law for the Prevention of Offspring with Hereditary Diseases of 26 June 1935 – *Reichsgesetzblatt* I p. 713.

(2) As reports have become available at home and abroad about the success of emasculation and its consequences, and as it is clear that the aim of such measures has been achieved in most cases, total supervision and care of the persons in question is necessary to prevent a relapse in isolated cases.

(3) To this end examinations must be carried out in full at the scheduled dates. To make this easier, a list should be drawn up of all compulsorily and voluntarily emasculated persons. In very large health departments such lists may be replaced by a card index.

(4) In para. 7 of the directive of 30 November 1936 I explained that a request of the health department to attend for follow-ups does not have the force of an obligation for emasculated persons. Since the police have made the preventive combating of crime a special task, however, the acceptance of follow-ups can now be enforced on the basis of the provisions issued for this purpose. Thus, if an emasculated person does not appear for follow-ups, the competent (regional) headquarters of the Criminal Police should be informed and it will have the emasculated person brought in for examination as requested under the preventive combating of crime.

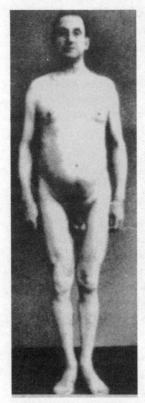
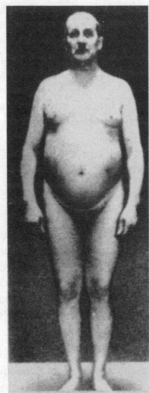

Before and after castration. From N. Jensch, *Untersuchungen an entmannten Sittlichkeitsverbrechern*, Leipzig 1944.

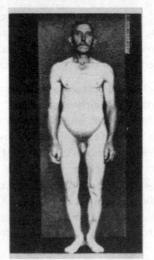

Letter of 9 February 1943 from the Reich Minister of Justice to the Jena Public Prosecutor concerning the criminal case against Max B.

'Having regard to the seriousness of the offence I consider it inadvisable, despite the guilty man's poor state of health, to grant partial suspension of his sentence. I therefore ask you to dismiss the plea for clemency.

In the directive you mention of 12.7.1940 – V B. 1 Nr. 1143.40 – the Reichsführer-SS requested that in future his subordinate authorities should take all homosexuals who have seduced more than one partner into preventive police detention after they have completed their sentence. As there can be no question of clemency in the case of B., I have refrained from contacting the Reichsführer-SS for the purpose you suggested. I would stress, however, that the question of whether clemency should be granted to a homosexual who has seduced more than one partner calls for especially thorough examination. In the interests of public safety, there will not normally be any question of clemency in such cases.'

p.p.
Signed: Dr Vollmer

BAK R 22/970 fol 90.

Persons who request a certificate from a medical officer or court doctor for voluntary emasculation under §14, cl. 2 of the Law for the Prevention of Offspring with Hereditary Diseases (version of 26 June 1935) should be referred at their examination to their obligation to attend for follow-ups.

(5) (Regional) headquarters of the Criminal Police shall report to public health departments for follow-up those sex criminals who have voluntarily allowed themselves to be emasculated in order to be free of the preventive detention hanging over them. A request for an examination made of public health departments shall in all cases be complied with. The instructions of the previously mentioned directive of 30 November 1936 and of the directive of 1 April 1938 – IV b 6/38 – 1079 b (RMBliV. p. 595) – shall be applied accordingly.

(6) For their part, public health departments must report to (regional) headquarters of the Criminal Police:
  (a) all cases of compulsory emasculation,
  (b) voluntary cases of emasculation only if the persons arouse suspicion of acting in a criminal manner, or if they keep away from follow-ups.

(7) On scientific grounds it is desirable to collect material regarding the effects of emasculation on people who have been emasculated not for criminal-biological reasons but as a result of an illness or accident. There can be no question here, of course, of follow-ups in the sense of the directive of 30 November 1936. Insofar as this is possible, however, in observing the condition of such men, material should be collected about any symptoms of disturbance, with special attention to whether major divergences present themselves in comparison with observations made in the case of sex criminals. I reserve the power to call in the material for scientific evaluation in due course. (Regional) headquarters of the Criminal Police shall be provided with instructions by a directive of the Reich Security Headquarters.

[92] Preventive police measures against 'emasculated' persons

Directive of the Reich Security Headquarters, 2 January 1942

Reich Security Headquarters   Berlin, 2 January 1942
V – A 2 Nr. 1039/41

Confidential

To:
Directors of (regional) headquarters
of the Criminal Police – or deputies
in [...]

Subject: Preventive police measures against emasculated persons

I enclose herewith a directive of the Reich Minister of the Interior dated 13.11.1941 – IV b 2248/41 -/- 1079 b – concerning the medical examination of emasculated persons.

   In order to assure the performance by public health departments of follow-ups required at certain intervals which are especially in the interests of the security police, the persons named in clause 6 of the enclosed directive should be *immediately* placed under regular police supervision – if necessary under A I 3 of the dir. of the Min. of Int. dated 14.12.1937 – even if it does not appear or no longer appears necessary for further measures to be taken by the security police.

   If these emasculated persons are already under supervision, they should in all cases be *further* required:

1 'to report any change of residence regardless of the general registration procedures of the local police' (cf. B I 1 (1) d of the directive dated 14.12.1937); and

2 'to comply with all orders of their relevant public health department'.

Where public health departments request the bringing in of emasculated persons who wilfully fail to attend obligatory follow-ups, such applications shall be granted.

The issuing of further conditions in the framework of the directive of the Reich Minister of the Interior dated 14.12.1937 shall, if this is necessary in individual cases, be left up to the competent (regional) headquarters of the Criminal Police; the (regional) headquarters of the Criminal Police are also at liberty to order preventive police detention *in exceptional cases* – e.g. if, on the evidence of the emasculated person's behaviour or the expert medical report, it can be assumed that, despite castration, he continues to present a considerable danger to the community and especially the youth.

I shall communicate to the relevant (regional) police headquarters the particulars of persons voluntarily emasculated in concentration camps, for further action in the sense of para. 5 of the enclosed directive of the Reich Min. of the Int. of 13.11.1941. Emasculated persons to be named by public health departments in accordance with para. 6 of the directive shall be directly reported to me in the form of lists broken down into the compulsorily and the voluntarily emasculated.

[93] 'A large number of homosexuals have withdrawn such applications . . .'

Routine report by the Hamburg High Court to the Reich Ministry of Justice, 5 January 1942 (Extract)

The President of the   Hamburg 36, 5 January 1942
Hanseatic High Court

Registered!

To State Secretary Dr Schlegelberger
Reich Ministry of Justice

Subject: Report on the general situation
Ref.   Your Nr. 1 a 11012/35

[...] It has often happened, especially when a preventive detention order is in prospect, that recidivist homosexuals on trial before the Hamburg courts have voluntarily applied for emasculation. After the health authority has initially arranged for emasculation on the basis of such applications, it then makes difficulties. A large number of homosexuals have withdrawn such applications after proceedings have been taken sufficiently far for the emasculation to be undertaken. The health authority will then carry out emasculations only after the main hearing has been duly completed in accordance with the law.

Such difficulties have generally allowed a wish to come out that judges should be given the legal possibility of imposing castration on homosexuals too in their sentence. Hitherto this legal possibility has not existed in the case of such homosexual criminals.

Connected with this in a way is the transfer to the public prosecutor of the authority to determine how long preventive detention will last. Unfortunately there can be no mistaking the fact that when the courts order preventive detention they exercise more caution and restraint than they used to do, for they no longer have a clear picture of the length of preventive detention. This attitude of the courts should not be condoned, but it is psychologically understandable. I fear that the reorganization has brought about the opposite of what was intended, which was a tougher use of preventive detention. [...]

[94] Compulsory castration of homosexuals demanded
From the files of the Reich Ministry of Justice

[94a] *Memorandum of the Reich Ministry of Justice, Ministerialrat [Assistant Head of Department] Rietzsch, 25 February 1942 (Extract)*

On 25.2 I called the specialist at the Reich Criminal Bureau, Dr Scheefe, and asked him how things stand with discussions of the draft law on social aliens, particularly whether he has already discussed any drafts at the Ministry of the Interior. Dr Scheefe said that he had first pursued the clarification of views within the Reich Criminal Police Bureau, and he now reported the following wishes:

In the text of the law one might dispense with any reference to the Penal Code.

On the question of emasculation, officials involved in the combating of homosexuality – especially Crime Adviser Jakob – would like to see emasculation allowed in all cases under §175a, but also under §175 of the Penal Code. Experience teaches us that most cases arise through seduction of a person aged between 21 and 25 by an older person; here emasculation should be introduced.

Sterilization or emasculation should be permitted by law for all anti-social elements; he also thinks that it would then mainly be used on failures and good-for-nothings. [...]

'For National Socialism the racial idea is one of the cornerstones of its world-view. It is certain that blood inheritance – i.e. inherited tendencies – overwhelmingly shape individuals in both body and mind. But to express this knowledge in reality is the goal of the racial legislation of the National Socialist government. It is fighting for the survival of our *Volk*. Its final aim is that, through appropriate measures, the precious hereditary stream of our *Volk* will flow ever more strongly, and that less valuable ones will gradually dry up' (p. 9).

'If one further considers that the legislator is to a large degree guided by the demand for a healthy race, to be achieved through the eradication of inferior and criminal elements, then we think we are quite right in claiming that emasculation should be employed alongside sterilization as a further means in the struggle for the racial interests of our *Volk*. Emasculation robs the criminal of his reproductive capacity and thus prevents further contamination of the *Volk* with this criminal tendency' (p. 12).

'It can remain open whether the *Volk* is already capable of understanding the elimination of inferior types by killing them. But today it certainly welcomes at least the extermination of sex criminals and thus the prevention of an anti-social progeny. But the whole of law should be in the service of racial regeneration' (p. 34).

H. Puvogel, 'Die leitenden Grundgedanken bei der Entmannung gefährlicher Sittlichkeitsverbrecher', legal dissertation, University of Göttingen, Düsseldorf 1937.

[94b] *Letter from Dr Rodenberg, SS-Sturmbannführer, then at the Reich Security Headquarters, to Ministerialrat Rietzsch at the Reich Ministry of Justice*   Berlin, 3 October 1942

Dear Ministerialrat,

May I thank you very much for your kind letter of 29 September. I am familiar with the Führer's general order embargoing legislation on matters not directly connected with the war, but I could imagine that exceptions would be quite permissible for such important questions as the combating of homosexuality. You are surely aware that the Führer attaches great importance to the danger of homosexuality and the combating of this evil. May I simply recall various internal directives and orders. The last leader-speech again clearly affirmed the Führer's attitude to dangerous habitual criminals. It does look as if the war will last a while longer, and in my view the whole question really must be solved during the war.

It is clear that emasculation also has a major impact on homosexual criminals. A whole series of homosexual criminals are currently in preventive detention centres (departments of lunatic asylums), as well as in concentration camps. These inmates cost the state a lot of money and do not work productively enough. If they are castrated they can be released in a shorter time, for then they are no longer a risk to the national community and can be put to good use again in the world. This being so, I think it is justified to try to solve the problem during the war. I would ask you to be so kind as to consider these points. Professor Mezger from Munich reported to me yesterday that my material strikes him as quite remarkable, and it emerged from his remarks that he too would like to see the matter resolved soon. He invited me to talk the matter over with him and touched on the question of how and where the exact boundaries might be drawn. It also emerged from the statements of Professor v. Neureiter-Strassburg that he would like to see a speedy settlement of the problem. As I personally discovered through Reich Minister Dr Frick, he is also having this set of questions examined by competent men at his ministry. I myself would like to try to win round the Reichsführer-SS, so that he too supports the idea of an early solution to the problem. It would appear highly desirable that legal experts should take up a position by publishing something on the whole business. Would it not be possible for you to get a lawyer working on this?

With best regards and
Heil Hitler!
Respectfully yours
Signed: Rodenberg

[94c] *Letter from Ministerialrat Rietzsch at the Reich Ministry of Justice to Ministerialrat Dr Linden at the Reich Ministry of the Interior*

Berlin, 9 October 1942

Dear Dr Linden,

Dr Rodenberg wrote me the letter which you will find enclosed. It refers to the essay published by Dr Rodenberg in No. 37 of *Deutsche Justiz* on the emasculation of homosexual criminals, and strongly advocates an early change to §42k of the Reich Penal Code. If the kind of change wished by Dr Rodenberg is to be made, it would in my view be desirable that the Reich Health Führer should declare that, given the present state of medical research, the time has come for Dr Rodenberg's desired extension of emasculation, and request the Reich Minister of Justice to bring it about at a suitable opportunity. It would not be out of the question that an opportunity for revising §42k might appear in connection with the law on social aliens. I should be grateful to hear your views whenever this is convenient.

With best regards and greetings
and Heil Hitler!
Yours
Signed: Rietzsch

'[...] From experience we are coming to the view that it is no longer possible to allege the ineffectiveness of castration on the perverted instinctual life of homosexuals, and that there is therefore no reason why the provisions of §42k should not be applied to sentences under §175 of the Penal Code. On the contrary, in sentences under §175 it no longer appears justified to refrain from a norm of emasculation where the corresponding police requirements are satisfied – for as in other cases involving sex criminals, this norm promises complete success with regard to crime therapy and at the same time is thoroughly beneficial from a personal and sociological point of view. According to our experience and the conclusions of the present analyses, the intentional gap which the legislator left among the provisions for crime-prevention measures (emasculation) no longer appears to be a justifiable restriction. In our view, rather, it is actually necessary to put this set of questions on a new legal basis and so make this important crime-prevention measure more complete and more effective' (p. 587).

C.-H. Rodenberg, 'Zur Frage des kriminaltherapeutischen Erfolges der Entmannung homosexueller Sittlichkeitsverbrecher', *Deutsche Justiz*, 1942/A No. 37, pp. 581–587.

[95] Authorization to castrate concentration camp prisoners
Secret directive of the SS Economic and Administrative Headquarters, 14 November 1942

Economic and Administrative   Oranienburg, 14 November 1942
Headquarters, Branch D
– Concentration camps –
D I/1 Az: 14h 7/OT.U.-   Secret

Subject: Sterilization of prisoners
Ref: Reich Criminal Police Bureau Tgb. Nr. 1158/41 A 2b 5
Enc: None

To:
Commandants of the
concentration camps of
Da., Sah., Bu., Mau., Flo., Neu., Au., Gr.-Ro., Natz., Nie., Stu.,
Deb., Rav., and Lublin P.O.W. camp[3]

As the Reich Criminal Police Bureau reports, on the basis of the Führer's special powers the Reich Committee for the Scientific Understanding of Serious Hereditary and Inherent Disorders has the right to authorize sterilization in special cases not covered by the law. In such cases it is not necessary for the Hereditary Health Court to make a ruling having the force of law.

In any cases that occur, the procedure should be in accordance with the above order.

[3] Dachau, Sachsenhausen, Buchenwald, Mauthausen, Flossenbürg, Neuengamme, Auschwitz, Gross Rosen, Natzweiler, Nieborowitz, Stuhm, Demblin, Ravensbrück. *Translator's note.*

Part VI
Homosexual Men in Concentration Camps
The Example of Buchenwald

(a) Pink-Triangle Prisoners at Buchenwald Concentration Camp

Not long after the establishment of the Nazi regime homosexual men were already being sent to concentration camps. In many cases this happened as an exemplary measure of terror. Corresponding regulations were only issued some time later to give an appearance of legality. Himmler's order of 14 December 1937 and his decree of 12 July 1940 defined the target groups as sex criminals, by which he especially meant 'corrupters of youth', 'rentboys' and those with related previous convictions. Thus, not every man convicted under Section 175 had to reckon with deportation to a concentration camp after the end of his sentence. And yet, where political considerations were involved, the provisions could be interpreted in such a way that an arbitrary attribution of one of the above labels opened the way to such a harsh punishment.[1]

Buchenwald concentration camp started operating in 1937 and was soon admitting its first homosexual men. By the end of 1938 28 prisoners were already wearing the pink triangle; the figure went up to 46 by late 1939 and stood at 51 two years later. As a result of Himmler's directive of 12 July 1940 – 'in future, after their release from prison, all homosexuals who have seduced more than one partner should be taken into preventive police detention' – the number of male homosexuals also rose at Buchenwald, passing a hundred for the first time in 1942. At the end of 1943 the camp held 169, and a year later 189. The figures were small in comparison with the total number of prisoners there – well below one per cent in every year.[2]

Deportation was justified on the absurd grounds that 'encouragement to perform regular work' would help to cure male homosexuals of their 'unnatural inclinations'. According to Heydrich's cynical classification of 1941, Buchenwald was a Category II concentration camp. This meant that, together with Flossenbürg, Neuengamme and Auschwitz, it was to be used for 'severely disturbed persons in protective custody' who were still 'capable of being educated'.

Their daily life was governed by the inhuman conditions of the camp. In addition there was the stigma of being a homosexual, which gave them a dangerous special status. They were isolated in many different senses: from their friends, who did not dare write for fear of themselves

[1] See in general R. Lautmann/W. Grischkat/E. Schmidt, 'Der Rosa Winkel in nationalsozialistischen Konzentrationslagern', in R. Lautmann, ed., *Seminar: Gesellschaft und Homosexualität*, Frankfurt/Main 1977, pp. 325–365.
[2] G. Grau, 'Homosexuelle im KZ. Buchenwald', in S. N. Rapoport and A. Thom, eds., *Das Schicksal der Medizin im Faschismus*, Berlin 1989, pp. 67–69; and W. Röll, *Homosexuelle Häftlinge im KZ. Buchenwald*, Weimar-Buchenwald 1991.

being registered as homosexuals; from their family, which out of 'shame' might disown father or son and might in the case of death – as we know from the file of Karl Willy A. – even refuse to accept the urn or hold a funeral; and from other groups of prisoners, who avoided men with the pink triangle both to keep clear of suspicion and because they shared the widespread prejudices against 'queers'. But the homosexual prisoners were also isolated from others like themselves, for gay men are seldom bound together by anything more than their sexual orientation. There was no question of the kind of solidarity that was evident among political prisoners or Jehovah's Witnesses. And they had correspondingly little influence in the prisoners' structure of communication and authority.

Until autumn 1938 male homosexuals were allocated to the political blocks. But from October they were sent en masse to do quarry work in the punishment battalion, where inhuman working conditions and the arbitrary violence of the SS claimed ever more victims. In the summer of 1942 they started to work with other prisoners in the war industry, and in the autumn or winter of 1944 were deported to the centres producing V-2 weapons in the 'Dora' out-camp near Nordhausen.[3] Catastrophic conditions of internment, heavy labour in the underground galleries and a generally poor state of health brought death to most of them. Thus, 96 homosexual prisoners died between 8 and 13 February 1945 alone – more than half the number interned in Buchenwald up to that time.

Reports of fellow-prisoners, such as Walter Poller who worked as a doctor's secretary in the sick-bay in 1939 and 1940, indicate that most of the homosexuals deported to Buchenwald were castrated.[4] But it has since become known that they were also used for the dreadful typhus fever experiments. As these were very incompletely documented, we cannot definitively gauge the scale on which they were carried out.[5] So far five homosexual men have been identified in this context; and the refusal to hand over the dead body of Karl Willy A. suggests that he too should be counted among the victims.

---

[3] For an account of the 'Dora' camp (but without any reference to the group of homosexual prisoners), see E. Pachaly and K. Pelny, 'KZ Mittelbau Dora. Terror und Widerstand', *Buchenwaldheft* 28, Weimar-Buchenwald 1987.

[4] W. Poller, *Arztschreiber in Buchenwald*, Hamburg 1947.

[5] On the typhus experiments in general see W. Scherf, 'Die Verbrechen der SS-Ärzte im KZ Buchenwald. Der antifaschistische Widerstand. 2. Beitrag: Juristische Probleme', diss., criminal law department, Humboldt University, Berlin 1987.

[96]   The situation of homosexuals at Buchenwald concentration camp

Report from spring 1945 (Extracts)[6]

[...] Until autumn 1938 homosexuals were divided among the political blocks, where they went relatively unnoticed. In October 1938 they were sent en masse to the punishment battalion and had to work in the quarry, whereas previously all other units had been open to them. Apart from a few recorded cases, every member of the punishment battalion had the prospect of being transferred after a certain time to a normal block where living and working conditions were significantly better, but this possibility did not exist for homosexuals. Precisely during the hardest years they were the lowest caste in the camp. In proportion to their number they made up the highest percentage on transports to special extermination camps such as Mauthausen, Natzweiler and Gross Rosen, because the camp always had the understandable tendency to ship off less important and valuable members, or those regarded as less valuable. In fact, the wider deployment of labour in the war industry brought some relief to this type of prisoner too – for the labour shortage made it necessary to draw skills from the ranks of such people, although in January 1944 the homosexuals, with very few exceptions, were still going to the 'Dora' murder camp, where many of them met their death. The striking fates of a few homosexuals at Buchenwald may afford some insight into the conditions.

L. Adloff, a librarian at the State Library in Berlin and a collaborator of the left-leaning periodical *Die Weltbühne*, was arrested as a political suspect in 1938; he was also under suspicion of homosexuality. In summer 1938 he was sent as a political to Buchenwald concentration camp. In October 1938, when all homosexuals and others under suspicion were sent to the punishment battalion, he had the sign of homosexuals, a pink triangle, put on him and went to work in the quarry. In January 1939 he was sent to Mauthausen concentration camp, where terrible conditions prevailed. While working in the quarry there he suffered a leg injury which developed into a huge inflammation, and in the same year he was shipped as an invalid to the concentration camp at Dachau. After severe mistreatment at the hands of the Dachau sick bay kapo 'Heathen Joe' [*Heiden-Sepp*], he was sent as an invalid to Buchenwald camp, then returned as an invalid to Dachau, then sent back

---

[6] Passages omitted here do not specifically refer to the situation of homosexual prisoners at Buchenwald. Cf. the unabridged version and commentary in *Zeitschrift für Sexualforschung*, Vol. 2, 1989, pp. 243–253.

to Buchenwald in autumn 1941 where he finally remained and died. This constant moving of broken people had the result that they died off like flies with every change of conditions. In Dachau in 1941 he picked up a sentence for some trifling incident, and although he was already punished in Dachau he received 25 lashes twice more in Buchenwald as well as a few weeks in a detention cell. Jail was then an absolutely deadly place to be: he had long been written off in his block before the sheer miracle of his return. But meanwhile the leg inflammation, which had never healed, developed in such a way as to cause serious damage to his heart. As he was a naturally strong person and had enormous will-power, he pulled himself along for another month until pleurisy prepared the end in April 1943.

In the spring of 1942 a Berlin writer called Dähnke was sent to the camp as a homosexual. The main reason for his internment, however, was political statements which had brought him to the attention of the Gestapo. One morning, after he had been working for several months in the quarry, he was taken by someone on fatigue duty to the sick bay and presented to the camp doctor as suffering from TB. As a matter of fact he was having chest trouble. The camp doctor at first wanted to put him in the TB unit for treatment, but when D., not knowing how things stood, mentioned that he was really there for political reasons, the doctor sat up and took notice, realized that he was dealing with a homosexual, and had him taken into the room reserved for the death list. Two days later he was given the lethal injection.

H. D., an office worker born in 1915, was arrested on 20.4.1938 because of an illegal trip abroad to Prague. He had tried to make contact with the Russian Consulate in Prague so as to get away from Germany; the Gestapo suspected him of being an underground Communist courier. At the same time, a friend with whom he had been in a relationship of trust was arrested and forced to confess. The charges of high treason had to be dropped, because nothing could be proved against D. and nothing could be got out of him. So he only received three-and-a-half years' imprisonment for unnatural sex acts. After serving his sentence, he was sent to Buchenwald in November 1941.

The first impression he had was of the bodies of various people who had died in the punishment battalion, which were thrown in front of the door like sacks of flour. On the same evening a young homosexual hanged himself – everyone calmly went on eating, nobody cared a jot about it. Still on the same evening, a prisoner who had already been there a long time told him that he would have to work in the quarry, that the kapo was a terrible man, that especially §176 people (relations with juveniles) were done for, and that he should be careful although there was no point in keeping quiet about anything. After an agonizing sleepless night, D. decided to prepare himself for every eventuality: he mentioned to the kapo that had been told such and such and that he did not want to hang himself, and asked him for advice about what he should do. But he got the exact opposite of what he wanted. The kapo, Herzog, was a former member of the foreign legion, extremely brutal, apparently homosexual-sadistic and with a frightening tendency to become frenzied; if someone was beaten by him it was all over. Herzog was determined to find out who had spoken to D. and he threatened him with some terrible things. But as D. realized that it would mean curtains for his comrade in suffering, he refused to reveal the name of the man who had warned him. The next day he was sent to work on the quarry wagon – an exhausting and dangerous job. Anyone who could not keep going was tossed on the wagon and then dumped on a heap of stones. Then Herzog either trampled them to death without further ado, or poured water down their throat for so long that they suffocated. If anyone still survived, Herzog treated him as a malingerer and crushed him underfoot. Although D. was young and strong, the work exhausted him so much that only the end of the day saved him from collapse. Next morning the friend who had warned him, now grateful for his silence, took him to another part of the quarry where the work was a little easier and where he was out of the kapo's line of sight for the next few weeks. After three weeks or so, however, Herzog remembered him, again asked for the name and presented him with an ultimatum: at a certain hour he would drive him through a cordon of duty sentries. D. knew this was deadly serious and he was ready for anything. He was saved by a sheer miracle. An hour before the appointed time, Herzog was called to the door and quite unexpectedly released from the camp. (The word later went round in the camp that he had been stabbed to death in his home area.) On 4.1.42 D. was sent to the typhus fever experimental ward, where young homosexuals were favourite guinea-pig material. He came through the illness but suffered from heart trouble as a result. On 15.7.42 he was discharged from the ward to perform light quarry work. Meanwhile things had become quite wild in the block. Assisted by isolation from the other camp and more supported than supervised by the SS, a number of bandits were completely terrorizing the workforce, stealing the packets they were supposed to receive since winter 1941, and holding real orgies of brutality and the most shameless sadism. Sexual abuse and the foulest murder were the order of the day. The battle still raging between politicals and the Greens [criminals] who wanted to get control still tied the hands of the Reds for the time being. Only after some months was it possible to clean out the Augean stables – which was made easier by the fact that some of the guys were sending each other to kingdom come. One incident described by D. throws a revealing light on the conditions. The punishment battalion was not allowed to smoke. But people on the typhus ward bought things like everyone else, and that included tobacco. As they had also not been allowed to smoke on the typhus ward, they all naturally had a small stock of tobacco and cigarettes. The first thing the block elder, a former SS man, did was to ask all those who returned to hand over their tobacco. When they hesitated for a moment, he singled one out, spread him over a table and counted out 25 lashes – whereupon the tobacco and cigarettes shifted double-quick into his pocket.

Balachowsky: [...] We had a lot of homosexuals at Buchenwald – I mean, people sentenced by German courts because of their vice. These homosexuals were sent to concentration camps, especially Buchenwald, and mixed in with other prisoners.

Dubost: Especially with the so-called politicals, who were really patriots?

Balachowsky: With all kinds of prisoners.

Dubost: Did everyone come into contact with homosexuals who were German nationals?

Balachowsky: Yes, you could only tell them apart by the pink triangle they wore.

Dubost: Were there precise rules for wearing the triangle, or was it all a big mess?

Balachowsky: I heard that right at the beginning, before my time, it was all neat and proper with the triangles. But when I arrived at Buchenwald in early 1944, the whole triangle business was completely confused and some prisoners weren't wearing one at all.

From the statements made by the former French prisoner Alfred Balachovsky on 29 January 1946 to the French deputy prosecutor, Dubost, at the Nuremberg war crimes tribunal. IMG, vol. 6, Nuremberg 1947, p. 346.

Selected groups of prisoners at Buchenwald concentration camp. Compiled from the 'strength reports' made on 30 December of each year, and for 1945 at the end of each month.

Year	Total prisoners	Of which political	Jehovah's Witnesses	Homosexuals
1937	2561	n/a	n/a	n/a
1938	11028	3982	476	27
1939	11807	4042	405	46
1940	7440	2865	299	11
1941	7911	3255	253	51
1942	9571	5433	238	74
1943	37319	25146	279	169
1944	63048	47982	303	189
Jan. 1945	80297	53372	302	194
Feb. 1945	86232	54710	311	89
Mar. 1945	80436	n/a	n/a	n/a

The liquidation methods had meanwhile changed somewhat. Until early 1942 a sorting of new arrivals had undoubtedly been carried out in the political department. People – especially §176 homosexuals – were called to the door a few days after their arrival and moved into the cells. Some days later came the announcement of death. From spring 1942 the cell murders stopped. But to make up for it the second camp Führer, Gust, turned to the now compliant quarry kapo, Müller, generally known as 'Waldmüller' [forest miller]: he came to see him nearly every day, shook hands and regaled him with cigarettes, and no doubt gave him instructions. The number of people 'shot while attempting to escape' was terrifyingly high in the summer of 1942. For the sake of appearances, it was felt necessary to post quarry trustees as sentries to hold people back. D., who stood out from the others by his human qualities, was made a sentry and witnessed some hideous scenes. [...]

In autumn 1942 these quarry shootings came to an end. The greater use of prisoners' labour forced the SS to be a little more sparing with its 'human material', and the forces of order in the camp finally managed to wrest away its instruments of murder. Later, when conditions eased a little, D. managed to get sent to a better unit, to hold on in the camp by keeping a clean slate, and to appear as a witness at trials as one of the few to have survived. [...]

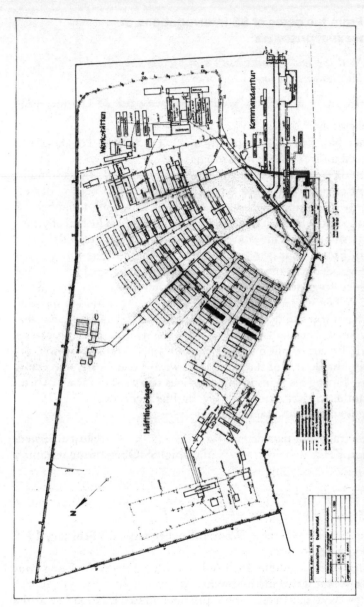

Plan of Buchenwald concentration camp, near Weimar. From Wolfgang Röll, *Homosexuelle Häftlinge im KZ. Buchenwald*, Buchenwald 1991, p. 29.

[97] From the notes of SS interrogations of homosexual prisoners

[97a] *'But the Jew's plan wasn't completely successful [...]'*
Prisoner Gerhard K. on 25 October 1938

Dept. III   Weimar/Buchenwald, 25 October 1938

Interrogation
Prisoner No. 7497, Gerhard K., b. [...] (19)10 in Potsdam, was produced and stated the following.

Eight days or so ago, after work when it was dark, I was standing in front of prisoners' block No. 22 to which I had been allocated. Suddenly a Jew approached and asked me how long I had been in the camp and whether I felt hungry. I replied that if he had anything over he should give me something to eat. So I got from the Jew a piece of bread, a sausage and a cigarette. Then I went with the Jew to the wooded part of the preventive detention camp. I knew it was forbidden to go into the wood, but the Jew knew how to talk me round. When we reached the wood he led me to a hidden spot and said: Now you can do something I'd like, seeing as I've done what you wanted. Then he said: Take your trousers down, no one can see us here; I want to put my penis in your anus. I refused at first, but then let him do it. But the Jew's plan wasn't completely successful, because having his penis in my anus was too painful for me. Then I got another cigarette from the Jew and he went away.

The Jew is not known to me.

Read, agreed and signed   Closed. Signed:
Gerhard K.   (illegible) SS-Obersturmbannführer

[97b] *'[...] and confess my guilt.'*
Prisoner Friedrich Sch. on 22 February 1939

                                   Weimar/Buchenwald, 22 February 1939
Interrogation
Prisoner No. 5727, Friedrich Sch., b. [...] (19)17 in Essen, was produced and stated the following.

A few days ago I met the BV prisoner Max H. No. 1919 at the barracks of block 11. It was after the end of work. We walked between the barracks and talked about one thing or another. Then I tried to get closer to H. I put my cheek against H.'s with the aim of finding relief for my feelings. The arrival of some other prisoners on the scene stopped me carrying out my intentions.

On 21.2.39 I again met H. At first I made a show of talking with

H. so as then to gratify my homosexual feelings. But as it was already quite late I again could not see my plans through. When I got to my barracks, the block elder Weitz immediately asked me what I had been up to with H. I told him that I wanted to try to make H. do my bidding.

I am aware that I have violated camp regulations and I confess my guilt.

Read, agreed and signed
Friedrich Sch.

Closed. Signed:
(illegible) SS-Obersturmbannführer

[97c] *'It hasn't happened to me that Sch. tried to do something to gratify his homosexual feelings.'*
Prisoner Max H. on 23 February 1939

Interrogation   Weimar/Buchenwald, 23 February 1939
Preventive detention prisoner Max H., b [...] (19)03 in Dresden, No. 1919, was produced and stated the following.
I have known preventive detention prisoner Friedrich Sch. No. 5737 since he arrived at the camp. Sch. worked with me in the SS settlement. Sch. already approached me then and asked for food. I always gave him some food. In return Sch. always kept my things in order. A few days ago Sch. again came and asked me for some food. Sch. took me by the head. I then pointed out to him that this was very dangerous.

On 23.2.39 Sch. again came to me asking for something to eat. I couldn't give him anything, because I didn't have any myself. He again took me by the head and said: 'You are so good to me.' I then gave him a couple of slaps. At the same time I told him that he shouldn't let himself be seen with me again.

I did not notice that Sch. tried to do something to gratify his homosexual feelings.

Read, agreed and signed
Max H.

Closed. Signed:
(illegible) SS-Obersturmbannführer

[98] Reports for punishment
To the preventive detention camp leader at Buchenwald

To the: Weimar, 10 April 1942
Preventive detention camp leader
of Buchenwald concentration camp

I am reporting the prisoner Rud(olf) R. No. 4828 for punishment.

On 8.4.42 and on preceding days R. abused a fellow-prisoner to engage in sexual relations with him, during which he took the person in question into his bed and committed illicit sex acts with him.

(Signature)

Stamp:
Age of prisoner: 31
Occupation: worker
Camp punishments: Note: Proceedings under way
    Smoking ban 5 X[7]   Still in custody
    Theft of food 10 X

To the preventive detention camp leader of Buchenwald concentration camp

I am reporting the BV Pole Johann G., No. 8818, for punishment. On 1.8.42 and previously G. attempted to commit illicit sex acts with young Poles from his block. The Poles in question, whom he touched on the genitals, carried out their duty and reported this. G. did not take responsibility for his offences but strongly denied it. I request assignment to the punishment battalion.

Signature

Stamp:
Age of prisoner: 30 years
Occupation: businessman   Note:
Camp punishments: none   Postponed/25 X

---

[7] 5 X means: 5 strokes on the buttocks, administered by SS thugs. The prisoner was tied to the punishment stand for this.

Transports with homosexual prisoners from Buchenwald to other concentration camps or to the Dora out-unit.

Date	Destination	Deported homosexuals	Total deported
15.4.1940	Mauthausen	27	311
24.10.1941	Natzweiler	3	150
12.3.1942	Natzweiler	12	350
13.3.1942	Ravensbrück	32	700
21.4.1942	Gross Rosen	2	200
6.7.1942	Dachau	17	300
15.9.1942	Gross Rosen	18	–
24.10.1942	Sachsenhausen	3	–
29.10.1942	Dachau	2	181
17.12.1942	Sachsenhausen	2	–
5/6.1.1943	Neuengamme	5	–
5.3.1943	Dachau	4	–
22.1.1944	Dora	77	1000
16.2.1944	Dora	5	250
18.2.1944	Lublin	6	1000
8.4.1944	Bergen-Belsen (from Dora)	13	1000

All details are taken from a private communication from Wolfgang Röll, the Buchenwald Memorial, 1991.

[99] 'She is making no application for transfer of the urn.'
From the files of the prisoner Karl Willy A. from Holzhausen near Leipzig

[99a] *Preventive police detention order, 17 May 1943*

State Criminal Police　　　　　　　　　Leipzig, 17 May 1943
Leipzig Criminal Police Headquarters
Daybook No. 33440/43

Preventive police detention order

Karl *Willy* A.

Born in Rehau/Bavaria　　　District of Hof/Bavaria　　　in 1914
Occupation: bricklayer/foreman
Last resident at: Holzhausen nr. Leipzig, Horst-Wessel-Strasse
ground floor
Citizenship: Reich German
Religion (incl. former): Evangelical-Lutheran
shall with effect from 11.5.1943, by virtue of decree of the
Prussian Minister of the Interior of 14.12.1937, -S-Kr. 3 Nr.
1682/37/-2098-,
　　be taken into preventive police detention as a habitual criminal.

Staatliche Kriminalpolizei   Leipzig, am ...17. Mai... 19 .43.

Kriminalpolizeistelle Leipzig

Tgb. Nr ..33440/43.......

Anordnung der polizeilichen Vorbeugungshaft

D .er. am ...1914.........   in .....Rehau/Bayern............

Kreis .....Hof/Bayern....   geborene ..Maurer/Vorarbeiter.....

                                                (Beruf)

.................Karl Willy A.................

                (Vor- und Zunahme)

zuletzt
wohnhaft in .Holzhausen bei Leipzig, Horst-Wessel-Strasse Erdg.

                (Ort – Straße – Platz – Nr.)

Staatsangehörigkeit: ....Reichsdeutscher.......

Religion (auch frühere) ..ev.-luth............ wird mit Wirkung

vom ...11.5.1943.... auf Grund des Erlasses des RuPrMdI. vom 14. 12. 1937

-S-Kr. 3 Nr. 1682/3/ – 2098 –

                als .Gewohnheitsverbrecher......

in polizeilicher Vorbeugungshaft genommen.

Reasons:

In the period from 1934 to 1940 A. was convicted four times of unnatural sex acts. In the last two cases he was sentenced to penal servitude under §175a Cl. 3 for, among other things, the corruption of juveniles. He has seduced more than one partner to commit sex offences and, according to the decree of 12.7.1940, is to be taken into preventive police detention. His last sentence of penal servitude of 1 year and 6 months was served at the penitentiary of Vechta/ Oldenburg. At the end he was taken back to the Leipzig police prison. As the last case occurred shortly after his marriage, one can hardly count on his reforming.

[99b] *'The prisoner is to be taken to Buchenwald on the next group transport', 28 May 1943*

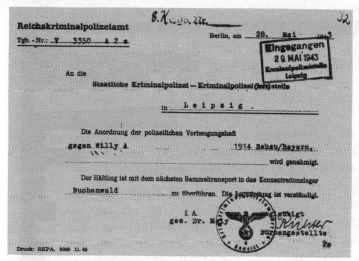

Reich Criminal Police Bureau   Berlin, 28 May 1943
Daybook No. V 3350 A2a

To the:
State Criminal Police
Leipzig Regional Criminal Police Headquarters
The preventive police detention order against Willy A. 1914 Rehau/Bavaria is approved.
The prisoner is to be taken to Buchenwald concentration camp on the next group transport. The camp leadership has been notified.

p.p.   Authenticated
Signed: Dr Maly   (signature)
                                              Clerk

[99c] *Confirmation of admission dated 10 June 1943*

To:
Leipzig Criminal Police Headquarters

The above-mentioned prisoner was delivered here today.

The camp commandant

[99d] *'Cause of death: purulent pleurisy'*
Telegram to Leipzig Gestapo, 24 November 1943

```
+ DR. KL. BUCHENWALD NR. 5513 24.11.43 1450 = SCHU=
AN KRIPO LEIPZIG. ---
DRINGEND - SOFORT VORLEGEN. ---
BETR.: ( HOMOS.) WILLY A              GEB.      1914
IN REHAU. AZ.: ROEM. 33440/43.---
DER VORSTEHEND ERWAEHNTE HAEFTLING IST AM  24.11.43 UM
05.10 UHR IM HIESIGEN KRANKENBAU VERSTORBEN. ---
TODESURSACHE: EITRIGE RIPPENFELLENTZUENDUNG LINKS. ---
UNTER BEZUGNAHME AUF DEN BEFEHL DES REICHSFUEHRERS- SS.
S. ROEM. 4 C 2. ALLG. NR. 40 454 - VOM 21.5.42 WIRD
GEBETEN. DIE ANGEHOERIGEN VON DEM ABLEBEN DES HAEFTLINGS
SOFORT IN KENNTNIS ZU SETZEN. UND IHNEN AUSSERDEM NOCH
FOLGENDES MITZUTEILEN: DIE LEICHE WIRD SPAETESTENS AM
27.11.43 HIER AUF STAATSKOSTEN EINGEAESCHERT. ---
EINE UEBERFUEHRUNG DER LEICHE ODER ERDBESTATTUNG KANN
Z. ZT. NICHT STATTFINDEN. ---
EINE BESICHTIGUNG DER LEICHE IST AUF ANORDNUNG DES
LAGERARZTES AUS HYGIENISCHEN GRUENDEN NICHT MOEGLICH. ---
BEZUEGLICH DDS TOTENSCHEINES UND DES NACHLASSES ERHALTEN
DIE ANGEHOERIGEN UNMITTELBAR VON HIER AUS SCHRIFTLICHE
NACHRICHT. --
ALS ANGEHOERIGE SIND HIER VERMERKT:
EHEFRAU MARTHA ANGERMANN. HOLZHAUSEN BEI LEIPZIG. HORST
WESSELSTR. 34.---

DER LAGERKOMMANDANT: PISTER, SS- STANDARTENFUEHRER ++
```

++ DR KL. BUCHENWALD NO. 5513 24.11.43 1450 = SCHU = TO CRIM. POL.
LEIPZIG.––– URGENT – IMMEDIATE DELIVERY.––– RE: (HOMOS.) WILLY A. B.
1914 AT REHAU, AZ.: ROEM. 33440/43.––– THE ABOVE-MENTIONED PRISONER
DIED AT THE MEDICAL CENTRE AT 05.10 HOURS ON 24.11.43.–––
CAUSE OF DEATH: PURULENT PLEURISY LEFT.––– WITH REFERENCE TO
COMMAND OF REICHSFUEHRER-SS. S. ROEM. 4 C 2. GEN. NO. 40 454 – OF
21.5.42 IS ASKED TO INFORM THE FAMILY AT ONCE OF DECEASE OF PRISONER
AND TO COMMUNICATE THE FOLLOWING: THE BODY IS TO BE CREMATED HERE
AT PUBLIC EXPENSE BY 27.11.43 AT LATEST.––– SHIPMENT OR BURIAL OF
BODY CANNOT TAKE PLACE AT PRESENT.––– BY ORDER OF CAMP DOCTOR
VIEWING OF BODY IS NOT POSSIBLE FOR HYGIENIC REASONS.––– CONCERNING
DEATH CERTIFICATE AND ESTATE THE FAMILY WILL RECEIVE WRITTEN NOTICE
DIRECTLY FROM HERE.–– THE FAMILY HERE REFERS TO: MRS MARTHA
ANGERMANN. HOLZHAUSEN NEAR LEIPZIG. HORST WESSELSTR. 34.–––

THE CAMP COMMANDANT: *PISTER*, SS-STANDARTENFUEHRER ++

[99e] '*Mrs Martha A. was sympathetically informed [...]*'
26 November 1943

8.K.44272/43   26.11.1943

To the:
Commandant's office at Buchenwald
concentration camp nr. Weimar

Subject: Homos. prev. det. pris. Willy A. b. 1914 at Rehau
Ref.:   Your telg. No. 5513 of 24.11.1943

Mrs Martha A., resident at Holzhausen nr. Leipzig, Horst-Wessel-Str., was sympathetically informed of her husband's decease and instructed by the municipal police as ordered. She is making no application for transfer of the urn, but asks for the estate to be remitted for the benefit of her child.

To avoid unnecessary costs I would ask you to remit the deceased's estate directly to Mrs A. or to the mayor at Holzhausen nr. Leipzig.

p.p.
(signature)

A punishment battalion working in the quarry

(b) Experiments in 'Reversal of Hormonal Polarity' at Buchenwald

In contrast to the compulsory castration and typhus fever experiments, the hormonal experiments on homosexual men at Buchenwald are quite well documented. They were conducted in strict secrecy on the orders of the SS by the Danish doctor Carl Peter Jensen, alias Carl Vaernet. He went to Germany in 1942 after being forced to give up a practice he had had in Copenhagen since 1934. His contact with the leader of the Danish Nazi Party, his colleague Frits Clausen, must already have cost him a lot of patients in the first year of the war. In summer 1943 he was brought to Himmler's attention by the SS Reich Doctor, Dr Grawitz. Vaernet's claim that his hormonal research in the thirties had made it possible to cure homosexual men aroused Himmler's undivided interest. He gave instructions for Vaernet to be treated with 'the utmost generosity', and to be given the possibility of continuing his research in a Prague cover firm coming under the Reichsführer-SS, 'German Medicines Ltd.' By July 1944 he was in a position to start the human experiments. Buchenwald concentration camp was instructed to place five prisoners at his disposal.

Surviving documents tell us about the choice and temporal sequence of the experiments. Together with Schiedlausky, the Waffen-SS garrison doctor at Weimar-Buchenwald, Vaernet first selected the five prisoners during a visit to Buchenwald in late July 1944, then nominated a further ten on 8 December. According to a memorandum (from the prisoners' sick bay?) four of the five selected in July were identified as homosexuals and one as an SV or *Sittlichkeltsverbrecher* [sex criminal]. Of the December batch all we know (from a memorandum drawn up in October) is that six of them had been castrated. It is very likely that these too were pink-triangle prisoners, so that altogether at least ten male homosexuals would have been subjected to Vaernet's experiments.

A total of fifteen prisoners were selected. Vaernet 'operated' on twelve men – if that term can be applied at all in the nightmarish conditions of the camp. What actually happened is that he made an incision in the groin and implanted a hormone preparation in the form of a briquette; the release of hormones was then checked through examination of the blood and urine.

What seems to us today a macabre experiment was heralded by Vaernet as a great success. But in his reports to the SS leadership he did not say a word about one effect which was nevertheless quite apparent to him. If the victims readily gave the answers expected of them, they did so partly at least in the hope that they would be pronounced 'cured' and soon released from the terrible reality of the concentration camp. To the SS Reich Doctor Vaernet suggested three results of 'direct importance to the war': the maintenance or restoration of a full capacity for work, the better possibilities of sustenance, and an increase in the birth-rate.

Little is known of the victims' fate. One prisoner was already dead by December 1944. But of those who may have survived, we do not know of any who applied for compensation after 1945. (This is true also of persons born after 1910, who might have been likely to take advantage of the new regulations for the compensation of victims of sterilization and castration that came into force in the late 1980s.)

As for the perpetrators, the experiments were not explicitly mentioned in the list of charges at the Nuremberg doctors' trial.[8] The SS doctors Schiedlausky and Ding were condemned to death for other profoundly inhuman experiments. Vaernet himself evaded responsibility by fleeing to South America.

[100] 'I request that you treat Dr Vaernet with the utmost generosity.'

Order from Himmler to SS Reich Doctor Grawitz. Memorandum from the Economic and Administrative Headquarters of the SS [Schutzstaffel], 3 December 1943 (Extract)

Stab W. Dr Hf/Mi   Berlin, 3 December 1943
Memorandum
Re: hormonal research of the Danish doctor Carl Vaernet

The matter was raised with us by the SS Reich Doctor and SS-Standartenführer Poppendick,[9] when SS-Oberführer Baier and the undersigned were discussing the matter of the V Research Institute with the SS Reich Doctor.[10]

There is an order from the Reichsführer-SS of 15 November of this year in which the Reichsführer-SS expresses his agreement with the proposal of SS-Gruppenführer Dr Grawitz to support Dr Vaernet. The Reichsführer-SS also expressed his agreement with a draft contract which Dr Vaernet has submitted. He writes: 'I

---

[8] On the dispute during the Nuremberg doctors' trial about responsibility for the experiments, see W. Scherf, *Die Verbrechen der SS-Ärzte im KZ. Buchenwald*, pp. 136ff.
[9] From 1943 Dr Helmut Poppendick was Head of the Personal Office of Reich Doctor Grawitz, and at the same time a leading doctor at the SS Race and Settlement Bureau.
[10] 'V' (= Vonkennel) was the cover name for an SS-supported research department at the dermatology clinic of Leipzig University, for which the clinic director, Prof. Dr Josef Vonkennel (1897–1963), was responsible. Vonkennel, who since 1943 had also been an adviser to the Waffen-SS on sexually transmitted diseases, must have been involved in the typhus fever experiments at Buchenwald. Kogon considers (incorrectly) that Vaernet belonged to this research department and merely had his official residence in Prague. See No. 1300, Prot. pp. 1224f., BArch P Film 28 725.

request that you treat Dr Vaernet with the utmost generosity. I myself would like a monthly report of 3 to 4 pages, because I am very interested in these things. At a later time I would also like to invite V. to visit me here.'

On the special aims associated with the promotion of Dr V.'s work, I shall give a verbal report because they are of an absolutely secret nature. The SS Reich Doctor's secret file has come in and is being kept in the VS office.

Following a brief overview of Dr Vaernet's research:

Since the beginning of the war Dr V. has been working on an 'artificial gland'. On the basis of numerous animal and human experiments, V. has developed a new kind of store substance – 'artificial gland' – for the implantation of drugs, especially hormone stores. A detailed account of his work is available to the Reich Doctor. [...]

Dr Vaernet does the following.

The drug in question is enclosed in his specially designed capsule that is fitted with an opening. This is implanted in any part of the body. This capsule then has the same effect as organic glands. In particular, in adapting to the organism as a whole, it only ever secretes the required amount of the drug into the body. This assures the necessary consistency and avoids what happens with the ingestion of pills, for example – i.e., the loss of much of the drug while it is being carried through the digestive system. [...]

In the consultations so far between Dr V. and the SS Reich Doctor's office, the starting-point has always been that the SS is interested in the matter because it relates to the needs of SS and Police medical experts.

In this light Dr Vaernet has also drawn up a draft contract in his letter of 2 November 1943 to the SS Reich Doctor. [...]

For his research activity, which is due to receive SS support by 31 December 1944, he is asking 1500 reichsmarks per month - RM 500 for himself in Germany and RM 1000 to meet his obligations in Denmark. In return he will concede to the SS free right of use over his patent for the area of SS and Police medical expertise. Should the Schutzstaffel make no use of this option, the research contract would lapse on 31.12.44. [...]

[101] Preparation of the experiments by the Waffen-SS garrison doctor at Weimar-Buchenwald, Dr Schiedlausky

Memorandum concerning Vaernet's visit to Buchenwald

The Waffen-SS Garrison Doctor   Weimar-Buchenwald
Weimar   29 July 1944

Subject: memorandum

SS-Sturmbannführer Dr Vaernet arrived at Buchenwald concentration camp on the evening of 26.7.1944 to inform himself about the possibilities for his experiments that have been approved by the Reichsführer-SS.

In the first discussion it was agreed to select five genuine homosexuals considered suitable for the testing of his theory. Before the operation is carried out, the level of hormone in the urine must be checked. An attempt was made to carry this out here in the camp, but it became clear that this was impossible owing to insuperable difficulties – particularly with regard to the procuring of test animals. [...]

The Waffen-SS garrison doctor
Signed: Schiedlausky
SS-Hauptsturmführer

[102] The selection of prisoners for experiments

[102a] *Memorandum (undated) on experiments of SS-Sturmbannführer Vaernet, Prague, Petergasse 10*

Notes:
10.8.44 No. 2282 (homos.) S., Hermann, b. 27.4.1901 in Dessau-Althen, unit: digging work[11]

List of prisoners who will be used for the experiment:
No. 33 463/3 (homos.) So., Johann, b. 24.2.12 in Lugau
No. 43 160/3 (SV)cast. K., Philipp, b. 1.9.08 in Duisburg-Hamborn
No. 21 686/4 (homos.) St., Bernhard, b. 6.8.89 in Oelde
No. 22 584/4 (homos.) Sch., Gerhard, b. 13.3.21 in Berlin
No. 21 912/4 (homos.) Sa., Karl, b. 21.9.12 in Falkenau

[11] It is not altogether clear whether this memorandum refers to notes for compulsory castration of a pink-triangle prisoner or for the experiments. The name of the prisoner, Hermann S., does not reappear in the files on Vaernet's experiments.

[102b] *Memorandum (undated), kapo of the prisoners' sick bay*

Block elder 4
Please arrange for the prisoners
No. 21 686   St., Bernhard   No. 21 912   Sa., Karl and
No. 22 584   Sch., Gerhard   No. 7 590   L., Ernst
to go at once to the prisoners' sick-bay offices. If you do not know
where the prisoners are, you must inform the messenger straight-
away.

Kapo (signed) Busse
Pr.-Sick-Bay
[Handwritten note:] Can't be done
                            At clearing work
Block elder 3
Please arrange for the prisoners
No. 33 463   So., Johann and
No. 43 160   K., Philipp

Letter of 24 August 1944 from Carl Vaernet to SS Reich Doctor
Grawitz (Extract)

Subject: Activity report No. 4, up to 24.8.1944

My work in the past focused on the preparation of 'artificial glands'
mainly in areas where it is of direct importance to the war.
This is the case with:

I   (a) *The maintenance of a full capacity for work*, above all in
    leaders who for years were subjected to enormous psychological
    and physical strain.
    (b) *Restoration of the capacity for work* in people where it has
    been reduced or completely disappeared for the above reasons or
    because of age.
    (c) *Prevention of the complaints* which, as we know from
    experience, are a result of the above-mentioned conditions.

II An increase in the birth-rate
    In I and II the 'artificial sex gland', chiefly the 'artificial male sex
    gland', is to be used.

III Possibilities for better nutrition.

The large number of existing experimental results form the basis for
increased meat, fats and milk production, through use of the
respective hormones in the 'artificial gland'.

BDC, Carl Vaernet

to go at once to the prisoners' sick-bay offices. If you do not know where the prisoners are, you must inform the messenger straight-away.

Kapo (signed) Busse[12]
Prisoners' Sick-Bay

[Handwritten note:]
Can't be done
At clearing work

[103] Notes on the 'operated' prisoners

[103a] *Letter and report from SS-Sturmbannführer Dr Carl Vaernet to SS Reich Doctor Grawitz, dated 30 October 1944*

Carl Vaernet   Prague IX, 30.10.44
SS-Sturmbannführer   Deutsche Heilmittel GmbH
Dr. med.   Podiebrader Landstr. 5

The Reichsführer-SS
Reichsarzt-SS und Polizei
SS-Obergruppenführer and Waffen-SS General Dr Grawitz

via
SS-Obergruppenführer and Waffen-SS General Pohl
Berlin W 15
Knesebeckstr. 51

Subject: Report on the implantation of the 'artificial male sex gland' at Weimar-Buchenwald. Report No. 6, up to 30.10.44

The operations at Weimar-Buchenwald were carried out on 5 homo-sexual persons on 13.9.44. Of these
2 had been castrated
1 sterilized
2 not operated on.

The purpose of the operations
1. To investigate whether implantation of the 'artificial male sex gland' can normalize the sexual orientation of homosexual persons.
2. To establish the support dose.
3. Control standardization of the 'artificial male sex gland'.

---

[12] Ernst Busse (1897–1952), KPD member, deputy in the Prussian Landtag from 1933 to 1936, detention in Kassel, from 1937 to 1945 at Buchenwald, from 1943(?) 1st camp elder, a kapo in the prisoners' sick-bay, member of the illegal camp committee.

The 'artificial male sex gland' is implanted in varying amounts, so that the absorbed quantities of hormone can be expressed as 1a, 2a and 3a.

The investigations are far from complete. But:

I. The provisional results show that the 3a dose *transforms homosexuality into a normal sex drive.*
The 2a dose reawakens the sex drive in a person castrated seven years earlier. *The reawakened sex drive* is without any homosexual elements.
The 1a dose produces a reappearance of erection among castrated persons, but no sex drive.

II. The absorption doses – 1a, 2a and 3a – supplied by the 'artificial male sex gland' transform severe depression and tension into optimism, calm and self-confidence. All three absorption doses brought about an excellent sense of physical and psychological well-being. [...]

[103b] *From the report by SS-Sturmbannführer Dr Vaernet dated 30.10.44*

[...]
Provisional results
An assessment of the operations is not yet possible, as the intervening period is too short and the various post-operative tests have not yet been completed. The case-book notes are given below, in the form used by the doctor at Buchenwald. They are supplemented with my own investigations and observations, but at the present time they are most eloquent in their original form. On 28.10.44 I checked them against my own investigations and found that

1 With the implantation of the 'artificial male sex gland' the desired results were achieved in patients 1, 2 and 3 – that is, the conversion of a homosexual into a normal drive.

2 Instead of a severe and pronounced depression, one finds in them optimism and confidence about life. They more easily master a number of difficult psychological problems bound up with their present existence.

3 Their physical strength is significantly better and there is less susceptibility to fatigue.

4 Sleep is better.

5 They look better. The other prisoners have also noticed this.

6 Patient No. 5 insistently asks for a new implantation, 'in order to do as well as the others'.

Case-book:
No. 21 686 St., Bernhard, born 1889, theologian, member of a religious order.

Previous history:
Constantly sick, more withdrawn, but good-natured and ready to help. Puberty at 18 years. From 1911 to 1912 attempts to get closer to a girl, but did not reach intercourse *out of anxiety*. At school was at first a poor learner because of unsettled conditions of life, then good. From 1924 to 1928 intercourse with young men, thigh intercourse, *no anxiety*. From 1932 to 1935 again with men, then normal intercourse with a girl. Same satisfaction. Last pollution in February 1944. Eight years penal servitude; nothing happened there.
On 16.9.44 *implantation of the 'artificial male sex gland'* (dose 3a). After the operation on:

16.9.44   pain – neurological negative
17.9.44   no pain
18.9.44   erection
19.9.44   stronger erection around morning
20.9.44   stronger erection a few times
21.9.44   again erection
22.9.44   erection, but weaker – no pain
23.9.44   erection in the evening and the morning
24.9.44   ditto
26.10.44   The operation wound is healing without any reaction. No reaction to the implanted 'artificial gland'. Is better and dreamt of women. Prospects have significantly improved. Looks younger. His features are smoother. Today he came laughing and uninhibited to the examination – at the first examination he was taciturn and only answered direct questions, but today he speaks freely and in detail of his previous life and of the changes that have occurred since the implantation.

Reported by patient:
Sleep has been better ever since a few days after the operation. Previously he felt tired and not in the mood for anything; he was depressed and his thoughts dwelt only on life in the camp.
The depression has disappeared: he looks forward to the time of his release, makes plans for the future; now he masters everything better, including psychologically, and feels freer in every respect.

Other prisoners have told him that he has changed and looks younger and better.

His erotic imaginative world has also completely changed. Previously all his erotic thoughts and dreams were of young men, but now they are of women. He thinks that camp life is unfavourable: he has thought of the women in the brothel, but he cannot go there for 'religious' reasons.

Blood cholesterol level on 12.10.44 190%
Blood cholesterol level on 24.10.44 210%

43 160 K., Philipp, b. 1908, miner, unmarried

18.IX.44 Family case history negative, normal development. Puberty at 15 years, first intercourse at 17. Never normal intercourse, always with violence. Has never danced. Twice convicted of rape. Emasculated 8 years ago. Never seminal emissions. Neurological negative.

19.IX.44 Feels nothing at all
20.IX.44 Observed nothing
21.IX.44 Erection around morning while asleep
22.IX.44 Erection around morning
23.IX.44 Ditto
24.IX.44 Weak erection during the night

[103c] *Memorandum. Visit by Sturmbannführer Vaernet on 8 December 1944*

On 7.12.1944 ten men were taken to Room 6 for urine samples (B. sick in Room 25).[13]

Of these 10, 7 were operated on:

R.	21 526	Room 6	L.	9 576	Room 6
Sch.	31 462	Room 6	P.	6 169	Room 6
K.	21 957	Room 6	B.	21 941	Room 25
H.	20 989	Room 6			

The last four should be photographed immediately (face shot) and again after one month, so that the pictures can be used to check any rejuvenation.

In the case of P. the planned castration will have to be postponed for at least a month.

In the case of the 3 not operated on,

13 Nothing further is known about the prisoners. One of the specifications of Vaernet's experiments was most probably that as many as possible of the men were (homosexual) 'habitual criminals' who in the past (while serving their sentence or at Buchenwald itself) had 'willingly' undergone castration.

M.   41 936   Room 6   V.   779   Room 6
K.   6 186   Room 6
the 24 hours of urine collected so far will be enough.

[103d] *Letter of 3 February 1945 from the Waffen-SS garrison
doctor, Schiedlausky, to SS-Sturmbannführer Dr Vaernet*

Enclosed herewith are records of the prisoners operated on so far
(total of 13).[14]

Those who had the operation on 8.12.44 are numbered as follows:

R.   (21 526)   No. 1   H.   (20 998)   No. 3
Sch.   (31 462)   No. 4   K.   (21 957)   No. 6
L.   (9 576)   No. 5   P.   (6 169)   No. 5a
B.   (29 941)   No. 5b

Prisoner H., No. 20998 (3) died 21.12.44 at 8.00 hours from heart
trouble combined with infectious enteritis and general bodily weak-
ness. No records were kept of this prisoner.
The urine samples are waiting here to be collected. [...]
Pokorny[15] will question and examine these seven post-operatives
once a week for the first three weeks and then just once a week, and
also once a week the first five to have had the operation. The results
will be sent weekly to Stbf. Vaernet.

[104] Cleared off in good time

*Letter of 28 February 1945 from Deutsche Heilmittel GmbH, Prague, to
the Economic and Administrative Headquarters of the SS*

Deutsche Heilmittel GmbH   Prague, 28 February 1945
Prag IX
Podiebrader Landstr. 5

To the
Chief Waffen-SS Oberführer
SS Economic and Administrative Headquarters
Berlin-Lichterfelde West
Unter den Eichen 135

Dear Oberführer!

    With reference to the telephone conversation with yourself, we
report the following in the matter of Dr Vaernet.

---

[14] There was no trace of such observations. Schiedlausky's figure of 13 operations is
contentious. The first was performed by Vaernet on 13.9.44 on five prisoners, the second on
8.12.44 on a further seven. One of these twelve, the prisoner P., died on 21 December 1944.
[15] Dr Pokorny, the Czech doctor-prisoner active in the sick-bay.

On the basis of the contract signed between Deutsche Heilmittel GmbH and Dr Vaernet on 16.5.1944 (§3), Dr Vaernet has an obligation to present a detailed monthly report on the state of his work, which is sent to the Reichsführer-SS via the SS and Police Reich Doctor.

Dr V. delivered his last report in October 1944. In it he pointed out that he would have completed his scientific work by 10.1.45

'He [Vaernet – G.G.] went to a British prisoner-of-war camp and was interned with many other traitors at the Alsgade Skole in Copenhagen. A crude sorting of war criminals took place there. But no one knew anything concrete about Vaernet, except that he had been a doctor at Deutsche Heilmittel.

This obscurity only lasted a short time, however. Already on 29 May 1945 the chairman of the Danish Medical Association forwarded to the Justice Ministry a statement made by a Danish police officer. This officer, who had been detained in Buchenwald together with some two thousand other Danish policemen, had identified Vaernet in the camp wearing his black SS uniform. The chairman of the doctors' association never received an answer to his submission. In the autumn of 1945 the British handed Vaernet over to the Danish authorities. What they did then is not known today. On 2 January 1946 the Medical Association received a letter from Vaernet's lawyer stating that his client had resigned from the association – a step which, as the chairman of the association said in his reply, did not affect the disqualification proceedings initiated against Vaernet. The chairman thought that Vaernet was still in prison, but in fact he had been transferred to the public hospital because of a 'heart complaint'. Shortly thereafter, he vanished into thin air. He told fellow-doctors that his complaint could only be treated in Sweden, and somehow he managed to obtain official permission to travel there. It is not known who gave him that permission.

At any event Carl Vaernet thus said goodbye for ever. In Sweden he made contact with a Nazi escape network. From there he went to Argentina and not – as *Land og Folk* [of 22.6.1947 – G.G.] writes – to Brazil. [...]

The last anyone heard of Vaernet was from a reader's letter to the Copenhagen paper *Berlingske Tidende* [19.11.1947 – G.G.], in which a Dane living in Argentina expressed amazement that the doctor Carl Vaernet, despite the crimes attributed to him, held employment in the Buenos Aires health service.'

H. Foged and H. Krüger, *Flugrute Nord. Nazisternes hemmelige Flugtnet gennen Danmark*, Lynge 1985, quoted from K. Krickler, 'SS-Arzt Dr Vaernet', *Lambda Nachrichten* (Vienna) No. 2/1988, pp. 53–55.

and would not give any further report on his activity until that time. We did not receive activity reports, then, for the following months. It is not known to us what Dr V. did during that time.

Dr V. did not observe your instruction, Oberführer, that he must inform us where he was at any given time or where he could be reached.

Just once, on 17.10 of last year, Dr V. informed us in writing that he was temporarily working in the University library and that when he was busy elsewhere information could be obtained by telephone from his home address.

On a number of occasions when we wanted to speak to Dr V. on an important matter, we rang his home and received the information that he was not in Prague but in Berlin etc. From roughly the middle of December last until the present, Dr V. only once presented himself here and that was in the first week of February. On that occasion he told us that he wanted to take his family to Copenhagen for three weeks, as he himself would be going to Berlin. He said that if the Reichsführer gave his consent, he would probably go as regimental doctor to a unit in the field, and that 'someone else' would come here and continue his work during that time. Who that is, and what are the conditions under which he will work, are not known to us. Dr V. also said that if the Reichsführer did not give his consent, he would return to Prague.

In the recent period Dr V. has generally developed a high degree of independence. For example, we know next to nothing about his plans for the acquisition of new machines which are supposedly being made by a body of the SS.

Probably Dr V. discusses these matters with some offices in Berlin, which are presumably acting in ignorance of the contract signed between Dr V. and ourselves. In this way he disregards Deutsche Heilmittel so as to carry out his own will.

We are therefore convinced that Dr V. has no intention of keeping us informed about his activity.

It is self-evident to us that unless we subsequently accept the way in which Dr V. has been acting, we will not be liable for any financial commitments into which he might enter.

Heil Hitler!
Deutsche Heilmittel GmbH
Signed: [illegible]

Appendix

Sources of the Illustrations

The illustrations on p. xx (of Astel and Ding) and p. xxi (Rodenberg and Schiedlausky) were made available by the Document Center Berlin. The portrait photograph of Meisinger (p. xxi) and the illustrations on pp. 75 and 77 are reproduced from Walter Wuttke, *Homosexuelle im Nationalsozialismus*, exhibition catalogue, Ulm 1987. The pictures on pp. 167 and 177 are taken from Herbert Tobias, *Photographien*, Stuttgart (Parkland Verlag), 1987. All others, unless otherwise stated, come from the author's own archives.

Translations of lengthy documents appear adjacent to the original wherever possible. In some cases they are on the preceding or following page.

Sources of the Documents

Abbreviations for the libraries and archives cited here are given on page xxvii.

1. BAK R 22/973
2. Printed in *Volkswart. Monatsschrift zur Bekämpfung der öffentlichen Unsittlichkeit*, vol., 5, 1933, pp. 56f.
3. Ibid., p. 57
4. Printed in *Braunbuch über Reichstagsbrand und Hitlerterror*, facsimile of the original 1933 edition, Frankfurt/Main 1983, pp. 151–154
5. Humantities Research Center, University of Texas at Austin. A copy of the letter was kindly made available by Manfred Herzer, Berlin.
6. Sachsen-Anhalt Landesarchive, Magdeburg. Rep C20 Ib, No. 1839
7. Ibid.
8. Printed in A. Ebbinghaus/H. Kaupen-Haas/K. H. Roth, *Heilen und Vernichten im Mustergau Hamburg. Bevölkerungs- und Gesundheitspolitik im Dritten Reich*, Hamburg 1984, pp. 83f.
9a. IfZ Munich, MA 131
9b. Ibid.
10. BAK R 58/1029, fol 12
11. BA – MA NS 17, LSSAH/57
12. BArch P Film 2428/AN 2950373
13. BArch P Film 2428/AN 950423
14. BArch P Film 1842/AN 5525 555–558
15. BArch P Film 1842/AN 5525 559
16a. BA – ZPA PSt 3–271, fol 50
16b. Ibid., fol 51
17. IfZ Munich, FA 119/2
18a. Quoted from BAK R 22/973
18b. RGBl I, 1935, pp. 839f.
19. Printed in *Deutsche Justiz*, 1935/28, pp. 994–999
20. Printed in F. Gürtner, ed., *Das kommende deutsche Strafrecht. Besonderer Teil: Bericht über die Arbeit der amtlichen Strafrechtskommission*, Berlin 1935, pp. 116–118, 125f.
21a. BAK R 61/127
21b. BAK R 61/332
22. Printed in *Deutsches Recht*, 1936, pp. 469–470
23. Kindly made available to Claudia Schoppmann by Wolfgang Wippermann
24. Staatsarchiv Munich, NSDAP 1034
25. Printed in Kukuc, I. (i.e. Ilse Kokula), *Der Kampf gegen Unterdrückung*, Munich 1975, pp. 127f.

26. BAK R 22/970, 64
27. BA – MA H20/479
28a. Ibid.
28b. Ibid.
28c. Thuringia Hauptstaatsarchiv Weimar, MdI P113
29. Hessisches Staatsarchiv Marburg. Stock 120, LA Eschwege, 1718
30. BA – MA H 20/479
31. BArch P Film 1123/AN 2885836
32. OuMD, p. 37
33. BAK R 58/840, fol 196
34. OuMD, p. 60
35. BAK R 58/1085, fol 57
36. BAK R 58/1085, fol 58
37. OuMD, p. 101
38. Mecklenburgisches Landesarchive Schwerin. Min. f. Unterricht, Kunst, geistliche und Medizinalangelegenheiten, No. 967
39. Printed in *Jahrbuch des Reichskriminalpolizeiamtes für das Jahr 1938*, no date or place (Berlin 1939), pp. 20f.
40. Printed in *Jahrbuch Amt V (Reichskriminalpolizeiamt) des RSHA SS 1939/1940. Berichtsjahr 1939*, Berlin 1940
41a. BDC. Karl Astel
41b. Ibid.
41c. Ibid.
42a. Thuringia Hauptstaatsarchiv Weimar. MdI P 113
42b. BA – MA H 20/479
42c. Ibid.
43a. Printed in 'Hier geht das Leben auf eine sehr merkwürdige Weise weiter' [Here life goes on in a quite remarkable way], *Zur Geschichte der Psychoanalyse in Deutschland*, exhibition catalogue, Hamburg 1985, p. 155
43b. Ibid., p. 154
44. Printed in H. G. Stümke, 'Vom "unausgeglichenen Geschlechtshaushalt". Zur Verfolgung Homosexueller', in *Verachtet, verfolgt, vernichtet. Zu den vergessenen Opfern des NS-Regimes*, edited by the Project Group for the Forgotten Victims of the Nazi Regime in Hamburg, Hamburg 1986, pp. 47–63
45. BArch P Film 4168/AN 9375910ff.
46. BArch P – AH 925 A 10, fol 318f.
47. IfZ Munich, doct. 17.02
48. BArch P Film 1123/AN 2885 838–844
49. Sachsen-Anhalt Landesarchive, Magdeburg. Rep C20 Ib, No. 1839
50a. BAK R 22/1460, fol 22–26
50b. BAK R 22/1460, fol 38
51. Thuringia Hauptstaatsarchiv Weimar. Chief Prosecutor Jena No. 438
52. BAK R 22/970, fol 9f.
53. BAK NS 2/57
54. BA – MA H 20/57
55. BA – MA H 20/474
56. BA – MA H 20/479
57. Ibid.
58. IfZ Munich. FA 146, fol 70/71

59. Kindly supplied by Dieter Schiefelbein, Frankfurt-am-Main
60. BA – MA H 20/479
61. Ibid.
62. BArch P Film 2782/AN 2741216
63a. BArch P Film 382268/AN 19604
63b. BAK NS 19/2376
64. BAK NSD 41/49
65. Printed in *Das Schwarze Korps*, 15 February 1940
66a. BAK R 22/970, fol 27
66b. BAK R 22/970, fol 20
66c. BAK R 22/970, fol 21
67. BAK R 22/970, fol 47
68. Taken from RGBlI 1942, pp. 568–569
69. Hessisches Hauptstaatsarchiv Wiesbaden 463/1117, fol 6
70. BAK R 22/850, fol 462
71. BAK R 22/850, fol 464–468
72. BAK R 22/850, fol 469–470
73. BAK R 22/850, fol 472
74. BArch P Film 41870/AN 0190/91
75. Printed in J. Rogier, 'Homoseksuele emancipatie. Historische context van de Nederlande vereniging van homofielen C.O.C.', *Dialoog* No. 5, 1966, pp. 173–209 (from p. 200)
76. Printed in *Crimineele statistik, uitgave CBS*, from the abridgement in P. Koenders, *Homoseksualiteit in bezet Nederland*, Amsterdam 1984, p. 88
77. BArch P Film 40168/AN 9380 011–12
78. BArch P Film 40168/AN 9380 015–16
79. IfZ Munich, MA 438/962993 1
80. IfZ Munich, MA 438/962991–2
81. Printed in *Kriminalität und Gefährdung der Jugend. Lagebericht bis zum Stande vom 1. Januar 1941*, published by the Youth Führer of the German Reich, edited by Bannführer W. Knopp, no date or place (Berlin 1942), pp. 116–120
82. BAK R 22/1175, fol 55a
83. BAK R 22/1197, fol 18/19
84. BArch P Film 14653
85. BAK R 22/1197, fol 93
86. BA – MA H 20/557
87. Sachsen-Anhalt Landesarchive, Magdeburg. Rep C141, No. 231
88. IfZ Munich, doct. 17.02
89. Ibid.
90. Ibid.
91. Ibid.
92. Ibid.
93. BArch P Film 55492/AN 1078
94a. BAK R 22/943, fol 301
94b. BAK R 22/943, fol 262
94c. BAK R 22/943, fol 263
95. Archiv DA/BA NS 3 collection of decrees
96. Stefan Heymann materials, Archiv Buchenwald 53, 1–7
97a. Archiv Buchenwald 57

97b. Ibid.
97c. Ibid.
98. Ibid.
99a. Staatsarchiv Leipzig PP-S 27
99b. Ibid.
99c. Ibid.
99d. Ibid.
100. BAK NS 3/21
101. BAK NS 4/50
102a. Ibid.
102b. Ibid.
103a. BAK NS 4/21
103b. BAK NS 4/50
103c. Ibid.
103d. Ibid.
104. BDC. Carl Vaernet

Index

Entries for illustrations are in *italics*.